the
FRAGILE

by

MITRA DE SOUZA

Wild Ink Publishing

wild-ink-publishing.com

Copyright © 2024 Mitra De Souza

Edited by Amy Nielsen & Brittany McMunn

Cover Design by Abigail Wild

ISBN (paperback): 978-1-958531-67-9

ISBN (epub) : 978-1-958531-68-6

Any references to historical events, real people, or real places are used ficti-tiously. Names, characters, and places are products of the author's imagina-tion.

To my dad who never got the chance to finish his story
To my mom who helped me finish mine
To everyone who has ever felt like the world was not built
for you,
I see you.

Content Warnings

This novel contains the following themes and content that may be sensitive or triggering to some readers. Reader discretion is advised.

Substance Abuse: References to underage alcohol use, including scenes depicting characters consuming substances while under the legal age.

Violence: Depictions of violence, including but not limited to physical altercations, battles, and instances of self-defense. While these scenes are integral to the storyline, they may be distressing to some readers.

Domestic Violence: Character backstory includes references to domestic violence.

Chapter 1

MAYA KNEW SHE WOULD never be enough, but that didn't stop her from trying. She'd been in the testing room countless times and wasn't any tougher, stronger, or braver. As usual, Dr. Nix glared at her from the head of the long metallic table, the single fluorescent bulb in the ceiling casting a sallow glow on her harsh features. She nodded toward the cage.

A tiny mouse trembled in the cage, dark eyes filled with panic. The electrodes strapped to his head obscured his tiny ears. His fear gnawed at Maya's insides, weakening her resolve to hurt him.

Maya shook out her hands and rubbed them against her faded coveralls. She turned to Dr. Nix. "I'm ready now."

Dr. Nix rolled her eyes and rapped her pen against the table.

Tap. Tap. Tap.

Maya's insides churned. She glanced at the mouse and back to Dr. Nix.

Tap. Tap. Tap.

The mouse's terror pounded in Maya's chest. His adrenaline shot through her veins. They were the same—but only one of them had the chance to be free.

Maya pushed away the mess of thick dark curls that clung to her forehead and focused on the switch. Just one flip and she would pass her test.

Don't look at him. You don't have to feel his fear. She swallowed the lump in her throat. *You don't have to feel his pain.*

As soon as Maya placed her hand on the switch, Dr. Nix's thin lips twisted into a triumphant smile.

Maya froze.

Somewhere deep within her burned an ember of compassion that refused to go out. An ember that held her prisoner in a world where she would never fit. Tears filled her eyes as she returned her gaze to the mouse. She dropped her hand from the switch. Dr. Nix scowled. Her shiny black boots clicked across the linoleum like so many black boots had done before.

"You know what comes next. Either shock the mouse or–" She slapped the electrode on Maya's arm. It was Maya or the mouse, but either way, she'd feel it.

She felt everything.

All the time.

Dr. Nix's frustration, the mouse's terror. There was nothing she could do.

She was a Fragile.

And she wasn't getting any better.

Despite the pain of the shock radiating up her arm, Maya refused to rub it until Dr. Nix left the testing room.

A nurse with a clipboard opened the door. "Need a painkiller?"

Maya grabbed her backpack off the floor. "I'm fine. Do you have my results?"

The nurse's eyebrows drew together with concern—a look Maya knew well. She got "concerned" looks from nurses and teachers at the Arc all the time. This one was steeped in pity. More often they bordered on revulsion, as if being a Fragile was contagious. Somehow pity stung worse.

The nurse handed her the paper. "I'll give Dr. Barrow the copy for your annual review tomorrow."

The red ink from the "failed" stamp seeped through the paper. Dr. Nix must have enjoyed slamming it down on the page.

Maya let out a heavy breath and shoved the paper in her backpack. She was about to leave when she turned to the nurse. "Can I have a reference form?"

The nurse's eyes widened. "For Professor Prim?"

"Yes." She gritted her teeth. It wasn't the best idea, but since she failed, she didn't have much of a choice.

She handed Maya the form with a tight-lipped smile. "I guess it can't hurt to try."

Maya placed the form in her notebook, being careful not to crease it. She lugged her backpack onto her shoulders and headed down the dark corridor to the lab exit.

Once outside, she squinted as her eyes adjusted to the sunlight. Though the mid-day sun warmed her skin, darkness clung to her insides. She shuddered and pulled her arms to her chest as she crossed the concrete terrace with her head down. Despite knowing better, she couldn't help but check the cracks in the worn pavement for sprouts of life fighting to reach the sunlight. It was spring, after all.

At the end of the terrace, she heaved open the dining commons' door to the low hum of muted conversations and clinking silverware. The thick scent of dirty dishes steam cleaning in the kitchen churned her stomach, but she grabbed a tray and scooped what was left of lunch on her plate. She scanned the sea of kids in gray coveralls until she spotted Jacob's mop of wavy brown hair across the room. He was hard to miss. The Arc assigned older Fragiles to tables along the back wall. Most kids passed their reviews by the time they hit twelve or thirteen, so only the highly dysfunctional ones—like Maya and Jacob—remained at seventeen.

When Maya reached Jacob's table, he smiled. "How'd it go?"

She set down her tray and slumped into her chair. "Don't want to talk about it."

"I saved you grilled cheese since all they have left is scraps of meatloaf." He glanced at the dining monitor chatting with a cleaner and slid the sandwich onto her tray.

The cooks never made enough food and encouraged people to take as much as they wanted, so they often ran out before everyone ate. It was supposed to teach the Fragiles how to "get ahead." When Maya reached for the sandwich, another monitor came up from behind her and grabbed it. He glared at Jacob and pointed to the sign on the cracked wall — "Sharing leads to idleness. Competition breeds excellence." He tossed the sandwich in the trash. Jacob's pale cheeks flushed red, his shame boiling across the table into Maya.

"Don't worry about it." Her stomach growled as she poked at the green mush of canned peas on her plate. "I'm not really hungry."

He studied her face. "Are you sure you're okay? I know that test can be—"

"I'm fine." To prove it, she scooped a spoonful of peas into her mouth and tried not to gag.

He cocked his head and narrowed his eyes on her. She choked down the peas. "Ok, I failed. But I think I can still pass my review. Like if Prim gives me a good reference letter that should help."

"Yeah, maybe." He took a sip of his water. "Have you ever considered that maybe becoming a lifer isn't the worst thing?"

Her body stiffened. "Be locked up forever? You can't be serious."

"I'm sure the adult ward isn't any worse than here." He dropped his eyes and fidgeted with his tray.

"If you're trying to make me feel better, it's not working."

"I'm not saying give up. I just mean things are unpredictable out in the Republic. It's hard for people like us out there. You know that."

"I know." She smashed the peas with her fork. How is this even food? She pushed her tray away. Before the silence got too awkward, she asked, "How did labs go this morning?"

His face brightened. "I spent the whole time in the scent lab. Based on my testing, they confirmed the scent of vanilla makes people spend money. Imagine people in the Republic walking through vanilla-scented stores because of me."

"I told you you're a scent lab savant." She grinned. "Can I get your autograph?"

"Ha. Very funny." He pushed aside his tray. "You know what's weird though? There were barely any kids in the lab building. Even the emotion lab was empty."

The words "emotion lab" sent a chill up her spine. Last week, Dr. Nix had made her watch a recording of an execution to measure her emotional reaction. The image still haunted her. She wrapped her arms around her stomach as it filled with darkness.

"Earth to Maya. Isn't that strange?"

"Oh, yeah. Sorry. I was just thinking about something. Hey, did you get the results of your review yet?"

He glanced at the clock on the wall. "Uh, no, not yet."

"Didn't you finish your tests last week?"

"Yeah, sometimes it takes a while." He got up and reached for his backpack. "We should head to class."

"Okay, but—"

"Is it cold outside?" He pulled his scarf out of his backpack.

"No, it's fine." She got up to clear her tray. "Dr. Barrow gave your scarf back? That was quick."

"Yep. His theory about it interfering with my ability to overcome my sensitivity to temperatures was short lived. After my latest stint in the infirmary, Director Williams made him give it back." As he wrapped the scarf around his neck, a comfortable nostalgia enveloped her.

Fragiles were forbidden from talking about their families, but she liked to think his mother knitted it and that it reminded him of home. Pressing him about his review results could wait.

They set their trays on the counter and waited in line at the exit door to receive their morning medication. The nurse gave the little kids in front of them fruit-flavored gummies. Maya used to love the purple ones even though they made her head feel funny. After a while she got so used to taking them that she didn't even notice a difference. When she and Jacob reached the front of the line, the nurse handed her a small paper cup with a blue pill and a cup of water. Once they had swallowed their pills, they headed to class.

Maya's shoulders tensed as soon as they entered the classroom. Professor Prim perched on her stool and glared at the class over her gold-rimmed glasses. Her anger barreled into Maya like a freight train. Hoping Prim would be in a good mood was as useless as expecting fresh fruit in the commons, but Maya couldn't help it. She forgave hope each time it betrayed her.

Maya grabbed a seat next to Jacob. The class had dwindled to less than a dozen. Everyone sat in silence with their Modern History of the Republic textbooks open on their desks, their eyes on Professor Prim. Maya placed her book on her desk and slid her reference form beneath it in case Prim's mood improved. The classroom door flung open, and Tully strolled in, oblivious to Prim's disapproving stare. Taking her time, she tossed her backpack on the floor and rolled her eyes before stretching out in a chair in the back row. Tully had only been at the Arc a few years, and everyone knew she didn't belong there.

Fragiles were hypersensitive, and Tully had the sensitivity of a sledgehammer.

Maya returned her gaze to her desk. Even looking at Tully felt like an infraction, and too many infractions were a one-way ticket to the adult ward. She tucked the edge of her reference form back under her book and clasped her hands in her lap.

Prim rose from her stool. "Today we–" Her laser eyes locked on Tully who was busy defacing her textbook. Tully's bright red hair fell against her clenched jaw as she scribbled on the page. In an instant, Prim loomed over her desk and cleared her throat. Tully continued to draw. "Ahem." Professor Prim tapped her ruler against her well-manicured hand.

Tully's fierce blue eyes glared at Professor Prim, her freckled face twisting into a smirk. "You need a glass of water or what?" She went back to drawing.

Prim's ruler struck the center of Tully's book, barely missing her hand. "To Director Williams's office. Now. And you will report to the media room at eight on Friday morning to assist with the preparations for Commander Abigor's visit."

Tully slammed her book shut and rose from her desk. Even though Prim stood in heels, Tully matched her height and scowled at her before storming out of the classroom, hair blazing behind her. As a surge of Tully's anger flowed through Maya, she ran her fingers over the edge of her textbook and lifted it. What would it feel like to slam it shut? To let the anger out instead of holding it inside. The instant the click of Prim's heels approached her desk, Maya released the edge and smoothed the open page.

Prim continued to the front of the class. "As I was saying, today we'll be watching a documentary highlighting the accomplishments of our illustrious Arc founder, Commander Abigor, in preparation for his visit. You should all be familiar with this documentary already, but I expect you to take copious notes to ensure you're paying attention. Before we start, one of your classmates has an announcement." She turned toward Bethany in the front row. "Bethany?"

Bethany got up from her chair, patted her blond bun, and straightened her already perfect posture. She turned to the class. "As you know, I'm head of the Welcoming Committee for Commander Abigor's visit." She glanced at Professor Prim. "But I need some additional volunteers to finalize our preparations."

"Thank you, Bethany," said Professor Prim. "How many more volunteers do you need?"

"So far the committee is just me, but I'm confident I can execute a welcome worthy of the Commander."

"That won't do." Professor Prim scanned the room until her gaze rested on Maya. "Maya, you're short several lab hours, so you'll make them up on the committee."

Maya stifled a groan. Group work was bad enough without Bethany being in charge.

Jacob's hand shot up. "I'd like to volunteer." He grinned at Maya.

She got that weird warm feeling she'd been sensing from him lately. Maybe it was puberty? Did guys still get that at seventeen? Their life skills teacher had told them to ignore the feelings and they would eventually go away.

"Thank you, Jacob. With Tully that makes four on the committee. How does that sound, Bethany?"

Bethany smiled through gritted teeth. "Yes, thank you Professor."

"Thank you for your leadership, Bethany. Even though rehabilitated Fragiles can never hold office— for obvious reasons—I'm sure you will make the Council proud upon your release."

Professor Prim dimmed the lights and turned on the projector. "I want all eyes on the screen."

Maya's head began to throb, but she resisted resting it on her desk. If she wanted any chance of passing her review, she had to stay on her best behavior. She would risk closing her eyes when the Republic forces annihilated the rebels. She hated that part. When she glanced at Tully's empty chair, a lingering spark of anger that didn't quite feel like

Tully's bubbled in her gut. Startled by the feeling, she returned her attention to the soldiers marching across the screen. Soon her eyelids became heavy, and she nodded off.

Suddenly, a scream echoed through her head, jolting her awake. Pain ripped through her body. She clutched her stomach, unable to breathe. An image of a young girl tore across her mind. The girl's dark hair pulled back from her face, revealing ice-blue eyes filled with terror. Maya cried out in agony as an invisible force sucked the life out of her. As the pain intensified, her body urged her to fight. She thrust herself away from her desk, flinging her book across the floor while her chair crashed behind her. As she gasped for air, she strained to focus on her surroundings.

She took a deep breath and recalled Dr. Barrow's words, *Just because it feels real, doesn't mean it is.*

The documentary droned on in the background, but all eyes were on her, including Prim's very real, venomous glare. Still trembling, Maya picked up her chair and straightened it behind her desk. She was about to snatch the reference form off the floor when Prim's red pump came down on it. Prim held out her hand and released the form just enough for Maya to ease it out from under her shoe.

Maya handed her the paper. "It's a reference form. But you don't have to fill it out."

Prim fixed her gaze on Maya's book, still strewn across the floor and scoffed, "Oh, but I do."

Chapter 2

MAYA LEANED HER HEAD against the wall. The buzzing of the electric clock vibrated in her chest as she sat in the empty corridor. Her review should have started ten minutes ago. Although the scent of ammonia stung her nose, the roach scurrying across the hallway didn't seem to mind. Apparently, roaches are so resilient that they can survive in the harshest environments.

Must be nice.

Her stomach grumbled. She never ate breakfast before her reviews. At least not since the first one. Before her first review, she had gobbled down pancakes with grape jelly. Who knew purple vomit would stain a lab coat? As an expert in her neurotic hypersensitivity, Dr. Barrow should have known better than to show her such a gruesome photo. She still didn't understand why she had to look at violent images every time. Even though Dr. Barrow said it was to improve her "mental toughness", it never got easier. She only pretended it did.

Despite failing her practical exam yesterday, she was determined to pass her review this year. The countless hours she spent studying to maintain her high grades had to be worth something. In addition to earning the top mark in her Divinity of Capitalism class, she had only one behavioral infraction the entire year. She had been sure the physical fitness monitor was out of sight when she helped up her fallen classmate, but he had used binoculars from the tower. As for yesterday's outburst in class, she would explain it as a stress-induced nightmare. According to Prim, performance-related stress is acceptable because it fosters high achievement.

Dr. Barrow opened his office door, so she took a deep breath and squared her shoulders. His salt and pepper hair had thinned over the years and appeared particularly disheveled today. "Hello, Maya. I'm ready for you now." He held the door open for her to enter.

Maya squeezed past the hutch overflowing with books on psychological disorders and glanced at the portrait of Commander Abigor hanging above the desk. The extravagant painting dominated the wall, overshadowing Dr. Barrow's diplomas in their cheap frames. Avoiding Abigor's judgmental stare, Maya eased into the tattered leather couch which still let out a tired squeak.

Dr. Barrow straightened his tie. He always wore a bright green tie with his lab coat. It brought out his eyes, which must have helped him feel less ordinary. "Now Maya, you understand we are here today to complete your annual review, correct?"

She clasped her hands in her lap. "Yes, Dr. Barrow."

"Good." He pulled out a thick, worn file from the pile on his cluttered desk and opened it. "I see here you failed your practical exam yesterday. Would you like to explain what happened?"

"Well, I didn't shock the mouse, but I think I've been improving. My hand was on the switch. Maybe it stopped working or something?"

He narrowed his eyes on her. "Improving?" He pulled out a stack of papers from her file and fanned them out on his desk, the word "failed" stamped in various shades of red ink on each one. "Can you tell me which one shows the improvement?"

She chewed on her bottom lip as she scanned the papers. "Um, they're all the same test. Maybe if they gave me a different one?"

Raising his brows, he huffed. "A different one? The neurotic hypersensitivity assessment tool was designed by Commander Abigor himself. It's the gold standard for the early detection of Fragiles." He shuffled through the papers and pulled out a page so worn the "failed" stamp had faded to pink. "This is from your Fragile assessment day when you were seven. Normally, we don't discuss them with patients, but it might shed some light on why you haven't been improving. What can you tell me about that day?"

She shifted on the sunken couch. "Uh, well, there was a mouse in the cage and a button I was supposed to press to get a new toy."

He peered over the rims of his glasses. "Do you remember anything else?"

Of course, she remembered, no matter how hard she tried to forget. She shook her head.

"Perhaps it's because you lost consciousness during your assessment? Oftentimes, Fragiles don't have the mental fortitude to earn the prize, but no one else has ever blacked out. I also find it curious you attempted to free the mouse." He stared at her as if waiting for an answer.

Her seven-year-old self had tried to free the mouse but got him killed in the process. She winced as she relived the pain of his bones shattering beneath the doctor's black boot and the wave of darkness that overtook her. "Yes, they told me I fainted. I hadn't eaten breakfast, so maybe it was low blood sugar or something?"

He stared at her and then scribbled in her file. "Very well. Let's move on." He glanced through her file. "You've been getting good grades in your classes, so that's promising."

He continued shuffling through the papers. "Last week the nurse upped your normal medication due to nightmares. Is that correct?"

She fidgeted with the coarse curl that had escaped from her braid. "Uh, yes, but I'm okay now." Except for the nightmare in class yesterday, the ones brought on by the execution video had stopped.

"Good. Just in case, I already wrote you a prescription for something to help you sleep. You can get it from the nurse when we finish your review." He wrote more notes in her file. "You know, it's quite typical for Fragiles to have sleep issues. It is just a symptom of a hypersensitive mind. Imagine what it must have been like for Fragiles before Commander Abigor created the Academy for the Rehabilitation of Children."

She gazed at the wall behind him. "Yes, I'm thankful for the Commander and for the Arc." Wringing her hands in her lap, she returned her eyes to his desk. "Are we going to look at the photos now?"

"No need for those today. I examined your emotion lab results. Your reactions have become even more hypersensitive, which is the opposite of what should be happening. I can't possibly pass you."

His words punched her in the gut. "I failed my review? Maybe if we looked at the photos or my papers? I got the highest—"

"I'm sorry, but that won't make a difference at this point." He closed her file and leaned back in his chair. "You know, the genius of the Arc is that it identifies children at a young age. While it's nearly impossible to rehabilitate adults, young minds can be molded to make the tough decisions needed to get ahead and keep our economy growing. But I digress, I bring this up because you're moving closer to adulthood, and we simply aren't seeing enough progress. In fact, one of your professors reported an abnormal outburst yesterday. You may be regressing. I'm afraid we must consider the possibility that your neurotic hypersensitivity might be terminal."

"What do you mean by terminal?" Deep down she knew, but needed to hear him say it.

"In most cases, children who display certain dysfunctional traits, like heightened sensitivity, can be rehabilitated through intensive interventions like those offered here at the Arc. However, other children are so afflicted that conventional methods aren't effective. It's possible you may never get better."

Never get better.

Never go home.

Darkness constricted her insides. It swam through her head and spun it in a million directions. The room started to sway. She grabbed the armrest to steady herself.

He furrowed his brows. "Is something wrong?"

"No." She released the armrest. "I'm just feeling a bit lightheaded." Maybe she should have eaten breakfast. Maybe next time she would eat fruiti-os. Would they make rainbow stains on his lab coat?

He sighed and reopened her file. "Is that a new symptom?" He scribbled without waiting for an answer. "It's most likely spontaneous anxiety related to your condition–or just bad genes."

Bad genes. Particularly severe. Terminal. The knot in her stomach tightened.

"So, if it's genetic does that mean that it's, uh" – she choked on the word– "incurable?"

"Incurable? Well, I haven't given up yet so neither should you. We're working on new treatments, so who knows? You do have one more year after all." He forced a smile before checking his watch. "I apologize, but I have a meeting to get to. But don't worry, worst case scenario you can still live a productive life in the adult ward." He closed her file. "Don't forget to get your medication from the nurse."

On her way out, she eyed the medication waiting for her on the nurse's counter. Maybe the pills could soothe the dread gnawing on her insides. She grabbed the bottle which had "To be taken at bedtime-will cause extreme drowsiness" printed on it in big bold letters. Crap. She had lab hours and skipping wasn't an option. The last thing she needed was an infraction on her record counting toward next year's review. Her next and final review—her last chance. She slipped the bottle into her pocket and hurried out the door.

Chapter 3

When Maya arrived at the scent lab, Jacob and Liam, the lab attendant, huddled over a row of test tubes. Jacob glanced over his shoulder to give her a nod and then returned his focus to the test tubes.

Liam handed Jacob two of the tubes. "Let's see if you can tell the difference between these two. One is synthetic rose, and one is real."

Maya slouched down into the seat across from them.

Jacob opened the first tube, waved it in a circle by his nose, and closed his eyes. Despite Jacob being in "the zone," she couldn't stomach being a lab rat for the next two hours.

She glanced at Liam. "Didn't you once tell us that having a headache can interfere with our sense of smell?"

Liam focused on Maya for the first time since she arrived. "Yes, the slightest cold—and even hormonal changes—can affect your olfactory system." He nodded at Jacob. "That's why males make better test subjects."

"In that case, I should probably let you know I have a headache." It wasn't a complete lie, and if it got her out of the lab, all the better. Still reeling from her conversation with Dr Barrow, she needed time to process.

"A headache? We can't use your nose today. You'll ruin our data. I'll write you a referral for the infirmary." He bustled across the room to his cluttered desk. "I just need to find my referral pad." His hands sifted through the papers, but his eyes were on Jacob. "Tell me what you think of the scent in the largest test tube. There's a questionnaire there for you to record your responses and—" He glanced down at his desk. "Where's that darn pad?" Maya joined him by his desk and handed him the pad from on top of a stack of papers. "Thank you." He grabbed a pen and began to complete the form. "Time of first symptom?"

"Well, I think it started when—"

"Jacob, not that one. The one with the white label." His eyes returned to the form, and he turned it over to reveal more questions. "Why do they need all this information?"

"If it's easier, you can just give me a hall pass for the garden." The infirmary nurse would just give her more pills, and what she needed was to be alone.

He lowered the pad, his eyes drawn back to Jacob and his precious test tubes.

"Or we can sit here and go over all these questions," said Maya. "You should probably include a paragraph about the history of my headaches. Like ever since I was small I—"

"I'll write you a pass." He scribbled on a notepad and shoved it at her before joining Jacob by the test tubes. Maya slipped out the door without as much as a look from either of them.

The only living thing in the Arc's "garden" was an old tree, its gnarled branches cut short by groundskeepers tired of cleaning up fallen leaves, but it was still her favorite place. When she had first visited the garden as a child, she had thrown off her shoes eager to feel the grass beneath her feet. Back home, she loved how the damp soft blades caressed her toes. She would play barefoot on their front lawn for hours, dancing in the sprinklers and practicing cartwheels with her dad. However, the stiff "grass" of the Arc garden had pricked her skin. As it turns out, artificial turf is much cheaper to maintain than grass. She learned the old tree survived only because it was more expensive to cut it down than to let it live.

Maya ran her hand along the low stone wall that sur-
rounded the garden until she reached the entrance. Some-
how being in the presence of the old tree grounded her.
She approached the trunk and placed her hands on its
rough bark, inhaling the stillness in the air. "Hello old
friend," she whispered to the tree and took a seat beside it.
She closed her eyes and allowed her muscles to relax into
its sturdy trunk.

If only she could be as strong as the tree, to be unmoved
by her surroundings. But she was weak—weak like the
yellow flowers her dad had tried to grow in the window
box. While her dad had said the flowers' sensitivity made
them special, her mom called them impractical. As soon
as the flowers had begun to wither, her mom dug them up
and replaced them with bugleweed. Bugleweed can grow
anywhere, even when the soil is polluted. It's that strong.

In spite of their differences, her parents seemed to have
loved each other. She hadn't seen them since her assess-
ment day. On the drive to the testing center, her mom tried
to hide her fear behind a cheerful voice and told her to be
strong. But Maya knew she wasn't coming home. Even at
seven, she understood she was a Fragile. The teasing from
the kids at school and the concerned looks from adults
reinforced how flawed she knew she was.

One summer evening about a year before her assess-
ment, she watched the neighborhood boys catch fireflies.
The jars lit up like lanterns as the sky faded into darkness.

To her horror, the tallest boy with messy blond hair took a firefly between his fingers and smashed it until his fingers glowed with the firefly's light. As the other boys gathered around to try, she screamed at them to stop. But they just laughed and continued to crush the fireflies. She lunged at the blond boy who shoved her to the ground. While the other boys laughed, one spat at her and mumbled "stupid Fragile" under his breath. Her bruises healed, but the words left a permanent scar.

Although her thick curls and dark brown eyes resembled her mother, her sensitivity came from her father. He did a good job hiding it, but she knew it was there. Right before she entered the testing room on her assessment day, she had met his tear-filled eyes. He smiled and mouthed "I'll always love you." It had been so long that she barely remembered what his love felt like.

Maya pressed her hands to her face and wiped her tears with her fingers. As soon as she moved her hands, a burning pain seared from her eyes to her temples. Had she put something in her eyes? She checked her hands and wiped them against her coveralls as the pain intensified. She rose and stumbled toward the drinking fountain, each footstep sending bolts of pain through her head.

When she reached the fountain, she doubled over in pain. Her fingers slid off the handle and she collapsed below it. An image of the girl with the ice-blue eyes tore across her mind. The girl's scream echoed in Maya's head and pounded against her temples—the pain sending a wave of nausea through her. Maya fought to pull herself up to the fountain. If she could just splash water on her face or rinse her eyes, she might stop the pain. She steadied herself with one hand, while the other pressed down on the dispenser. No water. She pressed again, harder this time, but nothing came out.

Maya gripped the metal edges of the drinking fountain. Though the girl felt trapped inside her, Maya saw her dark hair, pale skin, and blue eyes like she was staring her in the face. The girl clutched her head in anguish and continued to scream.

"Leave me alone!" What Maya intended as a whisper came out as a scream. Just as the pain became too much to bear, it made a violent retreat. She gasped for breath as she bent over the fountain.

"What's going on here?" A campus security officer approached her from the garden entrance.

Maya fumbled in her pockets and stammered. "Uh, I have a pass."

"Who were you yelling at?" He kept his eyes on her.

She retrieved the pass and handed it to him. "It was ants. I was yelling at the ants. I think one bit me. I was trying to wash them off, but there wasn't any water." She pressed the dispenser. "See?"

The CSO raised a brow. "Ants?"

"Yes."

He shook his head and muttered, "Fragiles," under his breath. He motioned toward her. "Come on, your time in the garden is over."

Maya followed him out of the garden with her head bent and her hands in her pockets. Her fingers curled around the bottle of pills Dr Barrow had given her. Maybe they could stop the visions. Unless she really was incurable.

Chapter 4

It was almost 8 am, so Maya rushed into the Brickstone administration building and headed for the media room. Bethany would never let her hear the end of it if she arrived late to help with the preparations for Commander Abigor's visit. At least Jacob would be there to make it more bearable.

The media room was just a shared space with cabinets and a photocopier outside the Arc faculty offices. Maya hurried past the empty offices. All classes and labs had been canceled so faculty could prepare for Abigor's arrival the next day. He hadn't visited the Arc since Maya was a child. According to Prim, it was a momentous occasion.

Jacob rose from the floor where he was painting a rendering of the Republic seal. "Hey, Maya. You wanna help me?"

"Sure, I–"

Bethany swooped in. "Actually, I was hoping Maya could write a tribute to the Commander. Maybe Tully could help with the–" Her eyes darted to the clock. "Where is Tully?"

"I'm here." Tully sauntered in and plopped down on the armchair in the corner. She picked up a magazine.

Bethany glared at Tully. "You're late."

Tully raised her middle finger in the air without looking up from her magazine.

Bethany huffed and returned her focus to Maya. "So, as I was saying, in the tribute it's important you express our undying gratitude to the Commander. You can do that, right?"

Seriously?

Maya shrugged. "Yeah, I think so."

"You must use words worthy of the Commander. You can use his memoir for inspiration. I have it right here." She reached into her backpack.

"It's okay. I'll be fine without it."

Bethany's face tensed, her lips pursed so tight that they almost disappeared. "I better write it."

Maya tried not to smile. "Good idea. I'll help Jacob paint."

After making sure they were painting, Bethany carried a poster board over to where Tully sat. "I know you do not want to be here, but I think if you just try, you could draw something amazing. I can share a couple of my favorite stories about the Commander for inspiration."

"Can you shut up already? It's like you want to have his baby or something." Tully put down the magazine and went in for the kill. "Oh, but wait. You can't, can you? None of us can."

Bethany froze except for a slight quiver of her chin.

"Tully, come on." Jacob glanced at Bethany.

Bethany smoothed the front of her coveralls and straightened her posture. "That's okay, Jacob. We would just reproduce weakness. The Commander knows what's best for us."

Tully scoffed. "You seriously believe that?"

The tension in the room pounded in Maya's head. "Can we just work on the posters? I'm getting a headache."

"Of course, Maya. That's what we're here for, to honor the Commander. You know, you seem to get a lot of headaches. You should really see the doctor about it. It could be some sort of weakness."

"It's just because she's an empath," said Jacob.

"What did you call her?" Although Tully enjoyed a good insult, she clearly preferred to be the one making it.

"An empath. It's why the two of you arguing gave her a headache. I overheard the nurses talking about it during my allergy treatment this morning."

"Dude, you have allergies, too? I thought you just couldn't handle being cold."

Jacob loosened his knit scarf. "I'm allergic to dust and pollen and have other environmental sensitivities, but aren't we talking about Maya?"

"You mean about me being an empath? I don't even know what that is." Whatever it was, Dr. Barrow never mentioned it. Could that be why she wasn't getting better?

Tully got up. "You know, it's probably in your file. They keep files on all of us. I saw them in Director Williams's office." She gestured toward the office as she walked toward it. "I've always wanted to read mine. I totally passed my first Fragile test, and I'm sure the second one was rigged. Who even gets re-tested at fourteen?"

Bethany put her hands on her hips. "If you're not a Fragile then why haven't you passed your review?"

"Apparently I have too many behavioral infractions or some bullshit." She tried the lock and then walked toward the photocopier. "Anyone else wanna see what's in their file?" She grabbed a couple of paper clips from the dish on the copier and returned to the office door. After straightening the paper clips and bending one at the end, she went to work on the lock. Moments later, she watched in triumph as the door swung open.

Bethany's eyes widened. "You don't dare go in there."

"Well, now that you dared me, I kinda have to, don't I?" Tully grinned and then narrowed her eyes on Bethany. "And don't dare narc on me if you know what's good for you." Tully strode into the office and called over her shoulder, "Hey Maya, you coming?"

Maya stood in the doorway. The filing cabinet beckoned from just steps away. A quick peek at her file would only take a minute. But if she got caught, an infraction on her record could be devastating. Without her good behavior, she had little to help her on her next review—the review that could make her a lifer. The heaviness in her legs anchored her to the ground, despite her mind's attempt to coax them forward.

Tully used one of the paper clips to pop the file cabinet lock and began rifling through the files. An overwhelming desire to know what was in her file lodged in Maya's gut. All those years of Dr. Barrow's notes had to be there—everything he knew about her—everything he might have hidden from her. Tully's confidence must have seeped in because she took a deep breath and stepped into the room.

An ornate portrait of Commander Abigor in his military uniform hung on the wall above the desk. Maya walked toward it, studying his strong jaw and piercing eyes. Though he had the chiseled features of a handsome man, the intensity of his gaze sent a chill up her spine. As she turned from the portrait, she bumped into Director Williams's desk knocking a file to the floor. She dropped to her knees to gather the contents of the folder which had "Reconditioning Center Phase 1" printed across it. Her hands shook as she placed the folder on the desk, causing a photo to slip out. As soon as she grabbed the photo, a splitting pain pierced her head and her lungs constricted. She shoved the photo into the folder and stumbled back against the wall, gasping for breath.

Tully's voice rang out. "I knew it. I don't belong here. They messed with my test scores." She gripped a file in her hand.

Not so loud, Tully. We'll get caught. The words remained lodged inside her.

Director Williams appeared in the doorway, her tall frame squared toward Tully. "What are you doing in my office?"

Maya's stomach dropped as she froze against the wall.

"Maya was just studying the portrait of our benevolent Commander to inspire the poem she's writing for him." An attempt at an innocent smile spread across Tully's face.

"And you?" The steadiness in her voice masked any emotion. Her dark eyes locked on Tully.

"I found out what I already know. That I don't belong here. My scores got changed. I was cheated." Tully's voice rose with anger. "And look at this. My Dad gave two hundred thousand dollars to this place. What the hell? Did he pay you to take me away?"

The director approached Tully and put her hand out for the file. "Because you're trespassing in my office, I have no obligation to explain anything to you. But, if you must know, your assessor was new and made some errors, so your score had to be corrected. Please give me the file."

Tully held on to the file. "And the money? Why'd my dad pay you?"

"I'm not at liberty to discuss the charitable donations the Arc receives. Now, give me the file." She took the file and turned to Maya. "I'm disappointed in you, Maya. You should really be careful who you associate with. I have no choice but to note this infraction in your files which will impact your next review."

Still reeling with pain, Maya winced at the director's words. An infraction on her record? Just two more and she would never go home. Avoiding the director's stare, she mumbled, "I'm sorry," and headed for the door. As the walls closed in, heat rose in her chest and tears burned her eyes.

Maya barely noticed Bethany's "I told you so face" as she sprinted to the bathroom. She could taste the bile rising from her stomach. Jacob bounded after her saying something about trying to stall Director Williams and Bethany's telling, but his words dissolved into a blur as she flung open the bathroom door and vomited in the sink. Shaking, she splashed cold water on her face and tried to steady her breathing. As a whirlwind of emotions surged through her, one thing was clear. Something happened when she touched that photo, and she needed to know why.

Chapter 5

THE GREAT HALL BUZZED with anticipation and a whisper of fear. Even the loud red, blue, and gold decorations Bethany insisted upon using were no match for the chaotic emotions invading Maya. Professor Prim paced the aisle barking commands at the staff as they shifted the red carpet to cover the cracked floor. Two of the dining monitors worked feverishly to straighten the enormous portrait of Commander Abigor that had been unfurled behind the stage. For once, the Fragiles' coveralls provided the only gray in the room. And they only filled three rows behind the faculty and staff.

Maya clasped her hands in her lap unsure, if she should be excited or afraid.

The March of the Republic blared through the hall, jarring Maya from her chair as everyone around her rose. Tully remained seated until Professor Prim's icy stare brought her to her feet. As Commander Abigor made his way across the red carpet with his chin held high and his chest thrust forward, his presence filled the room. When the music subsided, he took a seat on his golden throne at the front of the stage, smiling and waving to the audience. The gleam of his teeth matched the bright white of his officer's jacket, and his hair was styled to perfection.

"That's gotta be a wig," said Tully.

Maya stifled a giggle and tensed when Professor Prim's glare seared through her.

Bethany stood at the podium, bubbling with excitement. She cleared her throat before reading her tribute. "We give thanks to Commander Abigor for his military service and his role in quelling the terrible insurrection that nearly destroyed our great economy. In his infinite wisdom, he created the Arc to rehabilitate the most fragile in society, and for this, we are eternally grateful."

Commander Abigor took the stage, his array of medals glinting in the bright light, and beamed at Bethany. She clasped her hands to her chest and gazed at him with a grin until Prim ushered her off the stage. Maya barely remembered Abigor's first visit, but he looked so much older than his portraits. Even his thick dark hair and winter tan couldn't hide the years carved on his face.

As he scanned the room with a tight-lipped smile, beads of sweat glistened off his forehead. "It warms my heart to see so many administrators and Fragiles here today to honor me."

"As if we had a choice." Tully elbowed Maya. "I bet Director Williams made the staff come, too."

Maya stiffened and glanced at Prim. Maybe Tully didn't care about getting in trouble, but she did. She shifted her body away from Tully and tried to focus on Abigor's speech.

Despite her best efforts, her mind wandered to what Jacob had said about her being an empath and her growing obsession with visiting the library to research it. Dr. Barrow was an expert, but he might be concealing the truth about her disorder. With her luck, it was probably something even worse. She had freaked out from simply touching a photo after all. She would head to the library as soon as they were dismissed.

"—we're getting closer to being able to cure Fragiles in a matter of days instead of years." The words caught her attention. "As founder of the Arc and the Nationwide Initiative to Rehabilitate Fragiles, I'm excited to share that our hard work is paying off. We'll soon be moving out of the experimental phase and into the widespread and immediate rehabilitation of all Fragiles." His voice reached a powerful crescendo as his eyes panned the Fragiles. "Who knows, maybe you can be our next success." His eyes rested on Maya. Could she really be cured?

Although his mannerisms were steeped in confidence, Maya sensed an uneasiness she couldn't place. As if on cue, a member of the Commander's entourage began to clap, triggering a roar of applause to burst forth from the audience.

Once Director Williams dismissed them, Maya hurried through the winding passages that led to the library. Although it was easy to get lost in the maze-like corridors, she could have found her way there in the dark. The quiet solitude of the library suited her. Having read all the storybooks years ago, she still enjoyed re-reading her favorites. Curled up in the reading nooks, she would get lost in stories about brave adventurers who never let anything stand in their way. She would fantasize about what life would be like if she was strong like the heroes in the stories—what life would be like if she wasn't a Fragile.

Within minutes she reached the library entrance. She approached the search console and wiped the sweat from her forehead. She glanced over both shoulders, typed "empath" into the search bar, and held her breath. The search console returned only one item: "The Modern Manual of Psychological Disorders and Diseases, Volume 3." Her shoulders dropped. The book was in the restricted section.

She took a deep breath and approached the library attendant counter with the search console print-out. The attendant glanced up from his magazine with a pinched expression. "Yes?"

Avoiding eye contact, she handed him the slip of paper. "I'd like this book, please."

The attendant studied the paper, stared at her, and then returned his gaze to the paper. "Reason?"

She cleared her throat. "Uh, it's for a research project." She wiped her sweaty palms on her coveralls.

He narrowed his eyes on her and wrote in his logbook. "Wait here." He disappeared behind the door marked Authorized Personnel Only.

As the minutes ticked by, Maya's heart started to pound. She glanced at the door and backed away from the counter.

The attendant returned with a large, thick manual and handed it to her. "You have ten minutes."

She lugged the massive book to the back of the reading area. Just how many psychological disorders were there? She took a seat in one of the cubicles and stared at the cover, unable to open it. Torn between wanting to know the truth and fearing it, she lifted the cover. As she turned the pages one by one, her desire to know grew. She thumbed through the book until she found the section on 'empathic disorders' between 'depressive sensitivity disorders' and 'erratic behavior disorders.'

According to the manual, empaths were once thought to be able to sense the feelings of others, but modern psychology discovered it was a narcissistic delusion that caused some people to blame their own emotional and physical pain on others. While empaths had historically used meditation, spending time in nature, or creating a physical routine to empty themselves of negative feelings, these "folk remedies" were not based on science and could be dangerous. The only acceptable modern treatment for empaths was psychotropic medications.

Psychotropic medication.

Her pills.

Maybe Jacob was right about her being an empath. Strong emotions had always overwhelmed her, but the manual called it a narcissistic delusion. Wasn't a narcissist someone who only cared about themselves? Although she often got other people's feelings tangled up with her own, sensing other's pain felt so real. She leaned back in her chair and let out a deep sigh. Instead of answers, she had more questions. Before returning the book, she copied the information about the folk remedies into her notebook, just in case.

Maya made it to the dining commons just in time for dinner. She took a seat across from Jacob who smiled at her. "Where'd you disappear to after the Commander left?"

"The library." She fidgeted with her fork. "You know, just to relax from the stress of Abigor's visit. It was either that or a shower."

"I would have come with you." Jacob cleared his throat as he loosened his scarf. "Uh, to the library, I mean, not the shower."

"I know what you meant." Did she? She sensed that weird vibe from him again.

Tully slammed her tray down on the table "Ugh, I'm so sick of chicken." Maya breathed a sigh of relief. An expert in anxious Jacob, she had no idea how to deal with awkward Jacob.

"Actually, last night it was baked turkey with way too much rosemary." Jacob pushed aside his plate.

"All tastes the same to me." Tully grabbed a fistful of fries from Maya's plate and sat down. "I thought at least they would give us pizza tonight to celebrate Commander A-big-snore's visit. Can that guy talk or what?"

Maya reached for her last fry, but Tully grabbed it.

"Sorry. I usually snag a plate of fries from the little kids, but there are only a few of them left and those seem to prefer vegetables. Who does that?"

Jacob glanced at the little kids area. "There's been a lot less kids around lately. I think Ms. Petersen's class is completely gone." He fidgeted with his scarf. "We haven't gotten any new kids in a while either. I wonder what's going on."

Maya checked behind her before lowering her voice. "It might not be related, but when we were in the director's office, I saw a folder with 'reconditioning center' on it. Maybe kids are being sent there?"

"Reconditioning center? What's that? What else did it say?" Anxious Jacob was back.

"I'm not sure." The memory of the terror she had felt touching the photo came rushing back.

Tully picked up a chicken leg from her plate. She narrowed her eyes on Jacob with a sly grin. "I wouldn't be surprised if they're torturing kids there." She chomped on the chicken leg without taking her eyes off him.

"Tully." Maya glanced at Jacob.

Tully, oblivious to the dining monitor who had approached their table, turned to Maya. "You do realize they locked us up here so who knows what they are capable of? Don't think for a moment the Arc is not a prison."

The monitor rested his hand on Tully's shoulder. "Is everything okay here?"

"Yep, just enjoying the prison food." Tully shook off his hand and took another big bite of chicken.

He straightened his monitor badge and glared at Tully and then Maya. "Well, I observed you sharing food. Need I remind you that–"

"Yeah, I know, sharing leads to idleness, blah, blah, blah. But Maya wasn't sharing. I was taking. You know, like stealing?" Tully mimed grabbing a fry from Maya's plate with exaggerated flair. "You know, because competition breeds excellence?" A smirk spread across her face.

The monitor scowled. "I'll be keeping an eye on you both." He glanced at Maya and Jacob before heading back to his station.

Maya waited to speak until the monitor was across the room. She turned to Tully and whispered, "Do you really think they could be torturing kids?"

"You mean beyond forcing them to wear polyester coveralls and watch boring-ass documentaries about our glorious economy?"

Tully shrugged. "I doubt it."

Jacob got up. "Well, if there is a reconditioning center, it's probably just for kids who are really messed up so I wouldn't worry about it, Maya."

Aware that he was convincing himself, she mustered a smile. "You're probably right." She didn't have the heart to remind him that she was one of the most messed up kids of all.

Later that night, Maya lay in bed staring at the ceiling. Her breathing had returned to normal, but the nightmare burned fresh in her mind. Unable to close her eyes without seeing the girl with the ice-blue eyes, she kicked her feet loose from her blanket and threw herself onto her side.

It was bad enough having to feel real people's emotions without some girl haunting her sleep. As she adjusted her pillow, her eyes rested on the bottle of pills on her night-stand. She reached for the bottle and fiddled with the cap.

The cap to her psychotropic medication.

For her narcissistic delusions.

She tossed the bottle into the nightstand drawer and slammed it shut. With one hand, she fumbled for the flashlight on her nightstand and balanced it to illuminate the concrete walls. Aside from the thin window high above her bed, it provided the only light source until morning. While she longed to go outside and clear her head in the fresh night air, her room would not be unlocked for hours. She let out a deep breath and slung her feet off the bed onto the cold tile floor.

The tiles chilled her feet as she tiptoed across the room to retrieve her backpack. After rummaging through it, she returned to bed with a crumpled notebook page. She scanned the notes she had taken at the library until she found the line about connecting with nature to empty oneself of negative emotions.

Aside from the small plant on her nightstand, she was surrounded by concrete. She picked up the plant and set it beside her on the bed. Maybe it would be enough nature. Now she just needed to figure out how to empty herself. But how do you empty yourself of something that's a part of you? Was it in her head? Her stomach? She closed her eyes and scanned her body for the emotions trapped inside. She whispered, "Go away," and opened her eyes. Nothing.

She let out a heavy sigh and placed the plant on her lap. Slowing her breathing, she closed her eyes and imagined a wave of light flowing through her. She pictured the light washing the emotions through her and out her fingertips into the plant. Her body tensed as the pain flooded through her. but relaxed as she released the energy through her fingers. It felt good to let it go. When she opened her eyes, the stiffness in her neck and shoulders had subsided. She yawned and set the plant back on her nightstand, brushing aside the fallen leaves. Maybe she could get a few hours of sleep before sunrise.

Chapter 6

EVEN THOUGH SHE SLEPT the rest of the night without any nightmares, she couldn't shake the feeling that the girl from her dream was real— and in trouble. Either she was losing her mind, or the girl needed her help. If she mentioned the girl to Dr. Barrow, he would call her delusional and record it in her file. Jacob would have an aneurysm if she even mentioned it to him, and Bethany would probably report her for being unstable. The one person who might be able to help was also the person who could get her in the most trouble.

Maya scanned the dining commons for Tully. The tables in the little kid area remained empty, their metal surfaces glistening, untouched by the normal breakfast rush.

She spotted Tully alone in the corner, so she took a deep breath and approached her. At least Jacob had early lab hours. She didn't need him reminding her what a bad idea it was to go to Tully for help. Trouble followed Tully, and the last thing Maya needed was to get caught in its tailwind.

When Maya placed her tray across from Tully, she glanced up from her breakfast. "What the hell happened to you? You look like shit." Maya picked up her tray, drawn to the numerous empty tables that surrounded Tully.

She took a deep breath and told herself it was just Tully's way of saying good morning. "I didn't sleep well. Mind if I sit down?"

"Sure, go ahead."

"Thanks." Maya sat and picked up her fork.

Tully held up a piece of bacon. "You know, you might sleep better if you ate normal food instead of twigs and grass."

"It's called fruit." Maya poked the syrupy lump with her fork. Were canned pears even considered fruit?

"Whatever." Tully shoved the bacon in her mouth. "So, what's up?"

Maya shifted in her seat, unable to form the words.

As Tully continued to stare at her, Maya fiddled with her fork. Would it be too weird if she got up now?

Maya put down her fork. If someone was going to know what a freak she was, it might as well be Tully. She checked over her shoulder and lowered her voice. "I know this sounds weird, but I think someone's in trouble and needs my help. Like maybe here or at the reconditioning center."

"Here?" Tully rolled her eyes. "Nothing ever happens here. It's seriously my hell loop. Protect Fragiles from the outside world, my ass. More like protect us from having any fun."

"But didn't you say the Arc was like a prison? What if something bad is happening?"

"I was just messing with Jacob. Why would you think someone's in trouble?"

Maya picked up her fork and moved the pear around her plate without looking up. "Well, I…"

"Just spit it out already."

"I've been having nightmares…or maybe visions?" The floodgate burst open for her words to flow. "And I get this horrible feeling that something terrible is happening to someone. It's like I feel her pain. I can even see her face and her ice-blue eyes. I think she needs my help." It felt good to tell someone, despite that someone being Tully.

"You do realize how weird you sound, right? It's probably all those pills you take, making you hallucinate or something."

"You mean morning medication? You don't take it?"

"Let them drug me? No way. I just hide it under my tongue and spit it out later. The nurses never even check."

"But the visions just started." Maya dropped her voice. "The only other time I've felt like that was when we were in the director's office, and I touched the folder. There was a photo in the folder with information about the reconditioning center, but I didn't get a good look at it. Maybe if I could see it again it would—"

"Cool. I'm always up for a break-in."

"What? Break into Director Williams's office? After what happened last time? I thought maybe I could talk to her or something."

"We won't get caught this time. I have a plan. I never got a chance to finish reading my file. Besides, asking her is no good. Adults always lie."

Maya put down her fork. "Do you have any ideas that don't involve breaking and entering?"

"What fun would that be?" Tully grinned. "So, are you in?"

She chewed on her bottom lip. What if they got caught? She might get sent to the adult ward.

Forever.

The thought made her stomach churn. "It's too risky. Maybe the whole thing with the girl is nothing."

"Feeling some girl's pain doesn't sound like nothing to me. But suit yourself. I'm fine going solo." She pushed her tray aside and got up.

"Wait." Maya took a deep breath. "Say I decide to do it, when would you even want to?"

"Tonight's movie night, right?"

"Yeah. The second Saturday of the month."

"Then tonight it is." She put on her backpack. "I gotta go do something, but meet me at the terrace after dinner if you're in."

Tully's empty chair stared at Maya from across the table.

No matter how badly she wanted to find out the truth, it wasn't worth the risk. Last time she listened to Tully she ended up with an infraction, and the thought of never going home was unbearable. She cleared her tray and headed to the door.

While she waited in line for her medication, she thought about what Tully had said about the hallucinations. When the nurse handed her the pill cup, she dumped the pill in her mouth. She brought the water cup to her lips, but then shifted the pill under her tongue. Once the nurse glanced at her open mouth, she ducked out the door and spit the pill in her hand. She discarded it in a nearby trash receptacle and hurried to the emotions lab. Dr. Nix would be livid if she arrived late.

When Maya arrived at the lab, Dr. Nix sat typing at the computer console. The "tap-tap-tap" of her nails clicking on the keyboard echoed through the room. Maya slumped down in the evaluation chair and waited for Dr. Nix to notice her. The rapid tapping continued while Dr. Nix stared at the screen with her lips pursed. Every few seconds, she jerked her head to the side to glare at her notes before returning her focus to the screen.

Tap. Tap. Tap.

Maya rubbed her jawbone and stretched her neck.

After a few more minutes, Dr. Nix got up and approached Maya, her voice curt. "I'm examining logical decision making under the threat of an emotional response. You'll be given a series of forced choice questions after being exposed to a stimulus. Do you understand?"

Maya swallowed and wrung her hands in her lap. "Yes, Dr. Nix."

Dr. Nix rolled a tray in front of her containing a small keypad, a white packet, and what looked like a clunky pair of binoculars. "Once the viewing apparatus is in place and we start the test, you will use the keypad to record your responses." She tore open the packet and pulled out several electrodes. When Dr. Nix attached the electrodes to her head, Maya flinched. Dr. Nix huffed and continued attaching the viewing apparatus over Maya's head. "These electrodes just measure brain activity. They can't give a shock unless connected to a source."

With the apparatus in place, Dr. Nix returned to her computer. "During the test, you'll watch several short scenes. Immediately after each scene, you will be given a choice on what the outcome should be. Once the options appear on the screen, you must select one within five seconds. Understand?"

"Yes." Maya wiped her palms on her coveralls and placed her hand on the keypad. For years, she failed almost every forced choice test. She would do something stupid like choose to save a forest over the expansion of a corporation, harming the economy. As she got older, she learned to pretend she wasn't a Fragile and got better at the tests. Jacob once told her pretending to be something and being something aren't the same thing, but it was the best she could do.

As soon as the video in the headset lit up the screen, Maya's whole body tensed. A family dressed in torn, mud-caked clothing scavenged for food across a barren wasteland. The mother held a crying baby to her chest. Although the electrodes could only measure Maya's brain waves, they heated against her scalp.She rubbed her palms on her thighs as the heat intensified.

As the baby continued to wail, the pale face of the girl with the ice-blue eyes tore across its image. Pain surged through Maya's head. The girl screamed in terror as the electrodes on her own head lit up like flames. Racked with excruciating pain, Maya groaned and gripped her chair. Unable to bear it any longer, she tore off the headset and the electrodes, but the pain only intensified. Overcome by the girl's pain, Maya clutched her head in anguish.

"What the hell?" Dr. Nix snarled. "How dare you move my equipment."

Maya gasped for breath and struggled to compose herself. The pain had just begun to dissipate. "I'm so sorry. My head was hurting. I don't know what happened. Please don't tell Dr. Barrow. I'll do the test. Please, just let me try again. I promise." Her body shook as tears pooled in her eyes.

Dr. Nix checked her watch as Maya sobbed. "Fine, but only because I need this data today. But any more problems and I am reporting this as an infraction to Director Williams."

Maya nodded and held still for Dr. Nix to configure the equipment. Once it was back in place, Dr. Nix returned to her computer and started the video. Despite the ache in Maya's heart, she tried to shut out the crying baby and the parents' despair and focus on giving the correct answers. Another infraction was the last thing she needed now that she had decided to break into the director's office with Tully.

Chapter 7

LATER THAT EVENING, FRAGILES gathered on the terrace in front of the jumbo screen. Bethany had staked out a place in front, like always, with one of the blankets staff passed out during movie nights. Tully nodded at Maya, and together they walked toward Bethany.

When they passed her blanket, Tully turned to Maya. "But it's the perfect time for me to pull that stunt on the Abigor statue in the garden. I'll do it while Director Williams makes her boring speech before the movie."

They rounded the corner and waited. Sure enough, Bethany arose in a huff and stomped across the terrace to the campus security officer stationed at the administration building. She spoke with him and returned to her blanket by the screen. Because the garden was located on the other side of the compound, it would take the CSO at least fifteen minutes to get there and back.

While Maya waited with Tully for the guard to leave his post, her stomach knotted.

Jacob came up behind them. "Hey, I was looking for you. I saved a place for us to watch the movie."

"Um, I'm not …" Her eyes darted to Tully.

"We weren't going to watch the movie, were we, Maya? They all die in the end. No need to watch." Tully gestured with her head for Maya to start walking. The guard had just left his post.

"They all die? I thought it was supposed to be a comedy," said Jacob.

"It's a dark comedy." She nudged Maya forward. "Come on, it's time."

"I'll come with you. I mean if the movie isn't good anyway, right?" Jacob grinned at Maya.

Maya shrugged. It was hopeless to try to get rid of him.

"Okay, just be quiet. And no questions." Tully led them around the building.

Night had begun to fall, so Jacob took out his flashlight. He always carried it with him after dark "in case of emergencies".

Tully whipped around and grabbed the flashlight. "Seriously?" She turned it off and handed it back to him.

Tully approached the outer door and tried the lock. "Shit. It's locked."

"You didn't think the CSO would lock the door?" asked Jacob.

"The CSOs are idiots. You know how much crap I've gotten away with?" Tully tried the door again. "No reason to waste real guards on Fragiles."

Jacob crossed his arms, his back against the building. "I know you said no questions, but breaking into the admin building?"

Maya met his eyes. "I know it looks bad, but I'll explain later. It's really important. I promise."

Tully bent over to examine the lock. Maya peered over her shoulder. "Can't you use the paper clips you brought to use for the director's office?"

"Different locking mechanism." Tully stood straight and surveyed the building. "I got an idea. You're the lightest, right?"

"I guess." Maya followed Tully's gaze to a small half-open window about ten feet off the ground. "Why?"

"We'll boost you up. On our shoulders. You can let us in from the inside."

"Um." Maya glanced from the window to Jacob. "I guess we could try, right?"

Jacob shook his head.

"We don't have much time." Tully positioned herself against the building and next to Jacob.

Jacob scowled but grasped hands with Tully so Maya could use their interlocked hands as a stepping stool.

Using their shoulders for balance, Maya placed her foot in their hands. They lifted her until she could climb to their shoulders. Because they kept shifting, she nearly lost her balance when she reached for the window ledge.

"Just grab it," said Tully through gritted teeth.

Maya grasped the window ledge and pressed her feet against their shoulders for leverage.

"Someone's coming." Jacob's heavy whisper sounded from below.

Tully and Jacob's shoulders dropped from beneath her feet. Legs dangling, she struggled to pull herself upward through the window. She pulled with all her might until her upper body made it inside. As she balanced halfway through the snug opening, she scanned her surroundings. The tiled bathroom floor dropped too far down for her to land safely. She stretched her arms toward the top of the bathroom stall closest to her, but it remained out of reach.

While her legs continued to hang outside for anyone to see, she gripped the interior of the window and strained to pull more of her body through the opening. The window ledge cut into her stomach as she inched forward.

With one more lunge, she propelled herself through the window. For a moment, her fingers gripped the stall, but she couldn't hang on. She slipped down the side of the stall and fell to the floor on her backside, her bent arms barely preventing her head from slamming against the tile. Pain shot up her back.

Once she got her bearings, she crouched against the wall and listened. If they had been caught, there should have been noises. Aside from the ache in her tailbone, everything seemed intact, so she got up and headed for the door. She inched it open and listened. Silence. She slipped into the hallway and limped toward the outer door.

When Maya reached the door, she pushed it open just enough to peak out. Seeing nothing, she closed it. She inched it open again, but this time a little wider. Someone grabbed the door from the side and flung it open.

Maya froze.

"What took you so long?" Tully pushed Maya aside and entered the building.

Jacob followed Tully, gripping his scarf around his neck. Outside the Director's office, Tully fiddled with the lock. She struggled to get it to open in the dark. Maya dug her nails into her palms. They were running out of time.

Jacob huffed and used his flashlight to illuminate the door lock for Tully. "I blame you if anything happens to us."

"And I blame you for tagging along." Tully shook the handle and the lock clicked.

Inside the office, a light outside the window cast a shadow on a portrait of Commander Abigor. The dark shadows twisted his face into an image so sinister it took Maya's breath away. As Maya approached the director's desk, her stomach clenched. Just as she feared, the folder was gone. "It's not here," she whispered. "We should go." She inched away from the desk.

Tully stopped rummaging through the filing cabinets. "Check the drawers." She glanced at the clock. "We still have four minutes until the guard gets back from the garden."

Maya slid open the top drawer and Jacob approached to help her search with his flashlight. Dread crawled up her spine as she sifted through the contents. Under a stack of papers, she found it. The words "Reconditioning Center Phase I" in ominous black letters stared up at her. She placed it on the desk, unable to open it.

Jacob nudged her. "Is that it?"

She nodded and inched open the cover. A memo dated earlier that week caught her eye. "Jacob, look at this. It's an update on the progress of the reconditioning center. It says, despite collateral complications resulting in irreparable psychological and/or physical damage to some of the younger test subjects, they have been approved to advance to phase two early next month." She raised a hand to her mouth as the words sank in.

"What the hell? Let me see that." Tully ripped the memo from Maya's hands.

Irreparable damage?

Maya's search became frantic as she riffled through the folder, freezing when she came to the photo. She recognized the girl from her visions instantly. "It's her." Maya picked up the photo with the words SUBJECT A written across it. As she cradled it in her hands, an ear-splitting scream tore through her skull. Her whole body burned with pain. The girl's pain. Her trauma. Maya doubled over on the verge of collapse, clutching the photo. To keep from fainting, she forced a few long exhales. Once she steadied herself, she willed the pain to flow out of her body through her fingertips like she had practiced. As the pain moved through her, she dropped the photo and reached for the desk for balance.

"Are you okay?" Jacob grabbed her hand and immediately recoiled. "Ow! What the heck, Maya? What did you do?" He rubbed his hand as if he were in pain.

Maya struggled to catch her breath. "Nothing. What are you talking about?"

"My hand, you did something to my hand. As soon as you touched me. It still stings." Jacob shook his hand.

"We got to go. NOW!" Tully headed for the door.

Maya ran out of the office behind Tully with Jacob right behind her. By the time they reached the terrace, Director Williams had finished her speech. They made their way to the place Jacob had saved with blankets and sat together in silence. When the movie began, Maya stared at the screen, but her mind continued to race. Had she really hurt Jacob?

But how? She pulled one of the blankets across shoulders and tightened it around her.

A moment later, Maya sensed a presence nearby and turned to find Director Williams standing behind them. "The three of you. Come with me. Now.

Chapter 8

"Uh, Director, I wasn't really a part of it. I mean, I was just—" Jacob stumbled on his words when Tully shot him a glare.

"You'll have plenty of time to explain yourself." Director Williams motioned for them to follow her to one of the classrooms adjacent to the terrace.

When they entered the room, Maya's throat tightened, and Jacob appeared to be on the verge of hyperventilation. Tully strode in beside them with a smug smile on her face. Director Williams motioned for them to take a seat at the table across from where Bethany sat with her hands in her lap. Once they were all seated, Director Williams dropped a balled-up piece of white fabric onto the table.

"Do any of you recognize this?" Director Williams motioned to the Arc-issued underwear displayed on the table.

Tully sat back and crossed her arms with a gleam in her eye. "Looks like underwear to me."

"Yes, Tully. And do you know where this underwear was found?"

"Were you going through my clothes again looking for something to wear?"

If Director Williams was annoyed, she didn't show it. "It was found in the garden—" She paused and cleared her throat, "—On the head of the statue of Commander Abigor."

Bethany twisted her face into a grimace, while Tully bit her lip, shaking with stifled laughter.

Maya tried to keep her voice steady. "To be fair, Director, that underwear could belong to anyone. All the girls have them."

"Yes, Maya is right. Some of the boys, too," Jacob added. "You know because boxers can cause chafing. I mean, uh, at least that is what I heard."

Director Williams's gaze shifted to Bethany who sat with her eyes focused on her lap.

"Bethany, would you like to share what you reported to me earlier?"

Bethany straightened her shoulders. "I overheard Tully tell Maya she was going to deface the statue of our glorious Commander, so I immediately reported it to the CSO."

"Thank you, Bethany. Would you like to add anything, Tully? Please keep in mind, I did see the three of you arrive together at the terrace after my speech."

"Okay, you caught me. I did it." Tully glanced at Maya. "But Maya was only trying to stop me. I ran into her and Jacob when I was walking back and told them I never made it into the garden."

Director Williams stared at Maya. "Is that correct?"

"Uh, yes. That's correct." Her mouth was so dry she choked on the words. "But Jacob didn't know anything about it."

Director Williams stared at Jacob who nodded. She then turned to Bethany, "Thank you, Bethany. You may go."

Bethany hesitated. "Excuse me, Director, but will I be getting a commendation in my file?"

Director Williams raised a brow. "A commendation?"

"Yes, for reporting this infraction and not being swayed by any pity I might feel for Maya?"

"Yes, of course. I'll be sure to note it in your file."

"Thank you, Director." Bethany rose and rushed out the door, avoiding Tully's death stare.

Director Williams turned to Tully. "Tully, because of your willful disregard for Arc property and your disrespect for the Commander, you will be assigned to one month of laundry duty." Her eyes locked on Maya. "Because you failed to alert Arc authorities of a potential act of vandalism, you will be prohibited from entering the garden for two weeks. These infractions will be noted on your permanent records. As you know, three infractions lead to an automatic failure of your next review, so you are on very thin ice." She turned to Jacob. "Jacob, please consider this a warning. You are all dismissed."

Maya followed the others out of the meeting room and back to the blanket to watch the movie in progress. Tully was right, they had already seen it, but at least everyone didn't die in the end. Not that it mattered since she barely paid attention. A two-week ban from the one place that made her feel whole was bad enough, but the second infraction on her record could prevent her from ever going home.

After the movie, Maya walked with Jacob and Tully back to their rooms for lights out. When they approached the dormitories, Maya turned to Tully. "I thought telling Bethany you were pranking the statue was to throw off the CSO. Did you really put the underwear there?"

"Yeah, I did it earlier. I've always wanted to and thought it would be good to give the guard something to do when he went to check the statue. So, basically a win-win." Tully laughed. "Cool how it worked out though, right?"

Jacob scowled. "It didn't really work out. Director Williams wasn't happy with us."

"Yeah, and now I have two infractions." Maya stopped walking. "What if I get sent to the adult ward?"

Tully scoffed. "Adult ward? You know that's not really a thing, right?"

"What do you mean?" asked Maya.

"They dump adult Fragiles out in the wasteland, like in a dungeon or something. The kid of the Council Chairman who went to my school used to blab about it."

Jacob tightened his scarf around his neck. "That can't be right. He probably made it up to get attention."

"Believe what you want. I couldn't care less since I'll be breaking out of the Arc."

Maya exchanged glances with Jacob. "Breaking out?"

"Did you read the rest of the memo? For phase two, they are going to start sending teenagers from the Arc to a reconditioning center in the Republic to be cured. And I, for one, do not want to be cured of anything. I've been planning to escape since I got here anyway. I already found a map in the security booth and lifted a compass from the science room."

"I don't want to be sent there either," said Jacob. "But escaping is not an option." His eyes shifted to Maya. "Maybe we could alert someone on the outside to help?"

"Alert who?" asked Tully. "We can't even send letters to our families. And Maya, think about the girl in the photo. Remember what the memo said about permanent damage? Don't you want to help her?"

Jacob's voice rose. "Tully, we can't do anything crazy based on some memo and a photo." He turned back to

Maya. "What is it about the girl in the photo? What happened in the office when you hurt my hand?"

"I told you I didn't mean to hurt you, Jacob." Maya struggled to hold back the tears. "I don't want anyone to be hurt. I just can't take the pain anymore. It's killing me." She covered her face in her hands, wiping her eyes. When no one said anything, she glanced at Jacob. "After you said I was an empath, I researched it. I've been practicing letting bad feelings pass through me, and I think I somehow passed them into you."

Jacob frowned. "That's impossible. Maybe it was static electricity or something."

"But I was focusing on the pain going out my hand when you touched me. I know it sounds crazy."

Tully's voice softened. "Maybe this place is making you crazy."

"Tully, you're not helping. She could be getting worse." He looked at Maya with an expression she'd seen countless times, just not from him. The one person who never looked at her like she was a freak— just did.

Chapter 9

THE HALL MONITOR STOPPED Maya as she headed to class. He held out a pass, "You need to report to Dr. Barrow's office."

"Me?" Her throat tightened. Why would Dr. Barrow need to see her? Unless he knows.

The monitor shoved the pass into her hand. "Yes. You need to go now."

"Okay." She gripped the pass and headed back down the hallway.

When Maya arrived at the office, Dr. Barrow glanced up from where he sat across the desk from Director Williams.

Director Williams motioned for her to enter. "Maya, please come in and have a seat."

Maya took the empty chair next to Director Williams and clasped her hands in her lap. Commander Abigor's gaze bore into her from his portrait above the desk. Her stomach knotted, another infraction would send her straight to the adult ward.

Dr. Barrow leaned across her desk toward Maya. "I called you into my office because we have some concerns about you."

"Okay," she nodded and squirmed in the rigid metal chair.

"Director Williams told me about some behavioral incidents. For example, trespassing in her office—" Every muscle in Maya's body stiffened. Her fingers dug into her thighs. "—when you were supposed to be preparing for Commander Abigor's visit."

She let out a heavy breath.

Director Williams furrowed her brows. "Dr. Barrow suggested these incidents may be due to a worsening of your condition. How you may be acting out as a coping mechanism. Is that right, Doctor?"

"Yes, that's correct. In some instances, neurotic hypersensitivity can lead to deviant behavior. Because your affliction is so extreme, you may be at greater risk."

Deviant behavior.

Greater risk.

Is that why she had hurt Jacob's hand? Was she dangerous?

"Maya?" Director Williams stared at her. "Do you understand what Dr. Barrow said?"

"Yes, I think so."

"It's important you understand the severity of this matter. You only have one more chance to pass your review, and you already have two behavioral infractions. If you break any more rules over the course of the year, you will be transferred to the adult ward. Is that clear?"

"Yes, Director."

"Good, now Dr. Barrow has some recommendations for your treatment."

"Yes, Maya, there are some excellent new treatments. Quite exciting actually." His face lit up. "You may have heard the Commander refer to it during his speech?"

Maya shuddered. "You mean the center?"

Dr. Barrow raised his eyebrows and glanced at Director Williams. He cleared his throat. "I don't recall the Commander mentioning anything about a center. What center are you referring to?"

Maya's palms began to sweat as she racked her brain. How could she be so stupid? Abigor never mentioned the center. "Uh, I mean the cure," she stammered. "The center of his speech was about curing Fragiles." Maybe he would buy it.

Dr. Barrow narrowed his eyes on her. "Yes, that is correct. There's a promising new procedure that may be able to help you. Minimally invasive, of course." His desk phone rang so he picked it up. "Hello? Yes, of course. I'll be right there." He hung up the phone. "I'm needed urgently in the lab." He got up and spoke to the Director. "Can you make sure Maya gets to class?"

"Of course." Director Williams watched him as he headed out the door.

After Dr. Barrow left, Director Williams stared at Maya and brought her hand to her mouth. A heaviness consumed Maya. If she wasn't mistaken, part of the dread searing through her flowed from Director Williams.

Catching herself gazing, Director Williams got up. "Thank you for coming, Maya. You should get to class now."

Unable to move, Maya cleared her throat. "Excuse me, but I was wondering what the adult ward is like. In case I'm remanded. Like, is it here near the Arc or..."

Director Williams walked to the door and closed it. She stared at Maya, her face stern. "You don't want to be sent to the adult ward. It's—"

Interrupted by the door swinging open, Director Williams froze. Dr. Barrow poked his head in. "I forgot my keys." He glanced at Director Williams standing by the door and then to Maya.

Director Williams offered a thin smile. "I was just telling Maya that she needs to get to class now."

Maya's knees threatened to give out, but she rose from her chair and made it to the door. She stumbled out into the hallway and headed for the bathroom. On the verge of tears, she couldn't stomach Professor Prim's icy demeanor at the moment. They were going to send her to the reconditioning center.

She slumped down on the bathroom floor and rested her head against the cold, tiled wall. The words from the memo flooded her mind.

Irreparable harm.

Permanent damage.

She desperately wanted to be cured, but not like that. Not like the girl in the photo. The pain she shared with her was already too much to bear. As her mind drifted to the girl's haunting face, a scream tore through her.

Help us!

The words echoed through her mind as if she had screamed them herself. As the scream dissipated, an image of a soaring building glinting in the sunlight flashed in her mind.

Help us!

In that moment, she became part of the "us" whether she wanted to be or not. She had to escape before it was too late. For her and for the girl.

Now she just had to convince Jacob to come with her.

"I can't believe Tully talked you into leaving." Jacob kicked a rock as they walked the dusty track during physical fitness hour. "Do you know how dangerous it will be? Where will you even go?"

"Remember the map Tully found? She says there's a settlement not far from here. Once we escape, we can get help. Besides, Tully knows a lot about the outside world. She was fourteen when she came here, remember?" She paused and lowered her voice. "I was hoping you would come with us."

"Come with you? I already told Tully I think it's a bad idea. You know if you get caught you fail your final review, right?"

She struggled to swallow the lump forming in her throat. "Jacob, I'm never going to pass my final review. Dr. Barrow says I'm getting worse. That my condition might be terminal. I feel things just as much now as I did when I got here. Maybe even more. I'm–" her voice broke. "Incurable."

"You don't know that for sure. There are other treatments."

She stopped in her tracks and stared at him. "Like the reconditioning center? You know what the memo said about permanent damage. And the pain. I've felt the pain. And what if..."

"What if what?"

"What if"—her voice trembled— "what if I don't want to be cured? Is it so bad not to want to hurt a mouse?" She raised her hand to her lips, shocked by the words that had escaped.

His eyes widened. "You don't want to be cured? I know you're scared, but Dr. Barrow—"

"Dr. Barrow is sending me to the reconditioning center!" Noticing his pained expression, her tone softened. "Why can't you understand I have to leave?"

"I do understand." He hung his head and then glanced up at her. "But why do you need me to come with you?"

"Jacob, you're my closest friend and the smartest person I know. I'm not sure if we could do it without you." She sighed. "And what if you stay here and they send you to be reconditioned or whatever? Wouldn't that be worse?"

Instead of answering, he resumed walking with his head slumped forward. She walked beside him, but he felt miles away. Only the crackling of the gravel beneath their feet disrupted the painful silence. She knew he needed time to process and that she shouldn't rush him, but time was running out. She nudged him with her shoulder, but he scowled and kept walking. After several minutes, he turned toward her. "Do you remember when we first met?"

She was only seven and had just emerged from her three-day, new arrival, confinement period. He had taken her hand and told her it was okay to cry. They had been best friends ever since. Her eyes met his. "Of course. Why?"

"When I met you, I knew everything would be okay." He kept walking, looking straight ahead. "Like, as long as we were friends, I would be okay. And now you're leaving, and I don't—" He let out a deep sigh. "I just, I can't..."

She absorbed his emotions as waves of fear and sadness crashed against her resolve to leave. Her eyes welled up. "You know I can't stay. I told you about what Dr. Barrow said. And I have to try to help the girl. I share her pain. There could be others."

"I know." His shoulders drooped as he continued walking. Moments later, his posture stiffened. "So, there's nothing I can say or do to make you stay?"

She shook her head. "I'm sorry."

"But what if something happens to you?"

"It might. But I'm not safe here. Neither are you. I know you're worried about the outside world, but how bad can it be? We used to live there. I'm sure we can find people to help us."

He kicked at another rock but got more dirt than rock. The stone held its position as the dust settled around it. He scowled at the rock and then turned toward her. "Okay, I'll come. But only because I know you're leaving with or without me."

"Jacob–"

"I know." He let out a deep sigh. "It's okay. I want to come. I can't stay here."

"Are you sure?"

"Yes. I don't want to be experimented on. And if we can help that girl, it might be worth it, right?" He forced a weak smile.

"I hope so." She straightened her posture and tried to sound confident enough for the both of them. "Let's go find Tully."

Chapter 10

MAYA AND JACOB WALKED toward Tully who stood on the far side of the track throwing rocks at a metal trash can.

Jacob nudged Maya. "Are you sure this is a good idea? She seems to have some anger management issues. Like what's with all the stone throwing?"

"It'll be fine. We need her."

Tully hurled another stone. It clattered against the can and fell to the ground. "Just working on my aim. You wanna try?" She handed a stone to Maya.

Maya turned over the small, smooth stone in her hand. "Maybe later."

"You should keep it."

Maya shrugged and slipped it into her pocket. "Jacob's coming with us—to escape I mean."

"Cool, he'll need a rock, too."

"So, we bust out wielding rocks as weapons? Have you lost your mind?" Jacob turned to Maya, eyes wide.

Tully laughed. "I hadn't thought of that, but the CSOs only have nightsticks so maybe with enough rocks—"

"Tully," said Maya. "What's the actual plan?"

"We use the stones to jam the automatic locks on our doors when they engage at lights out. I tried it one night with a piece of wood and it almost held. I think a rock would do the trick."

Jacob crossed his arms. "You think?"

"It'll work. But we'll try it first just in case." She scanned the ground and picked up a small stone. She handed it to Jacob. "This one's perfect. Don't lose it."

Jacob smirked and shoved it in his pocket.

Tully kneeled and began to draw in the dirt with a sharp stone. She grabbed a smashed aluminum can from the foot of the trash can and placed it in the corner of her drawing. She placed larger stones in various places and added a couple of discarded bottle caps.

Maya and Jacob exchanged glances as she worked.

Once she had finished, she stood and pointed to the can. "This is the dormitory." She bent back down and ran a line with her finger between two of the larger stones. "This is the dining commons, the administration building, and the labs and classrooms are over here. There is a wall around the entire compound, so the main entrance seems to be the only way in or out."

"I could have told you that without the map," said Jacob.

Tully ignored him and continued her presentation. "By the main entrance, there is a security booth." She placed a bottle cap in the booth. "During the day, I've never seen more than one CSO. But that's during the day, so we'll need to check at night. Like after lights out."

"So, we use the stones in the locks and sneak out?" Maya bent over the map and pointed. "If we stay along the backside of the admin building here, we might be able to get within sight of the entrance without being exposed, right?"

Jacob rubbed the back of his neck. "'Might' being the operative word."

Tully dusted off her hands. "Only one way to find out." The bell rang and signaled the end of physical fitness hour. "So, we'll meet tonight behind the admin building after lights out." She turned to Jacob. "And no flashlights."

Jacob frowned. "Noted."

Maya sat on her bed and waited. She checked the clock for the tenth time. 9:54. One more minute. She slipped her hand into her pocket and felt around for the stone and stretch of masking tape Tully had taken from the media room. Tully made breaking the rules look easy—she was good at it.

Maya wasn't.

Beads of sweat formed on the back of her neck.

9:55 pm

From behind Maya's door, the floor monitor made her final checks. "Lights out in five minutes."

As the monitor's voice descended the hall, Maya crept to her door and waited.

9:56 pm

She eased open the door just enough to expose the door's lock receptacle. Her hands shook as she tried to insert the stone into the receptacle. It wouldn't fit. As she struggled to force it in, she lost her grip and it dropped to the floor. Her heart raced and her breath hitched in her chest.

Breathe.

She took a deep breath and picked up the stone. She examined the sides, rotated it, and then slid it into the receptacle. With her other hand, she retrieved the masking tape and secured the stone.

9:59 pm

She closed the door and waited for the locks to engage.

When the clock turned ten, the familiar clicking sound echoed down the hall as the automatic deadbolts engaged. She placed her hand on the doorknob.

It worked.

Out in the cold night air, Maya hurried alongside the back of the dormitory building in darkness. When she reached the end of the dormitory, the exterior light of the admin building illuminated the space between the two structures. It was about fifty feet of space she'd have to cover with no shadows. There didn't appear to be anyone around, but someone could be watching. She pressed her body against the edge of the building, hidden by the last sliver of darkness.

If she ran, her sneakers would beat against the pavement. She could tiptoe, but that would take forever. She could yell and turn cartwheels and get sent to the adult ward. What was she thinking? Tully breaks the rules, not her.

She glanced back the way she had come and wiped her hands on her coveralls. That's when she heard it. A rustling coming from behind the admin building. She stepped back deeper into the darkness and looked across to where the sound had originated.

Tully peeked from behind the dumpster and beckoned to her with her hand.

Maya nodded but didn't move.

Tully beckoned again more aggressively.

"Okay," Maya mouthed. She took a deep breath and race-walked toward Tully. Once she was safely behind the dumpster, she stopped to catch her breath. "Where's Jacob?"

"Must have chickened out. Come on." Tully led her along the back of the admin building until they could see the ARC entrance. Tully pointed to a low wall behind the security booth. "We can get a good look from there."

Maya followed Tully and ducked down beside her when they reached the wall. "Now what?"

"We watch."

Maya peered over the wall at the security booth. The CSO appeared to be reading the paper. "What are we watching for?"

Tully scooted up beside her and pointed. "See that one? The blond one? I've seen him there during the day, too. He's the one with the flask. I figure he drinks to cope with the boredom."

"Okay, so?"

Tully pointed to the other side of the entrance gate. "See the Abigor statue over there? I was thinking we could do something to the statue so when he goes to investigate we could sneak out."

"Like put underwear on it?"

"More like blow it up, but I haven't been able to find any dynamite."

Maya locked eyes with Tully, not sure if she was serious.

"Or I could throw rocks at it to get his attention." Tully rummaged around in her pocket and pulled out a stone. She drew back her arm.

Maya grabbed her arm. "Wait, we're too far."

She lowered the rock. "You're probably right. Wait here." Tully glanced at the security booth and then bolted across to some shrubs about twenty feet from the statue.

After a moment, a clang rang out and the CSO stirred. He left the booth and walked toward the statue with his flashlight. When the shrubs lit up, Maya gasped, but Tully remained hidden. The CSO illuminated the statue and then headed back to his booth. Maya ducked as low as she could as his flashlight lit up the low wall hiding her. She stayed flat on the ground until Tully joined her.

"I guess he's not drunk after all." Tully settled in beside her. "But I don't think that'll give us enough time to unlock the gate, get out, and close the gate without him seeing us."

"Yeah, it won't." Maya peaked over the wall again into the booth. The CSO got up and poured himself a cup of coffee from the coffee maker. "He's drinking coffee."

"So?"

"Coffee keeps you up, but what if we make him sleepy?"

Tully's face lit up. "I could break into the infirmary. I bet they got a shitload of drugs in there."

"Or we could just use my sleeping pills."

"That works."

Chapter 11

MAYA SENSED JACOB'S FOUL mood even before she reached his table. She set down her breakfast tray and took a seat across from him while he poked at his pancake. He glanced at her plate which contained only a blob of applesauce and went back to picking at his food.

"What happened to you last night? Did the stone not work?"

He rummaged in his backpack and then placed the stone on the table. He slid it across to her. "I didn't try."

"Why not?"

"You know why. Aren't you the one who can tell how everyone feels?"

Her jaw tensed. "I can tell you feel angry, but I don't know why. You told me you wanted to come with us."

Jacob put his finger to his lips and glanced over his shoulder, but there were no monitors nearby. "You should keep your voice down," he whispered.

She lowered her voice. "It worked, you know. The stones. And Tully and I came up with a plan. I think we can really do it."

He leaned back in his chair with his arms crossed and let out a heavy breath.

When he didn't say anything, she continued. "I know you're worried. There are a million things that can go wrong. It's true. But I have to try, okay? If you've changed your mind, that's your right. But I'm leaving. No matter what."

Jacob ran both hands through his hair. "Can we talk about this later?"

"Okay, sure." She smashed her applesauce with the back of her spoon. "We can talk at break."

She choked down a few bites of the half-rancid applesauce while Jacob started packing up to leave.

A hand came down on her shoulder. "Are you Maya from Professor Prim's class?"

She turned to face a dining monitor. "Yes."

"Dr. Barrow instructed me to give this to you." He handed her an envelope and walked away.

Maya opened the envelope and took out a notice.

Jacob peered over her shoulder. "What's it say?"

She scanned the notice and let it drop from her fingers. "I'm being transferred to the reconditioning center. Tomorrow."

Jacob grabbed the letter. "Let me see that."

Maya got up and put on her backpack. She leaned toward Jacob and slipped the rock into his pocket. She whispered in his ear. "We leave tonight."

Later that night, Maya sat on her bed staring at the clock. As soon as the floor monitor's footsteps echoed away down the hall, Maya pulled the stone from her pocket. She approached her bedroom door, gripping the smooth stone in her fist. Without a sound, she eased the door open just enough to secure the stone into the lock receptacle with masking tape. Once it was in place, she returned to her bed and put on her backpack. Tully had told them just to bring their towels, water bottles, and any snacks they could swipe from the commons, but she had slipped in the handkerchief her mother had given to her to wipe her tears on her assessment day. Her only possession from her life before the Arc.

Maya took one last look at the concrete chamber surrounding her. Except for the plant, she wouldn't miss a thing. The room was now nothing more than a prison cell—one that would no longer contain her if everything went according to plan.

When the clock turned to ten, she listened for the locks to engage. The stone held. As soon as the lights went out, Maya slipped into the empty hallway and closed the door behind her. She hurried to the exit and pushed the door open into the cool night air. Walking as fast as she could, she tried to stay in the shadows and ignore the fear gnawing at her gut.

She reached the hiding spot by the security booth where Jacob agreed to meet her. When she explained the plan to him during break, he said he would come. But he had changed his mind once already. And Jacob was never late. She crouched down with her back to the low wall behind the booth and gripped her knees to her chest. She'd do it alone if she had to.

When Jacob didn't show, she peeked over the wall to get a glimpse of the CSO. It wasn't the blond one with the flask. Hopefully, this one was a coffee drinker. She eased back down behind the wall and waited.

After what seemed like forever, a faint thump echoed in the darkness as Tully started throwing rocks at the statue of Commander Abigor. The thumps continued. She must have struck the copper bust of the Commander directly in his face because the loud clang caught the CSO's attention.

Maya held her breath as the CSO got up to investigate. When he was far enough away, she crept out from behind the wall but stopped before stepping toward the security booth. Once she entered the booth, the walls would block her view of his return. Without Jacob as the look-out, she'd have no way of knowing if the CSO was on his way back. She glanced back toward the safety of the wall.

Another clang rang out from the direction of the Abigor statue.

Now or never.

She took a deep breath and headed for the booth. Once inside, she removed the bag of crushed pills from her pocket. Her eyes locked on the coffee mug on the desk. Empty.

Crap.

Maya gripped the wooden chair. Her pulse raced as her eyes panned to the door. The faint scent of coffee toyed with her stomach—its sharp, rich scent increasing her nausea.

Think.

In the corner, the old coffee maker's stained carafe contained remnants of its last brew. Maya grabbed the pot and poured the crushed sleeping pills into the coffee. She swirled the pot a few times until the powder disappeared. When she turned from the coffee maker, she slammed into someone.

Before she could utter a syllable, Jacob put his hand over her mouth and whispered, "He's on his way back." He ushered her out of the booth.

When they were safely behind the wall, Maya nudged him. "I thought you weren't coming."

"Yeah, me too." He tightened his scarf around his neck.

Tully joined them behind the wall. "You do it?"

Maya nodded.

"I'll keep watch first. He's gotta drink it at some point." Tully positioned herself to keep her eyes on the CSO.

As the minutes crawled by, Maya gripped her arms to her chest. Jacob shivered beside her with his arms wrapped around his knees and his head down. She shifted away from his quivering body and pulled herself up to join Tully who was laser-focused on the guard booth.

The CSO got up and stretched his arms out wide. He turned his neck from side to side and stretched again. He folded his newspaper and picked up his coffee mug. Maya kept her eyes on him as he walked over to the coffee maker and filled his mug. Once he returned to his chair, he sipped his coffee and set it down.

Maya and Tully watched until he had taken several more sips. They had to have been sitting there for at least an hour. After several more minutes, the CSO's head jerked forward, but he straightened himself and took a long swig of his coffee. His head slumped forward again, this time for longer. Maya elbowed Tully, but he straightened his head again. Finally, he slumped all the way forward with his head resting on top of the desk.

Maya nudged Jacob and motioned for him to get up.

While Tully positioned herself by the solid metal gate, Maya and Jacob hurried into the guard booth. The CSO sat snoring with his arms sprawled over the desk, his face planted on top of the newspaper. Maya searched for the gate release switch on the desk panel.

Jacob tapped her arm and pointed to the switch—below the CSO's hand.

Maya bit her lip. When she placed her hand lightly on the CSO's wrist, he groaned and twitched. She gasped and jerked her hand away.

The CSO resumed snoring, so she carefully reached for his wrist again. When he didn't flinch, she lifted his hand off the switch and set it on the desk.

Jacob flipped the switch and allowed the gate to open about a foot before switching it to manual. They rushed to join Tully by the opening in the gate.

Tully pushed her way through the opening first. "If I knew it was this easy, I would have left a long time ago."

"Maybe they don't expect anyone to leave?" Jacob peered around cautiously and followed Tully out the gate with Maya right behind him. Once outside, they slid the heavy gate back in place until the lock engaged. Although the full moon lit up the sky, Maya was glad they had flashlights.

"Guys!" Jacob's voice rang out from where he walked several feet ahead of them.

"Hang on," Tully said. "I want to make sure the gate is locked."

"You have to see this." Jacob illuminated the space in front of him with his flashlight. "Look."

The ground in front of them dropped off into a dark abyss. Maya stumbled back as a wave of fear overtook her. The high walls of the Arc jutted out from the smooth stone surface of a mountain, leaving them surrounded by a sheer cliff on every side.

Chapter 12

Tully joined them by the cliff's edge. "How far down is it?" She shone her flashlight into the darkness.

"Far. Too far." Jacob shook his head. "What are we going to do?"

"Shit. How is this possible?" Tully paced the edge of the cliff. "They brought us up here, didn't they? Neither of you remembered there was no road?"

"Tully, you came here after us, so if anyone should have known, it's you." Jacob's voice rose. "And I wasn't even awake when they brought me here. I was only five."

"Five? Don't they test everyone at seven?"

"They tested me early."

"Figures." She turned to Maya, "What about you?"

"I blacked out at my test and woke up here."

"And they sedated me when I bit one of the transport guys." Tully scanned the area. "Hell, maybe they flew us up here."

"We need to go back." Jacob approached the gate. "We can go back to our rooms, and they'll never even know we were gone."

Maya kept her voice calm. "Jacob, we can't. It's locked. And even if we could, we could get caught sneaking back in. I'm sure we can figure something out."

"Figure something out? If we try to get down that cliff, we'll die. If they find us out here, what'll happen then?" Jacob pushed on the gate, but it wouldn't budge.

"Dude, chill. Just give me a minute to think." Tully walked to the far side of the clearing.

Maya motioned for Jacob to come away from the gate and they made their way toward Tully in silence.

"This can't possibly be the only way in or out. There must be another exit. Damnit, how could I have missed that?"

"It's okay, Tully," said Maya. "There's no way you would have known."

"Ugh. What's that smell?" Jacob placed his hand over his nose. "It's like when the sewer line backs up. I think I'm going to be sick."

Maya took a whiff of the night air. "I don't smell anything."

Jacob walked over to a flat grassy area. "Right here. It's really strong. You can't smell that?"

Maya shone her flashlight on the ground illuminating a metal grate obscured beneath the dirt and weeds. She got on her hands and knees and brushed the dirt away. "Tully, come look. I think we found something."

Once Tully joined them, they lifted the metal grate exposing a hole in the ground. Tully pointed to the metal ladder embedded in one side. "I knew there had to be another way down." She smirked at Jacob. "Looks like that nose of yours is good for something, huh?"

"Through there? It smells disgusting." Jacob aimed his flashlight down the tunnel. "How do we even know how far down it goes? I mean, I can imagine the engineers would have designed a viable emergency escape route, but—"

"Only one way to find out." Tully dropped a large stone into the hole. They waited to hear it land, but it vanished into the darkness. Tully stared at Jacob with her hands on her hips. "You have a better idea?"

Jacob shrugged.

When Maya peered into the tunnel, her stomach dropped. One slip on the rungs and she'd plummet to her death.

Tully slipped her flashlight into her backpack. "We'll need our hands to climb." She lowered herself into the tunnel and disappeared into the darkness as her voice rang out, "See ya at the bottom."

Maya placed her flashlight in her backpack and glanced at Jacob. "Do you want to go first?"

"No, you go first. I'll be right behind you."

She nodded and grasped the top rung before lowering her legs into the tunnel. Darkness enveloped her as she began her descent. The thin metal bars allowed little room for error as she inched her way down. As she continued into the abyss, her hands began to shake. She tightened her grip around the bar and dug her feet into the thin rung beneath them.

Jacob called down to her. "Are you okay?"

Not really. I'm about to die.

"Maya?"

"Yes, I'm okay. Just give me a minute."

She took a deep breath and released her right hand. Once she had a solid grip on the rung below her, she moved her left hand down to join the right one. Despite the weakness in her knees, she lowered her foot toward the next rung and shifted her weight once it made contact. As she extended her other foot, her planted foot slipped off the bar, a burst of weightlessness overtaking her. The thin metal bars dug into her sweat-drenched palms while her feet struggled to make contact. Her heart dropped to her stomach.

By the time she regained her footing, Jacob hovered above her. Frozen with fear, she coaxed her limbs to move. There was only one way down—one way to freedom—and this was it. She took a few deep breaths to thaw her muscles. Rung by rung, she'd make it to the bottom. Once her feet were firmly planted, she released the muscles in her hands and shifted them one after another to the bar below. As she continued her descent into the darkness, she focused on the rhythmic movement of her hands and feet instead of the dark pit waiting to swallow her.

Losing all sense of time, Maya's only indication of how long she had been climbing was her aching muscles. The faint sound of Jacob's movements above her had almost disappeared when a thud echoed from below. Maya froze until the gleam of Tully's flashlight signaled she had made it to the bottom. Maya navigated the last few rungs, threw the backpack off her cramped shoulders, and collapsed in exhaustion. Once she caught her breath, she joined Tully, whose flashlight revealed a steady stream of murky water flowing down the center of the tunnel. Jacob had just made it down from the ladder.

"You were right about the sewage, Jacob," Tully said. "It's foul." The sharp stench of sulfur permeated the air.

When Jacob didn't answer, Maya turned to where he hunched over the base of the ladder. "Jacob, are you okay?"

"Uh yeah, just give me a…" Jacob's voice trailed off to the sound of him retching. When he finished, Maya took a water bottle from her backpack and offered it to him. Jacob got up and straightened his scarf. "I'm okay now."

Tully pointed her flashlight down the tunnel. "I figure we should follow the shit stream and head that way. It's gotta be flowing somewhere."

Joining Tully, Jacob examined the tunnel. "It looks pretty cramped in there." He gagged at the stench. "But, unfortunately, you're probably right." He took a deep breath and pulled his scarf over his nose.

Although the portion of the tunnel where they stood had ample headroom, it narrowed as it jutted off from the junction. Tully ducked her head and led the way into the dimly lit passageway. At first, Maya tried to straddle the wide stream of filth that flowed through the center of the tunnel, but soon gave up and let it swirl around her calves as she trudged onward. The smell was nauseating and after only a few minutes she felt bile rising in her throat. The worst part was not knowing how long they would be down there. It could be miles.

She resisted the urge to turn around and check on Jacob. If she stopped moving forward, she might turn back. The sewer water level seemed to be rising and she could feel the dampness approaching her knees.

"Shit." Tully's voice echoed from down the tunnel.

"Yeah, we know. It's everywhere," Jacob called out from behind her.

"No, look."

Maya and Jacob caught up to where Tully stood knee-deep in sewage, her flashlight illuminating a set of vertical rusted bars blocking their path. The sewage flowed easily through the bars, but the bars were too close together for a person to squeeze between them. They had reached a dead end.

Chapter 13

TULLY PUSHED HER WEIGHT into the bars and stepped back when they didn't budge. "Do you see any bolts or where they might be connected?" Her flashlight illuminated the edges of the bars which were welded flush with the tunnel wall. She cursed under her breath.

"There's no way we can get through," said Jacob. "We need to head back. I know Director Williams will be mad, but she seems reasonable and—"

"Jacob, if I go back, I'll be sent to the adult ward, and what if Tully's right about it?"

He scowled, "That they throw us in some dungeon? You actually believe that?"

"I asked Director Williams about it. She didn't tell me where it was, but she warned me that it's not a nice place."

"Why didn't you tell me?"

She avoided his stare. "I didn't want to worry you."

"It's a little late for that." Jacob tugged on the bars before stepping back.

Tully shone her flashlight back down the tunnel. "It made sense to follow the current out, but maybe the other end of the tunnel leads somewhere."

"I doubt it. If anything, it leads back into the Arc," said Jacob.

Maya approached the bars and placed her hand on one of them. They'd come too far to turn back now. She ran her hand down the bar and continued to follow its descent below the surface of the water.

Jacob gagged. "Eww, you know you just stuck your hand in excrement, right?"

Just as she had hoped, instead of running to the bottom, the bars connected to a horizontal bar hidden just beneath the surface. "The bars don't go all the way down." She stepped back.

"So what?" Tully placed her hands on her hips. Her glare moved from Maya to the bars and then back to Maya. Her smirk faded. "Sooo," she drew out. "We go under?"

"Under?" Jacob shook his head. "You know sewage is a biohazard, right? It could get in our orifices. We could get dysentery or some other bacterial infection."

Maya took off her backpack and checked to make sure it could fit between the bars. "You both have extra water bottles, right? And the hand towels from your rooms? Once we're through we can clean our hands and face. I'll go first and you can hand me my backpack when I'm on the other side, so everything stays dry."

"Works for me." Tully gave an upward nod toward Jacob. "Just be sure to keep your orifices shut and you should be fine." She took Maya's backpack. "I think 'orifices' might be my new favorite word."

Maya wiped her hands on her coveralls and smoothed back the hair that had escaped her braid. As if her curls being out of place would matter once it was soaked in human waste. She took a deep breath, pursed her lips together as tight as she could, and held her nose.

I can't believe this was my idea.

Before she had a chance to change her mind, she lowered herself into the sewer water and under the bar. As soon as she emerged from the other side, she exhaled sharply before daring to breathe. She shook the muck from her limbs and spit several times to make sure nothing got in her mouth. The sludge dripped down the side of her face and filled her ears. Her whole body convulsed as she fought the urge to vomit. Jacob pushed her backpack between the bars so that she could reach it from the other side.

She grabbed the water bottle, rinsed her hands, and poured the rest over her face. By the time she finished wiping her face with her towel, Tully had gone under the bar.

Jacob pushed Tully's backpack through to her. He then placed his scarf in his before passing it through to Maya. He shook out his hands like a boxer psyching himself up for a match and let out a series of sharp exhales.

Tully smirked. "Ten bucks says he doesn't do it."

Maya locked eyes with Jacob, catching a spark of determination. "He'll do it."

After breathing in enough air for an army, Jacob held his nose and covered his mouth. He plunged beneath the bar and surfaced on the other side like a phoenix rising from the ashes. Instead of shaking off the muck, he stood motionless as if paralyzed. Maya rushed to his side with his water bottle and poured it over him. His body started to tremble, and his eyes remained squeezed shut. She took out the towel from his backpack and handed it to him. "Here, wipe your face."

When he still didn't move, she pressed the towel against his forehead. "Are you okay?"

He placed his hands on the towel and held it to his face. Maya and Tully exchanged glances as they waited. When he lowered the towel, his eyes opened with a vacant expression.

Maya placed her hand on his shoulder. "None got in your mouth or anything, right?"

"I'm sure he kept his orifices shut. Come on, we gotta move." Tully started down the tunnel.

Jacob balled the towel in his hands. "I can't do this."

"What do you mean?" asked Maya.

"This." He held up his arms. "Human waste. The tunnel. Escaping. Everything. I can't believe I let you talk me into coming."

Maya's body tensed. "I'm sorry, okay. But I didn't make you come." She squirmed in her filth-covered coveralls. "I know this is horrible, but we have to keep going."

"We don't even know where this tunnel goes. I'm going back."

Tully rejoined them and nodded toward the bars. "Yeah, good luck with that." She grabbed his backpack from Maya and shoved it into his hands. "We gotta go."

"It can't get any worse than this." Maya placed her hand on his shoulder. "Let's just keep going, okay?"

Jacob scowled but put on his backpack. As they started down the tunnel, he called out to Tully, "You owe me ten bucks."

As they trudged down the tunnel in silence, Maya's skin crawled. Her sewage-drenched clothes rubbed against her skin, and the stench increased now that it clung to her hair. To keep going, she allowed herself to indulge in thoughts of her life before the Arc: tall trees and sprawling lawns, fresh strawberries in the summer. Her parents.

After a while, her legs began to tire. Her pace slowed and Jacob butted up behind her.

"Are you okay?"

"Yeah." She lowered her head and plodded forward, quickening her pace.

"Hey, is that moonlight?" Tully's voice carried down the tunnel.

A faint light shone from the distance. As they continued walking, the pattering of running water echoed through the passageway. When the tunnel opened into a small clearing, the cool night air made Maya shiver. While Tully explored the perimeter, Maya walked to the edge of the clearing. The sewage line poured into a large body of water about thirty feet below.

"Looks like there's only one way down," said Tully.

Jacob joined Tully. "You find another ladder?"

"Nope." Tully gazed out over the water. "You can swim, right?"

"Yeah, I learned when I was little, but..." Jacob peered over the ledge and stepped back.

"We can jump from here." Tully pointed to a flat area closest to the ledge. "The water looks deep enough."

Maya noticed the doubt clouding Jacob's eyes. "I don't know. We're still up pretty high."

"And the cliff's jagged. It looks dangerous." Jacob backed away further from the ledge.

Tully crossed her arms and glared at him. "What do you suggest we do?"

"I don't know, but I'm not jumping." Jacob shivered and rubbed his arms. "We could hit our heads on the rocks or drown. Or get hypothermia. I'm already freezing."

"Can you quit complaining?" Tully's voice rose. "I'm just trying to get us outta here."

"Trying to get us killed is more like it. You may have a death wish, but I don't."

Tully's jaw stiffened as her eyes narrowed on Jacob. "I don't have a death wish. I'm just not chicken shit enough to be afraid of jumping."

Maya's neck muscles tightened as they argued. Her head started to throb, but she fought to find her voice. "Tully, it's easier for you to be brave. You don't feel things the same way. Some people are more sensitive."

"What's to feel? We're jumping into a lake. Big deal."

Maya sighed, "I think if you understood how he is feeling, maybe you—"

"Understand what? What it's like to be a wimp?"

If only she could make Tully understand. She placed her hand on Tully's arm. "Understand this."

Maya took a deep breath and imagined all the fear and anxiety she had taken in from Jacob flowing out her fingertips into Tully. Tully's eyes widened before she dropped to her knees. Even after Maya released her arm, Tully sat huddled on the ground shaking.

Jacob's voice rose in panic. "What did you do to her?"

"I just wanted her to understand." Maya crouched beside Tully, her arm still tingling. "Are you okay?"

Tully took a few deep breaths and got up. She stood silently for a moment and then turned to Maya. "First of all, if you ever do that to me again, I will kick your ass. Second, I have no idea how you did that, but that's a pretty hardcore trick. And third, if you EVER do that to me again, I will KICK. YOUR. ASS. Got it?"

"Got it. I'm really sorry." Maya held out her hands in front of her. How did she do it?

"Good. Now, I know it's scary, but we need to get down from here. The longer we take, the less time we have until they come looking for us. The drop is not much more than a high dive, so if we jump feet first, we should be fine." Tully gave Jacob a wry smile. "I'll go first, so if I die, you don't have to jump, okay?"

"Okay," said Jacob. "Just be sure you get a running start so you can clear the side of the cliff. I'd prefer it if you don't die."

Tully took a running start and launched herself off the ledge. After the splash, the darkness obscured the surface of the water. Maya's stomach twisted in knots. How long had she been underwater? Moments later, Tully's voice rang out, "That was awesome!"

Jacob glanced at Maya and then flung himself over the edge. He must have done it quickly for fear of changing his mind. When he yelled, "I'm okay," she took a deep breath and jumped. The fall only lasted seconds, but the impact of the frigid water below jarred her senses. The momentum pulled her deep below the surface. Exhaustion weighed down her limbs, but she fought her way to the surface, gasping for air. Tully and Jacob were already on the shore, so she swam toward them.

Once on shore, Maya tried to squeeze as much water as she could out of her coveralls and dumped the water from her backpack. At least the dip in the lake had removed the sewage from her clothes and skin. Although it was almost summer, Maya shivered as Tully rummaged through her backpack.

"Shit." Tully pulled out a drenched map from her backpack. As she tried to peel it open, it crumbled apart in her hands. "Shit. Shit. Shit." She pulled out the compass, checked it, and chucked it in the dirt. She got up and stomped the ground. "Damnit."

Jacob retrieved a knotted plastic bag from his backpack and took out his dry scarf. He wrapped it around his neck. He took out a couple of granola bars from the bag and held out one to Tully. "You want one?"

Tully scowled but took the bar. "You had a plastic bag this whole time? Why didn't you tell me?"

"I assumed you packed one. It's kind of common sense to protect valuables. I used a couple of trash can liners." He handed the other granola bar to Maya and then pulled out one for himself.

Tully peered into his backpack as she devoured the granola bar. "Any chance you got a map in there?"

"No." Jacob closed his backpack and sat on a fallen tree to eat. "You might want to save half. We probably won't have access to food for a while."

Tully threw the empty wrapper on the ground and dusted off her hands. She climbed up on a nearby boulder and surveyed their surroundings.

Exhausted, Maya joined Jacob and nibbled on her granola bar. She leaned her shoulder into his. "Thank you."

Jacob gave her a small nod and returned his half-eaten snack to his backpack.

Tully climbed down from the boulder and pointed to lights in the distance. "From what I can tell, the wasteland is that way."

"From what you can tell?" Jacob shivered. "You don't have a map or compass."

"Lights mean civilization. And from what I remember from the map, the wasteland isn't far from the lake, and this must be the lake." Tully put on her backpack. "And across the clearing, there's what looks like a trail. It's gotta go somewhere."

"And what's this about the wasteland?" Jacob got up and placed his backpack on the tree. "Maya said we'd head to a settlement."

"Yeah. A settlement in the wasteland. If we can make it there before dawn, we should be safe. From what I know, government employees aren't paid enough to risk venturing there."

Jacob flung his soggy backpack onto his back. "That's reassuring."

Chapter 14

As they walked along the dirt trail, Maya's whole body ached with cold. Although the cheap fabric of her coveralls had begun to dry, her feet sloshed in her wet shoes. At least the full moon and stars lit up the night sky, making it easy to navigate the terrain in the darkness. Instead of tall trees and a lush landscape, the trail led them through clusters of low shrubs and barren trees that appeared like jagged skeletons in the moonlight. Maya shuddered and clutched the straps of her backpack to her chest.

"Hey, Maya. Are you listening?" asked Jacob.

"What?"

"I asked what your family was like."

"Talking about your families? Isn't that—"

"Against the rules?" Tully scoffed. "We just busted out of the Arc, and you're worried about the rules? To hell with the rules."

Tully was right. It was too late now to worry. "Okay. Well, it was just me and my parents. I don't have any brothers or sisters." Unless they had another child to replace her. "I mean, I don't think I do."

"What were your parents like?" asked Jacob.

"Just normal parents. But my mom was adopted. She was found abandoned as a baby at a church. She is an engineer, I think. My dad is a teacher." Her dad's light brown beard would tickle her face when he kissed her goodnight. "What were your parents like, Jacob?"

"Mine? I don't know. I hardly remember my dad except that he was gone at work most of the time and seemed sad. I was home a lot with my mom. She gave the best hugs. It was so long ago, I can't really remember." He shrugged and looked at Tully. "What about your parents?"

"My dad sent me to the Arc to get rid of me. What else do you need to know?"

"What about your mom?"

Tully hesitated before answering. "She died when I was fourteen. In a car accident."

Maya brought her hand to her chest. "I'm so sorry." That must be why she seemed angry so much of the time.

"So, my dad couldn't handle me after that and fixed it so I'd get sent to the Arc."

"Are you sure that's what happened?" asked Jacob.

"Do you really think I belong in the Arc? Besides, my dad was always buying off people. Him and his jerk politician friends. That's what they do. He owns the Modern Republic Broadcast Service. My mom was cool though." Her tone softened. "The best part of our family." Her shoulders dropped before she shook off the emotion. "Look up there. The trail splits."

Up ahead the trail separated into two paths. When they reached the fork, Tully pointed to the right. "I say we go that way. It heads more in the direction of the lights."

"I don't know." Jacob rubbed the back of his neck. "We really have no way of knowing where it leads."

Maya glanced down the trail to the left which was significantly wider. "Jacob, did your flashlight stay dry?"

"Yes." He took it out of his backpack and handed it to her.

She took the flashlight and shone it on the ground. "This way looks more well-traveled." She pointed to indentations in the ground. "I think those could be tire tracks."

"Let me see." Tully yanked the flashlight out of Maya's hands and knelt to the ground. "Yeah, it could be." She got up, turned off the flashlight, and handed it back to Jacob. "But I say we stick to the right and head toward the lights."

Jacob shook his head. "I agree with Maya. If they're tire tracks it's more likely to lead to civilization. And the other path could easily bend away from the lights."

Tully stared at them with her hands on her hips.

"You're kind of outnumbered," said Maya.

"Okay, whatever." Tully huffed and started down the path Maya had chosen. "But if we end up back at the Arc, you're on your own."

As they continued to walk, the trail veered farther and farther away from the direction of the lights. When the lights were almost out of view, Tully stopped walking. "I told you we should have gone the other way."

Maya brought her palms to her face and rubbed her brows. Tully didn't need to say it, but the words "stupid Fragile" echoed in her ears. Her whole body hurt, and it took everything she had not to collapse on the ground. Doubling back would waste even more time and cut their chance of making it to the settlement before sunrise. She turned back toward Tully. "I'm sorry. I should have listened to you."

"Yeah, you should've. Let's head back." Tully turned to head back down the trail.

Jacob had gone on ahead and called out to them from around the bend. "There's something up here."

Tully pivoted and let out an exaggerated sigh. "It better be good."

"It is."

Maya and Tully hurried to join him.

The path opened into a clearing with a log cabin in the distance. An old truck caked in mud parked alongside the dilapidated shack that had cracked windows and a porch teetering on the verge of collapse.

"I say we check it out," said Tully. "Come on."

When they neared the cabin, Jacob stopped and turned to Tully. "Looks abandoned. What do you think?"

"Looks like it, but we'll need to get closer."

Maya followed Jacob and Tully as they approached the cabin. As soon as Tully stepped onto the porch, the wooden slat let out a loud creek. Maya spun around, but the sound dissipated into the darkness. She joined Tully and Jacob on the porch and peered in the dirt-covered window. The cabin seemed empty. And warm.

Tully placed her hand on the door handle.

Maya reached for Tully's arm. "Maybe we shouldn't."

A distinct "click" sounded from behind them. "I suggest you listen to your friend," said a deep voice.

Maya put her hands up and turned around slowly. Behind the barrel of a shotgun, a guy with dark hair in cornrows stared them down.

"Sit." He pointed the barrel of the gun to the edge of the weathered porch.

Tully put up her hands and lowered herself to a sitting position. "Sorry man, we didn't know the place was yours."

Maya and Jacob joined her on the edge of the porch.

The stranger looked them up and down. "You're from the academy? What're you doing out here?"

Tully's voice lacked its usual bravado. "We escaped the Arc."

"Escaped?" He threw his head back and laughed. "People do that?"

"I'm not sure why you find that funny." Her voice rose, "Are you gonna let us go or what?"

"Relax." His eyes panned to Maya shivering. "I'm not sure where you're planning on going, but the nearest settlement is at least five miles from here and none of you look like you could make it there in one piece." He lowered his gun.

Tully stood. "We'll be fine." She motioned with her hands for Jacob and Maya to rise.

Maya glanced at Jacob but remained seated.

"Suit yourself." He stepped up onto the porch. "But you should head back the way you came. If you follow the trail behind the cabin, you'll have to deal with a lot worse than a guy with a shotgun." He opened the door to the cabin. "If you change your mind, you can come in and get warm. I'm Ren."

Once the door closed, Tully hopped off the porch. "I say we try to make it to the settlement. We can't trust some weirdo we met in the woods. Especially one with a gun."

"Did you hear what he said about where the path leads?" said Maya. "And I don't think I can walk another five miles." She barely had energy to push herself up from the porch.

"And I'm freezing," said Jacob. "How about we just go inside and get warm and then figure out what to do?"

"Fine, but you are too trusting." Tully peered in the window. "We're not at the Arc anymore."

Just as Maya began to raise her hand to knock on the door, Ren opened it with a smug smile. He tilted his head to the side to motion for them to enter.

Inside the dark cabin, the glow of the space heater cut the chill in the air. Maya followed the others toward the tiny heater where they huddled around it like a bonfire. When Ren lit a kerosene lantern, it illuminated stacks of boxes and a mattress on the floor. In the glow of the lantern, Maya glanced at Ren who seemed to be in his late teens. Tall with a strong slim build, he had warm brown skin and a faded scar on his temple. There was also a kindness in his eyes she hadn't noticed before.

"There's a line out back to hang your wet stuff. The bathroom's out there, too, so you can clean up. No hot water though." Ren walked over to the boxes and opened one. "These clothes are for my delivery, but you can see if anything fits. Normally, I would charge you, but I'm guessing you Fragiles don't have any money."

"I'm not a Fragile." Tully walked over toward the boxes. "My name's Tully."

Jacob held out his hand to Ren. "I'm Jacob and this is Maya. Thanks for letting us come into your cabin."

Ren chuckled. "It's not my cabin, but you're welcome."

"Not your cabin?" asked Jacob.

"Don't worry, the owner shouldn't be back anytime soon." Ren removed his shotgun from the hook on the wall and opened the door. "I gotta go finish up something but make yourself at home. The battery in the space heater should last a couple more hours."

Once he left, Tully rummaged through one of the boxes. "I told you there's something off about him. Who wanders off in the night to 'finish up something'? As soon as we get cleaned up and changed, we can head out."

Maya joined Tully by the boxes. "He seemed okay to me. And it was nice of him to let us in. Plus, I'm exhausted. Maybe we could at least rest for a little while?" She turned to where Jacob stood glued to the space heater. "What do you think?"

"I know it's not the best idea, but I really don't want to go outside again."

Tully pulled out a handful of clothes from the box. "Okay, but we sleep in shifts and leave at dawn. I've got dibs on the shower." She headed out the back door toward where Ren had pointed out the bathroom.

Maya retrieved an oversized sweatshirt and jeans from one of the boxes. Her gut told her Ren was harmless.

Hopefully, her gut was right.

Chapter 15

Maya didn't remember falling asleep on the thin mattress, but slept until the morning sun shone brightly through the window. Tully, who was supposed to be on watch, lay snoring on a pile of clothes in the corner. Jacob warmed his hands by the space heater which had survived the night. Since she had slept in her "new" clothes, she went outside to check if her shoes had dried in the sun. Although she was glad to get rid of her coveralls, her worn Arc sneakers would have to do.

Once outside, she checked her backpack drying on the line. The handkerchief her mother had given her remained bunched up in the bottom of her bag. Though almost dry, the white wrinkled cotton had become discolored from the lake water. She smoothed out the handkerchief and hung it on the line to catch a few minutes of sunlight before she packed it. Her fingers lingered on the stitching, carefully tracing the purple embroidered emblem in the corner that reminded her of a flower. For a moment, she connected to something beyond herself.

Ren walked towards the faucet behind the clothesline and began to rinse the mud from his boots. He turned off the water. "So you all had a good night?"

"Yes. Thanks for inviting us in." She moved down the clothesline to check her shoes.

He hung up his boots and headed towards the back-door into the cabin. He stopped in his tracks. "Where'd you get that?" He motioned towards the handkerchief hanging in the sun.

"My mom. Why?"

"No reason." He narrowed his eyes on her and contin-ued inside.

Maya shoved the handkerchief in her pocket and grabbed the rest of her belongings. She hurried into the cabin, where Tully had found a pair of black jeans and a crop top in one of the boxes.

"That's more like it." Tully ran her hands down her hips. "Remind me to burn my coveralls, Maya." Her height and curves made her look like a woman from a magazine.

Maya eyed the box of clothes, but decided she was comfortable in her baggy sweatshirt. Jacob had changed into a pair of khakis and a green long sleeve shirt that brought out the color of his eyes. For a moment, they could have been regular teenagers.

Ren came back in through the front door and grabbed a box. "I'm leaving as soon as I load up these boxes. If you all want a ride into the settlements, there's room in the truck." He headed out the front door again with the box.

Once he was out of earshot, Jacob nudged Tully. "What do you think?"

"If he wanted to kill us, he would have done it already. And it beats walking, right?"

Ren continued loading boxes into the truck and then returned to the front door. "Okay kids. I'm heading out if you want to hitch a ride."

□Tully tied her hair into a knot on top of her head. "Kids? I'm seventeen. How old are you?"

"Nineteen. So, yeah. You're a kid." Ren grinned and walked around the front of the truck to open the passenger door. "Maya, up in front. You two, in the back with the cargo." Tully hopped up into the back of the truck and made herself comfortable between the boxes.

Jacob walked around the back of the truck and examined the cramped contents. "Can I ride up front with you two? I get motion sickness."

"Sorry man, but I need you in the back."

Jacob made eye contact with Maya who shrugged her shoulders. Jacob sighed and climbed up into the back of the truck.

Once Ren pulled down the door behind Jacob, Maya got in the front seat. She hadn't been in a vehicle since her assessment day, and never in the front seat. The old bench seat squeaked beneath her as she tried to get comfortable. Ren went around the front of the truck, hooked up the battery and after several attempts, got the sputtering engine to start.

Ren got behind the wheel and glanced at Maya. "You should put on your seatbelt. Rides a bit bumpy."

Maya nodded and searched for her seat belt. When she couldn't find it, Ren reached across her and pulled the lap belt from where it was wedged between the seat and the seat back. Maya pressed herself tight against the seat, his body inches from hers.

"Don't worry, I don't bite." Ren handed her the belt with a smile and positioned himself back behind the wheel.

As they drove away from the cabin down the bumpy dirt road, she gazed out the window and tried to relax against the cracked vinyl seat.

Once they had been driving for a while, Ren glanced at her. "So, why'd you leave the Arc? Isn't life there easy?"

She looked out the window. "Depends on your definition of easy."

"I'm sure you didn't have to worry about where your next meal was coming from, right? Life out here can be rough."

□"Yeah they fed us." *If you consider mashed peas a meal.* She glanced at him. "Is that what the clothes and supplies are for? Do you work for a charity or something?"

He laughed. "More like a smuggler. Charities are illegal in the Republic. Didn't they teach you that in Arc school?" He continued in his best Commander Abigor voice, "Charity work promotes idleness and is inconsistent with the values of the Republic."

□"I didn't know that." She liked his laugh. He seemed so comfortable in his own skin.

□"Yep. You know what rich people do when they don't want their clothes any more? Throw 'em away. My uncle runs a hotel in the Republic and saves clothes and household stuff from the dump. Some are like new."

□"What's it like? The wasteland, I mean."

□"First of all, we don't call it the wasteland. Only the Republic calls us that." He glanced at her before returning his eyes to the road. "We're headed to a settlement called Huruma. After the military destroyed everything out here, the Republic stopped recognizing it as part of the union.

Some of it's in pretty bad shape, but Huruma is great. We grow our own food." He paused for a moment. "You still haven't told me why you left the Arc."

"Have you heard of the reconditioning center?" She glanced at him. "We think they might be hurting kids."

"Yeah, I've heard of it. The Republic does a lot of bad things, you know."

"I guess we thought we could do something about it."

"Do something about it?" He scoffed. "Good luck with that."

As she turned back to the window, she chided herself for telling him. Of course, it sounded stupid. He probably thought she was just some silly Fragile. She should keep quiet and try to enjoy the scenery.

As they continued to drive, the land became dry and barren. A cloud of gray smoke billowed in the distance. As they neared the smoke, Maya's curiosity overtook her. She pointed out the window. "What's that over there?"

"That's the Jamesville settlement. They run a mining prison for the Republic in exchange for weapons."

Close enough now to see the high barbed wire fence with guard booths on every corner, Maya's eyes widened. Hills of black soot littered the compound, and an enormous pipe jutting up from the ground spewed black smoke into the sky. She shuddered. "Where are the prisoners?"

"They keep them underground."

Her chest constricted and she whispered under her breath, "The adult ward."

"The adult what?"

"Tully told us they send Fragiles who can't be cured to a dungeon in the wasteland. I thought maybe she was kidding."

"I wouldn't put it past them." Ren sped up as they drove past the compound. "I heard no one survives there very long."

"That's awful. Can't anyone help them?"

"It's not safe to set foot near Jamesville. The amount of guns and weapons they've got is insane."

She returned her gaze to the window. If that was the adult ward, she would rather die than go back to the Arc.

As they drove, the terrain became greener and soon they were driving past bursts of thick green foliage. Out of nowhere, Ren's arm shot out in front of her as he hit the brakes. "Hold on." Moments later, a small animal darted out across the road in front of them and disappeared into the brush on the other side of the road. It had appeared out of heavy shrubbery, so there was no way he could have seen it in time. He accelerated again as if nothing had happened.

She glanced at him. "Should we check on Jacob and Tully?"

"I'm sure Tully kept him from being hit by the boxes." He smiled as Maya studied his profile.

Her curiosity overtook her for the second time. "How did you know the animal was about to cross the road?"

He stared at her and then returned his eyes to the road without saying anything. She fidgeted with the edge of her sweatshirt. Maybe she shouldn't have asked him. He didn't seem mad, but he was hard to read. Or maybe the butterflies in her stomach were clouding her perception.

A few minutes later, he said, "Sometimes I see things before they happen. Like intuition. It's no big deal."

"Really? Like that animal in the road?"

"Yep, but it's usually only right before it happens and not all the time."

Her mind raced with questions. "And just now you saw that Jacob was okay in the back?"

"Nah, but I'm sure he is fine." His eyes twinkled with a wry smile. "A couple of boxes to the head never hurt anyone." The truck decelerated and he turned off the main road onto a narrower dirt road. In the distance, a chain link fence surrounded a compound. As they approached the gate, he slowed down. "We're here."

Ren stopped the truck outside the locked gate. A couple of men stood by the gate, and a lanky one with a short ponytail approached the driver's side. Behind the fence stood several tent-like structures, a few larger buildings and an expansive field with people tending to crops. One of the buildings resembled the old greenhouses in her his-

tory book. People of all ages milled around wearing bright-
ly colored clothing.

Ponytail bumped fists with Ren through his open win-
dow. "Hey man. Glad to see yuh in one piece." He gave
Maya a nod. "I'm Sean."

"Hi. I'm Maya."

Sean spoke to Ren. "Sorry, but you know the rules
about outsiders. I can't let you in."

Ren turned towards Maya. "I'll be right back." He
hopped down from the driver's seat, and Sean opened the
gate for him to walk through. Once inside the compound,
Ren approached an elderly woman seated outside a tent.
Maya could barely make out the woman's features, but she
wore a beautiful purple head-wrap that matched her sim-
ple dress. Ren greeted the woman and then bent down and
spoke into her ear. She glanced at the truck, nodded her
head, and signaled to Sean at the gate. Ren returned to the
truck and Sean opened the gate for him to drive through.
Once Ren parked the truck, he took a deep breath and
turned towards Maya. "Now I just have to figure out a way
to explain the two kids in the back."

Chapter 16

WHEN A HEATED DISCUSSION broke out about whether they should be allowed to stay in Huruma, Ren ushered Maya out of the front seat and opened the back of the truck. He pulled down the tailgate and motioned for Maya to sit. "Stay with your friends in the truck til I get back." He followed the woman in the purple dress, and a few other people, into a tent.

While Maya waited with Tully and Jacob, a group of settlement children gathered near the back of the truck. One of the older girls approached Tully. "Can I touch your hair? It looks like red bulrush grass."

Tully stood up and glared at the girl. "No one touches my hair, but me." She turned to Maya. "What's up with these kids?" A few of the children giggled.

A boy with a dusty ball under his arm approached Maya and Jacob. "Are you all from the Republic? How do you know Uncle Ren?"

Jacob glanced at Maya before answering the boy. "Uh, yeah, we used to live in the Republic."

A smile spread across the boy's face. "Do you play kick-ball?

Ren walked up to the boy and ruffled his head. "You can play kickball later. It's time to unload the truck." Ren turned toward Maya. "You all can stay until I make my next trip to the Republic this weekend. But Celia wants to speak with you."

"Me?"

"Yes." Ren pointed to one of the tents. "She's waiting for you inside."

Maya's chest tightened as she walked toward the tent. Stopping halfway, she glanced over her shoulder at Ren who motioned for her to continue. The canvas door of the tent was pulled slightly open, so Maya peered inside. The woman in the purple dress motioned for her to enter.

"I'm Celia. Please, come on." Her gentle smile lit up her entire face and helped ease Maya's nerves. Although her deep brown skin was wrinkled, it had the warm glow of someone much younger.

"You wanted to speak with me?" Maya asked softly.

"Yes, please have a seat."

Maya took a seat on a cushion covered in colorful patterned fabric. Tapestries hung from the walls, while burlap covered the floor. The freshly cut flowers in a vase on the tea table perfumed the room. Celia had been making tea and poured a cup for Maya.

As Maya sipped her tea, Celia took a seat across from her and studied her with a smile. The tea tasted unfamiliar, but Maya savored the warmth that comforted her insides. Once Maya had put down her cup, Celia said, "Ren explained why you left the Arc. We'll do our best to help you and your friends, but I hope you understand our concern about giving you refuge. We have a precarious relationship with the Republic. You being here could put our community at risk."

"I understand. We appreciate you letting us stay until we go to the Republic."

"I'm glad we have an understanding. And we're happy to share what we have with you while you are here."

"Thank you." Maya's stomach growled and her mind drifted to the half-eaten granola bar in her backpack.

As if she heard the rumbling, Celia took a small covered dish from the tea table and opened it for her. "Help yourself."

"Thank you." Maya took a handful of dates. She put a date in her mouth and stuffed the rest in her pocket while

Celia returned the dish to the table. The sweet, tender date melted in her mouth.

Celia sat back and stared at Maya with a smile.

Maya waited for Celia to say something, but she continued to stare at her. Maya cleared her throat. "Ren said you wanted to speak to me about something?"

"Yes. Would you like some more tea?"

Maya offered her cup to Celia.

Celia filled Maya's cup and then filled her own. She cradled the cup in her hands. "What do you know about the uprising?"

Maya put down her tea and racked her brain for the right words. "Well, there was a violent insurrection that threatened the life of the economy. A lot of people died before the military was able to restore order." She glanced at Celia and added, "At least that's what they taught us in school."

"You're correct. Many people did lose their lives. However, it was a peaceful uprising. There has always been injustice in the world and sometimes that injustice becomes intolerable." Celia rose and removed a small box from the bookshelf before sitting beside Maya on the cushion. After opening the box, she sifted through the contents and took out a photo. "Have you heard of Leonora Light? She was the leader of the uprising. The most kind and compassionate woman I ever met. I imagine they don't teach about her in school." She handed the photo to Maya.

When Maya touched the photo, a peaceful love passed through her. She handed it back to Celia. "What happened?"

"Leonora inspired the good in people. She was descended from the original inhabitants of this land. She understood our oneness with each other and the environment, values shared by the majority of cultures and peoples that have been oppressed. She fought to dismantle a perverse system that placed profit above all else. Hundreds of thousands of people joined her cause and there were uprisings in cities everywhere. Those in power refused to yield and turned to military force. Many communities were completely destroyed. During this time, Commander Abigor rose through the military ranks and eventually convinced the Council to execute Leonora for treason."

Celia removed a small piece of fabric from the box and handed it to her. Maya unfolded the cloth revealing an embroidered emblem near the corner. Maya's mouth fell open. It matched the one on the handkerchief her mother had given her.

"That was the secret symbol of the uprising. Only those closest to the cause knew. I have been told you might know something about it?" Maya felt faint, but Celia's reassuring voice calmed her.

Maya pulled out her handkerchief from her pocket and handed it to Celia. "This was my mother's. It was tucked in the basket with her when she was found as a baby. She was abandoned at a church and adopted by my grandparents."

Celia unfolded the handkerchief and ran her hands over the embroidery. "Her mother, your grandmother, must have given it to her."

"My mom was told her birth mother was probably a drug addict. Maybe she stole it from someone? Or found it?"

"Perhaps." Celia handed the handkerchief back to Maya. Maya's mind swirled with questions. Before she could choose one, a young girl peeked in through the door.

"Miss Celia?" The girl hesitated before entering the tent. She was about eight or nine and wore a bright yellow dress that must have been a hand-me-down, her skinny arms swimming in the loose sleeves. Her long jet-black hair was braided in pigtails with bows to match her dress.

Celia motioned for the girl to come inside. "Yes, Evie?"

"Uncle Ren asked me to show the visitors around. They told me their friend Maya might want to come too if that's okay?" Evie's lips formed a shy smile as she shuffled her feet.

"Sure. Maya and I can finish our conversation later if that is okay with you, Maya?"

Maya nodded.

"Good. I'll see you at dinner this evening." Celia's face lit up with a warm smile. "Welcome to Huruma."

"Thank you." Maya returned Celia's smile and followed Evie out of the tent.

Outside, Tully kicked a ball around with a few of the older kids while Jacob sat watching. Evie motioned for them to join her and Maya, and she began to show them around the settlement. They passed small structures designed for sleeping and a larger communal area for cooking and dining. Although many of the structures were tent-like, some were made of mud, bricks, and the occasional metal sheeting.

Jacob pointed to the greenhouse. "What's over there?"

Evie's face lit up. "Oh, that's where we grow flowers. I can show you. It's lovely." Evie led them into the greenhouse. The thick warm air inside greeted them with the scent of damp soil and fresh flowers.

"Achoo!" Jacob sneezed. "Must be my allergies." He sneezed again. Evie ran over to a flower with vibrant orange petals and broke off a few of the larger ones. She ground them between her fingers.

Evie held out the ground-up petals to Jacob. "Don't worry. It doesn't taste bad."

"You want me to eat that?" Jacob sneezed again.

Evie giggled. "Just try it." Jacob took the petals and held them suspiciously up to his nose before placing them in his mouth.

Evie smiled at Jacob who had stopped sneezing. "See?"

"Interesting." Jacob studied the orange petal residue on his fingers. "Even faster than antihistamine spray."

"Come on. I'll show you more." Evie skipped ahead as they explored the greenhouse. Stunning flowers of all colors sprouted up from planters everywhere and overflowed from hanging baskets. Everything was so alive and vibrant. Joy spread across Maya's face as she shared in Evie's delight.

Further into the greenhouse, they encountered an older gentleman who tended to a large bed of colorful flowers. The man bent over a patch of delicate purple ones that were withered and brown on the edges. Maya approached him. "What's wrong with them?"

The man got up and examined the dirt between his fingers. "Nothing's wrong with them. The problem is the soil."

Jacob pointed to the flowers growing next to them that appeared to be thriving. "If it's the soil, wouldn't it affect the other ones?"

"Not yet." The man smiled. "These are galeas. They are so sensitive they can sense the slightest pollutant in the soil or water."

"Kind of like a canary in a coal mine," said Jacob.

Evie turned toward Jacob. "What's a canary in a coal mine?"

"They used to take canaries into the coal mines before the miners to make sure the air was safe to breathe. If the canary died, they knew it wasn't."

Evie's eyes welled up with tears. "That's awful."

Tully huffed. "Only for the canary."

Maya knelt by the flowers. They had a similar shape to the flower on her handkerchief. The symbol of the uprising. She rose and turned toward the man. "Are they going to die?"

The man chuckled. "Not if I can help it." His kind eyes met Evie's. "Why don't you show them the pond?"

Evie beamed. "We have fish. Let's go see."

They continued walking through rows of lush plants and flowers until Evie stopped in her tracks. "Careful, Tully."

"What?" Tully continued walking and her shoe came down on an earthworm traveling across their path.

"Oh no!" cried Evie. She knelt and picked up the lifeless earthworm. Tears pooled in her eyes.

"Don't worry." Tully checked the bottom of her sneaker. "I didn't get any worm guts on my shoe."

"But the worm." Evie's voice shook. "He's dead."

Tully raised her eyebrows in disbelief and turned to Maya. "Uh, it's just a worm, right? What'd I miss?"

"Maybe she feels bad for it." Maya crouched next to Evie. "Are you okay?"

"Seriously? A worm? She's lucky she isn't from the Republic. She would've been sent to the Arc in a heartbeat."

Evie placed the worm in a patch of soil. After a moment, she took a deep breath and stood up. Brushing her hands off on her dress, she turned to Tully. "My mom said the Republic sends sensitive kids to the Arc because they are scared of how strong they are. Is that why you all were sent there?"

"Yeah, they send sensitive kids there," said Jacob. "But it's because we need to be rehabilitated."

Maya faced Evie. "Did your mom tell you why she thinks that?"

"Nope. But Miss Celia says that my compassion makes me strong, so I believe it." Evie broke into a smile. "Come on, we still need to see the pond."

After they viewed the pond, Evie led them to the tent where they would be sleeping. A man greeted them outside the door. "I left some wool blankets on the bed. It gets chilly at night."

Jacob studied the tent walls. "How come you sleep in tents when other structures are made of bricks and metal sheeting?"

"We used to build more permanent structures with whatever materials we could barter for, but even after the end of the war, the Republic kept bombing us. Every time we built something new, they would destroy it, so we eventually used temporary shelters like tents. They haven't bombed us in years. Probably figured we aren't worth the price of the bombs anymore."

"So it's safe here now?"

"It has been." He eyed the three of them. "We'd like to keep it that way." He turned to go.

"Do you mind showing me to the bathrooms?" asked Jacob. "Evie showed us, but I can't remember."

"Sure, follow me."

As the two of them walked off, Tully turned to Maya. "I'm gonna go play kickball. You wanna come?'

"No, I think I'm going to lie down."

Inside the tent, three cots had been made up with blankets, and a vase of colorful flowers sat on a small table. Burlap covered the floor, and a box with more clothes sat in the corner. Browsing through the box spurred her anxiety, so she lay down on one of the cots. She had been wearing what she had been told to wear for so long it was unnerving to have so many choices.

As she stared at the ceiling, she let out a deep breath and allowed her thoughts to flow. Ever since she had put Jacob's fear into Tully, neither of them had spoken to her about it. Did they think she was crazy? Or worse, dangerous? And now her mother had somehow ended up with a secret uprising handkerchief. How was that even possible? Her avalanche of thoughts was interrupted by the tent door opening.

Ren stood in the doorway. "Hey. Everything ok?" He smiled at her.

She sat up and smoothed her hair. The white sleeveless shirt he had changed into accentuated his muscular physique. Catching herself staring, she glanced away. "Yes, I'm fine. Everyone here has been really nice."

"They're good people." He turned to go. "Dinner's at six in the outdoor eating area. Just follow the noise."

"Ren?" her voice cracked. "Can I ask you something?"

"Sure."

"I know you said it's just intuition, but when you started seeing things, how did you feel?"

"It was a little weird at first, but I got used to it." He walked over and sat on the cot across from her. "Why?"

"Sometimes I feel things."

"Doesn't everyone?"

She fidgeted with her sweatshirt, avoiding his eyes. "Yes, but I think I can make other people feel them, too." She glanced up at him.

He leaned toward her. "What do you mean, 'feel them, too'?"

"I can put bad feelings into people with my hands. At least I think I can. Maybe other feelings, too. I'm not sure."

"Hmm." He rested his chin between his thumb and forefinger and stared at her.

She shifted toward the end of her cot away from him. "You must think I'm crazy."

"I'm the guy who sees things before they happen, remember?" he grinned. "So, you can just touch a person and wham! They feel it? Like pain?"

She shrugged. "I think so."

"Here, try me." He held out his arm.

She glanced at his perfectly chiseled arm. "I'm not sure..."

"Don't worry. I doubt you could hurt me." He shifted over to her cot and sat beside her, offering his arm. "Just try it."

She placed her hand lightly on his bicep and searched her body for an emotion. Maybe the anxiety she was feeling earlier? But all she could sense was the warm, tingly feeling of being near him. She released his arm. "Sorry. I think I have to take in a bad feeling first to make it work." She turned as someone entered the tent.

"Hey, Maya." Jacob's eyes darted between Maya and Ren sitting inches apart. "What's Ren doing here? Is everything ok?"

Ren got up. "I just came by to make sure you Fragiles settled in." He approached the door. "See you at dinner."

After Ren left, Jacob took a seat across from Maya. "It's nice of them to take us in, but we don't really know these people. It can't hurt to be cautious."

"Cautious?"

"Yeah, you know, like not getting too close. We just got here."

"You mean like Ren?"

He loosened his scarf. "Yeah, Ren, whoever. It's like Tully said, we aren't at the Arc anymore. We need to be careful."

They weren't at the Arc anymore, but for the first time in years, she felt like she could breathe. "Don't worry. I'll be careful."

Chapter 17

AFTER NAPPING THE REST of the afternoon, Maya met the others outside for dinner. The long wood tables with benches on each side were covered with food of all kinds and colors. She had almost forgotten what fresh vegetables looked like. As people took their seats at the tables, she glanced around not sure where to sit. Older people sat next to children, and babies were passed around from one person to the next while parents got settled in no particular order. Tully grabbed a seat next to some of the kickball players. Luckily, Jacob saved her a seat next to him and Sean from the gate.

Once everyone was seated, Celia walked toward the center of the four long tables which were arranged in rows, so that two tables were to either side of her. Strings of lights hung between wooden poles framed the perimeter of the dining area, and lit up as dusk approached. When Celia reached the center, she stopped and raised one palm. The area fell silent except for the hum of a generator in the background.

"I'm sure you're all eager to dive into this delicious food, but let's take a moment to thank the hands who made it and the fields that provided it."

Nodding heads, smiles and murmured thanks flowed through the crowd.

"We're also thankful that we are able to assist our three guests who are here for a short while." A few quiet thanks were met with hushed grumblings from the table where the man who had given them the blankets sat. Celia pivoted to address the table. "We remember we're all connected and that when one suffers, we all do." She smiled directly at the man and then returned her attention to the gathering, hands raised. "Let's eat."

Sean offered Maya a plate of grilled vegetables. "Would you like some?"

"Yes, please."

He scooped a large portion on her plate and handed her the dish.

She looked at him quizzically.

He nodded toward Jacob. "To offer to your friend."

As she held the dish out for Jacob, she half expected a dining monitor to snatch the food out of her hands. Once she had handed the dish to Jacob, Sean offered her a plate of fresh vegetables. By the time they had finished passing the dishes around, Maya's plate overflowed with fresh and cooked vegetables, roasted potatoes, and a thick spiced bean stew. Her stomach rumbled and everything she devoured was delicious. She glanced at Jacob who seemed to be enjoying himself, finally able to eat food worthy of his taste buds.

During the meal, peals of children's laughter blended with animated conversation in a beautiful, almost musical, chaos that warmed Maya's heart. She scanned the dining area for Ren and spotted him sitting next to the men from the front gate. Engaged in a lively conversation, he threw back his head and laughed, then caught her eye and smiled. Her cheeks flushed, but she mustered a smile before dropping her gaze.

After dinner, Maya suggested that the three of them help clean up to show their appreciation for the food, so they carried the dishes toward the large outdoor sink. The sun had gone down, and the chill in the air made Maya glad she had her sweatshirt. As they washed the dishes, Jacob shivered. "It's getting really cold out here. I'm going to get my scarf."

Tully rolled her eyes. "We're almost done. I think you'll survive."

Jacob rubbed his hands on his forearms. "I'm freezing."

"Why don't you give me those glasses to dry so you can go get your scarf?" said Maya. Jacob nodded and handed her the glass. Noticing a frosty smudge on the glass, she handed it back. "I think this one needs to be—"

A loud crash and scream exploded from a nearby tent.

Jacob pointed to the tent. "I think that's Evie's tent."

Tully sprinted ahead with Maya and Jacob close behind her.

When they reached the tent, muffled voices sounded from inside. Tully pulled open the canvas door to reveal a large man with a glass bottle in his hand. The man's sweat-stained shirt barely covered his belly, and he swayed in place as if trying to maintain his balance. A vase of flowers lay shattered on the floor by an overturned table. Evie cowered in the corner while a woman knelt near the broken glass attempting to pick up the flowers, her long, straight dark hair clinging to her tear-streaked face. A sour scent laced with body odor permeated the room.

The man stumbled toward the woman. "I told you to get up off the floor, bitch."

Evie darted toward Maya and clung to her. "Please help my mom," she whispered. Evie's fear jolted through Maya.

"Here, stay with Jacob." Maya released Evie's grip and guided her into Jacob's arms. Tully had placed herself between the man and Evie's mother, who remained on the floor fumbling with the broken glass. Maya approached the man from behind with Evie's terror coursing through her veins.

Tully stood dangerously near the man who had raised the bottle above his head. She glared at him. "You think you're tough? You're just a drunk dumbass."

The man swung the bottle at Tully, but Maya grabbed his other arm from behind. He spun around to face her, bloodshot eyes spewing rage. Grasping his wrist with all her strength, she willed every ounce of emotion she had taken in from Evie into her fingertips. His eyes grew wide, and he let out a terrified gasp. Pain seared Maya's arm, but she held on until he collapsed to the floor shaking. She stumbled back just as Ren, Sean, and another man entered the tent.

Sean nudged the man on the floor with his boot. "Dammit, Earl. Why'd you let him in the gate while the rest of us were at dinner? You know he's not allowed here."

Earl bent to lift the man off the floor. "A man has a right to see his child."

Earl and Sean slung Evie's father's arms over their shoulders to help him up. Once he stood, Evie's father raised his chin.

He lifted a finger toward Maya and mumbled, "She's one of them." Saliva dripped from his mouth and his eyes rolled closed as he stumbled against Earl.

Maya clutched her stomach and stepped back against the tent wall. *One of what?*

Residual pain pulsated in her arm.

Ren exchanged glances with Sean. He clenched his jaw and shoved Evie's dad toward the door. "Be sure you take him outside the gate. I don't want to see him back here." His face softened as he turned toward Evie's mother. "Are you okay, June?" He took her hand and helped her to her feet.

"Just a bit shaken up." June smoothed her hair and turned toward Maya and Tully. "Thank you for helping me." She smiled at Maya. "Can I ask how you did that?"

"I'm not really—"

"She's stronger than she looks," Ren caught Maya's eye. "Why don't you all take Evie to see Miss Celia? I'll help June clean up."

Evie gripped Jacob's hand as they walked toward Celia's tent. Every few paces, she sniffled and wiped her eyes.

When they approached the tent, Tully turned to Maya. "You must have used your power on him, right Maya? I mean, I could've taken him, but I'm glad to know you got my back."

Evie looked up at Maya. "What power?"

Maya glared at Tully but then smiled at Evie. "It's not really a power. I'm just glad I was able to help." She was not "one of them." Whatever that was.

Celia stood waiting for them outside of her tent. She reached for Evie's hand. "Why don't you come and join me for tea?" Evie wrapped her arms around Celia's waist and buried her face in her skirt. As Celia embraced Evie, she spoke to Maya. "Are you able to come see me in the morning? I'd like to finish our conversation from earlier."

"I'd like that. I still have some questions."

A lot of questions.

Chapter 18

THE NEXT MORNING, MAYA awoke well-rested for the first time in recent memory. She had slept soundly, and the nightmares seemed to have stopped. As she walked in the cool morning air to meet Celia, she passed Ren who was standing in the doorway of June's tent. June stood next to him, her body leaning into him with her hand resting on his arm. Ren seemed comfortable with the closeness and bent down to speak in her ear. Had he spent the night there?

Ignoring the tight feeling in her throat, Maya hurried on her way before he could see her.

Celia had tea and fresh strawberries waiting for her when she arrived. Maya took a seat on the soft cushion and tried to dismiss all thoughts of Ren. "How's Evie?"

"She's better now. Unfortunately, her father lost his job in the Republic and developed a drinking problem soon after she was born. June is originally from Huruma, so she moved herself and Evie back here when Evie was still a toddler." Celia handed Maya a cup of tea and sat next to her. "Evie told me how you helped them last night. She mentioned that you used a special ability?"

Maya gazed into her tea. Did Celia think she was one of whatever Evie's dad called her? "Oh that was nothing. I just helped Tully."

Celia stared at her as if trying to read her. "It's okay. It's nothing to be ashamed of. We all have unique strengths." The warmth of her smile wrapped Maya in a comforting embrace, lowering her defenses.

Maya took a sip of tea and placed the cup on the table. "Okay. Well, sometimes I get overwhelmed with emotions."

"Go on."

"And I think maybe I can put them into other people. I know it sounds weird, like I'm some kind of—"

Celia put up her hand to cut Maya off. "It's not strange at all when you consider we are all one. When one of us hurts, we all hurt. It makes perfect sense to me."

"I guess that sorta makes sense, but how's it possible? For me to put feelings into people, I mean."

"We're capable of so much more than we think. Most people's minds hold them back from their true potential, especially those born with the gift of heightened sensitivity."

"I've never thought of sensitivity as a gift."

Celia placed her hand on hers, her eyes stern, yet filled with kindness. "Maybe it's time to start thinking that way."

Maya swallowed and nodded her head, overcome by the strength of Celia's conviction.

Maybe someday she could.

Celia gave Maya's hand a gentle squeeze before releasing it. "Regarding your specific ability, it's really not that difficult to explain. We're all made of energy that can impact those around us, so you're just doing it in a more dramatic way. My guess is that over time, the trauma you endured at the Arc caused a shift in the way you process the energy and emotions that you take in and how you're able to release it. Some people develop abilities through enlightenment, some through trauma."

"Trauma?"

"Yes, painful things we experience, like being taken from your family. We all experience trauma in different ways."

Despite her best efforts, her mind returned to Ren. "Is that what happened to Ren? Like how he gets glimpses of the future?"

"His story's not mine to tell, but yes, his ability is another example of what's possible. It's really just an advanced form of intuition."

Maya let out a deep breath. It was all so much to take in. She definitely needed time to process.

Celia held out the bowl of strawberries. "I know it's a lot to consider, but who you are is nothing to be ashamed of."

"Thanks." Maya took a strawberry. "I feel bad about hurting Evie's dad, though. Is he okay?"

"He'll be fine. There's nothing wrong with using your strength to protect someone—especially when it comes from a place of compassion." Her eyes locked on Maya. "Even the gentlest spirit can become a warrior in the face of injustice."

Maya bit into the juicy strawberry. Celia seemed to think she was strong, but how could she be strong when she couldn't even handle normal emotions? She was still obsessing over seeing Ren with June, and even the sweet strawberry couldn't get rid of the sour taste in the back of her throat.

Celia put her hand on Maya's arm. "The most important thing you can do is accept your ability as a gift. It's what makes you uniquely you."

"I'll try to remember that." She picked up her tea and swirled it around in her cup focusing on the smooth ripples of the liquid. "Can I ask you something?"

"Sure."

"Do you think it is possible to hear someone's thoughts? Like someone you don't even know?"

"There are people who believe we all have access to a collective consciousness, so I imagine it could be possible. Why?"

"I've been sharing a girl's pain. Someone I don't know, and she asked me to help her."

"If she's accessing a collective consciousness, it makes sense that she might reach a highly empathetic person."

"You think I'm an empath? I read that empathy is a narcissistic delusion."

"Don't believe everything you read," she chuckled. "Especially if it's from the Republic. Empaths just share other people's feelings and emotions. It makes it easier for them to feel compassion and connect with others but can be overwhelming at times."

Maya sighed. Overwhelming was an understatement, but at least she wasn't a delusional narcissist.

"So, if this girl is asking for help, you might want to listen." Celia smiled at her. "Any other questions?

A lot more questions. And one she really needed the answer to. "Evie's dad called me 'one of them.' Do you know what he meant by that?"

Celia's face tightened. "I wouldn't worry about that. Some people feel the need to label those who are different."

Maya sensed a slight shift in Celia's normally open demeanor. She put down her tea. "But I mean like one of *what*?"

"He probably meant someone who cares about others enough to risk their own safety. That's rare nowadays." She got up and handed the bowl of strawberries to Maya. "I have some matters to attend to, but can you please take these to share with your friends?"

"Sure, they'd like that." Maya took the bowl and approached the door.

"If you see Ren, please tell him I need to speak with him."

"I will. Thanks for the strawberries."

As Maya headed back to her tent, Ren approached her from the opposite direction. He must have just left June's tent.

"Hey, morning." He smiled and eyed the strawberries. "Those look good."

She shifted the strawberries away from him. "Yes, they are. I was just talking to Celia about what happened with June's husband."

"Ex-husband."

So he wasn't an adulterer. He still wasn't getting any strawberries.

"So where are you headed with the strawberries?" The warmth in his eyes lit up his smile.

As perfect as he looked in the morning sun, she would not give him a strawberry.

"I'm going to go see if Tully and Jacob are up. Celia told me to tell you she wants to speak with you."

"Thanks, I will. Enjoy the strawberries."

"Ok. See you later." Maya started to head up the path, but then stopped and turned around.

Dangit.

She held out the bowl to Ren. "You want one?"

Ren grinned. "Nah, I'm good."

When Maya got back to the tent, Jacob and Tully were still asleep. She placed the strawberries on the table and sat on her cot. With her palms facing upward, she examined the lines in her hands. She turned over one hand and ran her thumb up the back to the end of her middle finger. She repeated the motion up her ring and pinky fingers.

One of them.

Her fingers recoiled as she recalled the pain shooting through her arm into Evies's dad. She balled her hands into fists and then slowly opened them. What was she?

A rustling at the tent door drew her attention.

Ren poked his head in and motioned with his hand for her to come to the door.

Maya rose and joined him by the door. "What is it?"

"We're leaving for the Republic first thing tomorrow."

"Tomorrow?" It seemed so soon—too soon. "I thought we weren't leaving till this weekend?"

"Things have changed. Celia's worried you aren't safe here. Tell Jacob and Tully. We'll leave at dawn."

Tully let out a groan. "Can the two of you be any louder?"

Maya turned to Tully, "Sorry."

"You can pack any clothes you might need from the box in the corner," said Ren. "I'll take you to my uncle's hotel. It should be safe there."

"Should be?" Jacob got up and stretched.

"I'm sure the Arc is looking for you, but I doubt they'd look there. It's not exactly the kind of place three runaway Fragiles would go."

Tully slung her legs over the side of her cot and sat up. "Can I at least get my own room? These two chatterboxes get up way too early."

"I'd worry less about your room and more about what you are going to do once you get to the Republic." Ren turned his attention back to Maya. "I need to go make preparations for tomorrow, but let me know if you need anything."

"Okay, thanks."

Ren made eye contact with Maya and tilted his head. His mouth opened slightly like he was about to say something, but his lips closed into a frown. He gave her a light nod and left the tent.

Maya stared at the tent door, not sure if the worry in her gut stemmed from Ren or her own.

That evening, Maya and Jacob sat on one of the wooden benches overlooking the fields to enjoy the radiant sunset while Tully skipped stones across a nearby stream. The strokes of yellow, pink, and purple brushing the sky became more vibrant as the sun threatened to disappear below the horizon. Maya's heart constricted with every shift in the skyline. It was slipping away too fast.

Jacob's voice snapped her back to reality. "Hey Tully, didn't you say your dad owns the Modern Republic Broadcasting Service?"

"You mean Mr. BS?"

"Is that what you call your dad?" asked Jacob.

"No, that's what I call the company, MRBS, 'cause they're full of crap. I guess it works for my dad though, too." Tully laughed. "It's the only television station in the Republic. But yeah, he owns it. Why?"

"I've been thinking about what we should do when we get to the Republic. Maybe we could get him to broadcast a story about how they're hurting kids at the center so people can learn the truth."

"That sounds like a good idea," said Maya.

Jacob got up and approached Tully. "You could take us to see him, right?"

Tully hurled a large rock at the stream. "The next time I speak to my father, it'll be to tell him to go to hell."

Jacob's jaw stiffened. "Tully, we have to have a plan. We can't just show up at the reconditioning center. They'd lock us up on the spot."

"I have a plan. I'm going to order myself a Gino's pizza and inhale the sweet stench of the Republic." Tully threw another stone.

Jacob turned to Maya. "You hear this? She convinced us to leave the Arc just so she could get pizza. Are you kidding me?"

Jacob's anger threatened to invade Maya, so she took a deep breath. "Tully, remember you said you would help us save the kids at the center, right? Maybe Jacob and I could go see your dad. You just need to tell us how to get there. You could do that, right?"

Tully let the stone slip from her fingers. "Okay, yeah, I can do that. He likes sensational stories, so maybe he'll bite. I can't guarantee he'll give a crap though."

"At least that's a start." Maya motioned for Jacob to join her on the bench. "How about we enjoy the sunset and work out the details later?"

"I guess so." Jacob slumped down next to Maya as Evie came up the dirt path carrying a small potted plant.

Approaching Jacob with a shy smile, Evie held out the plant. "Ren told me you're leaving tomorrow. I wanted to give you this in case you get allergies." Her eyes welled up, and her lip started to quiver.

"Thank you, Evie." Jacob took the orange flowering plant and set it on the bench. He stood and gave her a hug. "I'll miss you."

Evie's face brightened. "I hope you all come back to visit soon. I have to get back to help my mom, but I'll see you in the morning." Evie gave Jacob a wide grin before hurrying off.

Tully nudged Jacob. "Looks like someone has a crush."

Jacob shoved Tully back, nearly losing his balance. "She's eight."

"I think it's cute," said Maya. "She's such a sweetheart."

Jacob smirked. "Kind of like your crush on Ren?"

"What are you talking about?" Maya shuffled her feet in the dirt.

Tully chimed in. "Oh, come on Maya. You know he's hot. You've seen the way his jeans—"

"Okay, Tully, we get the point." Jacob adjusted his scarf around his neck. "It's getting dark. Let's head back. We have a big day tomorrow."

Chapter 19

WEARY FROM A FITFUL night, Maya welcomed the early rays of sunlight that peeked into the tent the next morning. She got up and put on a sweatshirt while Jacob crammed clothes in his already full backpack.

She joined him by his cot. "We can hand wash stuff like underwear."

"I know." He clenched his jaw and then let out huff. He turned his backpack upside down and dumped out the contents. Amongst the clothes, he picked up a plastic bag filled with blue pills. "I forgot to take one."

"You still take your medicine?"

"Of course. Didn't you bring any from the Arc?" Jacob took out a pill and swallowed it. "I took a bunch from the nurse's station before we left."

She lowered her eyes. "I stopped taking them when we were still at the Arc."

"You stopped? We're supposed to take it for life. We're about to go to the Republic. That's no place for Fragiles, especially ones that aren't cured like you."

"I'm fine. In fact, I feel better since I stopped."

He shrugged and began to repack the contents of his bag. "Whatever you say."

Tully groaned. "Can you turn off the light already?"

Jacob put on his backpack. "It's not a light. It's the sun—as in dawn. We gotta go."

While Tully gathered her belongings, Maya shoved an extra pair of leggings and a t-shirt into her backpack to use as pajamas and followed Jacob out of the tent.

Once they were all outside, they proceeded to the gate where Ren loaded flowers into the back of his delivery truck. Tully peered at the stacks of crates. "What's with all the flowers?"

Ren sat down the last crate. "It's our ticket into the Republic. You can't just drive across the border without permission."

Jacob inspected the containers. "Yeah, but flowers?"

"Yep. The Republic is so polluted almost nothing can grow there. But rich people love flowers. You'd be surprised how much they pay to get something other people can't."

Maya didn't remember the Republic being polluted. She scanned the rows of colorful flowers. "So, you take flowers in and smuggle out stuff?"

"Basically. It's illegal to trade with the settlements, but they look the other way if we keep the flowers coming." Ren motioned to the place he had cleared alongside the crates. "Try to get as far to the back as you can, and I'll pack the rest in around you."

Maya waited while Tully and Jacob climbed into the truck. Despite knowing they needed to leave, her feet anchored her to the ground. She inhaled the crisp morning air and gazed across the field at the colorful skyline.

Ren placed his hand on her elbow. "Climb up. We gotta go."

His touch brought her back to the moment, and she pulled herself up into the truck. As she headed to the back, Ren packed the remainder of the crates around them. Once he had closed the back, the thin, high window behind the cab provided relief from the darkness enveloping them.

Making the best of the cramped space, Maya curled up in the corner and rested her head on a bag of soil. When the bumpy dirt road met the smooth pavement of the highway, the hum of the engine lulled her in and out of sleep. At some point, she drifted into a deep sleep because when she awoke the truck had come to a stop.

Maya glanced at Tully and Jacob who were frozen in place. The sound of the back door opening pricked the back of her neck.

"All you got back there is flowers, right?" It must be a border guard.

The truck dipped as if he had climbed into the back. As he shifted the crates around, Maya held her breath. All that remained between them and the guard were a few rows of crates.

"I don't know what the big deal is about these stupid flowers," muttered the guard. The sound of shifting crates drew nearer to where they hid. Maya's chest tightened. Her eyes darted to Tully who had an unfamiliar concern in her eyes. The guard had made it to the row of crates that hid them.

Jacob pulled his scarf up to his face, his eyes wide like he was about to sneeze.

Crap! Please hold it.

Maya locked eyes with Jacob and tilted her head toward the plant Evie had given him. Noticing her movement, Jacob nodded before silently breaking off a petal and slipping it into his mouth. The crates directly in front of them started to shift.

"Are you almost done?" called Ren. "I have important people waiting for those flowers who I don't want to piss off."

"Yeah, I'm done. Can't stand the stench of 'em anyway." The guard withdrew and the back of the truck slammed shut. Maya waited until the truck moved forward to breathe.

Although most of the journey had been long stretches of road, Ren was now making numerous turns and stops. Because the hotel was located just outside the capitol in the business district, they must have been getting close. Finally, the truck made one last turn and came to a stop. The three of them stared at one another in silence.

After a few minutes, Ren opened the back of the truck and began to clear a path through the crates. "It's okay. We're here."

While Jacob climbed down from the back of the truck, Maya rose and stretched her cramped muscles. After Tully jumped down, Ren held out his hand to help Maya, but she ignored it. Maybe she was still annoyed about seeing him with June, but regardless, she didn't need his help. She thought she saw a small smile escape from Jacob's lips as he watched the interaction.

Ren rearranged the crates and closed the back of the truck. "We're in the parking garage of my uncle's hotel. I just spoke to him on the service phone and explained everything. It's fine for you to stay. He should be down here any minute."

"Ren!" A man approached them with a wide smile and gave Ren a hearty embrace.

"Great to see you, Uncle." Ren returned the hug and patted him on the back. After releasing his uncle, he turned to them. "This is my Uncle Alastair. He'll help you get settled. I'll be back later tonight." Tall like Ren, but slimmer, Alastair had a fuzzy gray beard that made up for what little hair remained on his head. He wore round glasses, a tweed sports jacket, and a cheerful smile that lifted Maya's spirit.

"Welcome to the Republic. Let's get you folks upstairs." Alastair led them across the parking garage to a service elevator and entered a code to open the elevator door. "We use this for our guests that require special discretion." He smiled and gestured toward the door. "After you." He entered behind them and pressed number twelve on the panel.

"What kind of guests require special discretion?" asked Jacob. "Other than us?"

"Oh, you would be surprised." Alastair chuckled. "Let's just say there are certain people who do things their mothers wouldn't be proud of." The elevator came to a stop and Alastair led them down a plush hallway with deep burgundy carpeting and gold wallpaper. "I put you in this room so you can have a view of the city." As he unlocked the door, he smiled at Jacob. "It's a suite so the gentleman can have his own room." He motioned for them to enter. "From what Ren tells me, it's best if you all stay inside for now. If you need anything, just pick up the phone on the nightstand. Be sure to keep the door locked." He closed the door behind him as he left.

Tully went straight to the window and pushed open the heavy drapes. Out the window, dozens of skyscrapers littered the hazy sky. Flashy digital billboards sprung up from the sides and roofs of buildings, offering splashes of color against the gray concrete that covered most everything else. Below them, the street was jammed with traffic, alive with a cacophony of honking horns and blasting jackhammers. Everything was so much bigger, bolder, and chaotic than Maya remembered.

Maya set her backpack on one of the beds and scoped out the room. The two single beds draped with thick quilts were separated by an antique mahogany nightstand. Across from the beds, a television rested on a thin table. The deep burgundy fabric padding the walls made the room feel smaller than it was. On the other side of the room, a door led to a bathroom with Jacob's room connected to the other side. Maya sat on the bed while Jacob went to investigate his room.

Tully peered out the window. "I would kill for a Gino's pizza right now. I wonder if they still deliver."

Jacob returned from his room. "We need money for that. Speaking of which, how're we going to get around without any?"

Tully stepped away from the window and retrieved her backpack from the floor. She rummaged through it before pulling out a wallet and tossing it proudly on Maya's bed. "I lifted it from Dr. Barrow's office the day we left. Thought it might come in handy."

Maya picked up the wallet and thumbed through the stack of crinkled bills.

Tully grinned. "Who knew shrinks made so much money?"

Jacob walked over to the window. "We might need some to get to your dad's building tomorrow. How far is it?"

Tully joined him by the window and pointed. "It's that tall ugly one over there. He keeps adding floors to make sure it's the tallest." She scoffed and turned away from the window. "Too bad it's too risky for me to come with you. I would've loved to rub it in his face that I busted out of the Arc."

"Maya and I'll be fine without you."

Placing her hands on her hips, Tully raised an eyebrow. "Have you ever even been in an office building?"

"No, but we did business etiquette and negotiation tactics in life skills class at the Arc. I got an A."

Tully shrugged, "I must've slept through that part. His office is on the top floor, so just act like you know what you're doing and you shouldn't get arrested."

Maya stared out the window to the tall, foreboding buildings. Life skills class or not, were they really prepared to go up against Commander Abigor?

Night had fallen and Ren hadn't returned. When someone knocked on the door, Maya sat up from where she lay on the bed. Ren should have been back by now.

"That must be the pizza." Tully rushed to the door and peeked out the peephole. She slid a few bills from Dr. Barrow's wallet under the door and waited a full minute before retrieving the delivery. Turning to Jacob, she smirked. "Don't worry, I used a fake name."

Tully set down a huge box of pizza and a six-pack of soda on her bed. "Oh, how I've dreamed of this. Come grab a slice. Best food ever!" Tully was already halfway through her first gooey slice when Maya and Jacob joined her on the bed.

Jacob picked up one of the cans and examined it. "What kind of soda is it?"

"O'Malley's. My dad used to buy cases of it to serve at his parties, but never let me drink it. I've always wanted to try it." Tully took a soda and then tossed one to Maya.

Starving, Maya bit into the big greasy slice of pizza. The soda had a fruity kick to it that warmed her insides. She gulped it down, enjoying the feeling.

"Uh, Tully." Jacob sniffed his soda. "Is this soda? It smells like alcohol."

"How would you know what alcohol smells like?" Tully opened her can and took a sip.

"The scent lab. I have a very refined sense of smell in case you forgot." Jacob put down his can.

Maya had almost finished hers, her warm insides starting to tingle.

"Guess that's why my dad wouldn't let me drink it." Tully grinned and raised her can. "Cheers to my dad, Fitzgerald Doyle."

Maya devoured her pizza. The grease was no longer her enemy as she savored every piece of pepperoni she had picked off with disgust only minutes earlier. As the lightness in her head spread throughout her body, a grin spread across her face.

Jacob frowned. "Maya, did you drink the whole can?"

Maya turned the can upside down. "Yep." She giggled.

"Don't worry. She'll be fine." Tully grabbed another slice of pizza.

"Thank you, Tully. You're really smart. And so strong." Maya patted Tully's arm. "I wish I could be like you. Don't you wish you could be strong like Tully, Jacob? Instead of being so weak?" The words tumbled from her mouth.

"No, I don't." Jacob got up and went to sit on the other bed.

"Don't be mad," Maya stumbled across to Jacob. "I just mean with your sensitivities to everything. Wouldn't you rather be normal?" She flopped down on the bed next to him. "And what about me getting overwhelmed with all these stupid feelings all the time? What good am I?"

Jacob gazed down at Maya lying beside him and sighed. He gently moved a piece of hair from her face. "You are good. You're the best person I know." The tenderness in his voice matched the warmth of his touch. She wanted to say something, but the words got swallowed by the fuzzy clouds in her head. Resting her head against his thigh, she fell asleep.

Chapter 20

MAYA PULLED HER HOODIE over her head as she and Jacob headed up the main street toward the Modern Republic Broadcast Service building. A torrent of pedestrians and blaring traffic crowded the streets. The polluted air burned her lungs, and Jacob had already pulled his scarf over his nose and mouth. As they made their way up the sidewalk dodging uptight commuters, Maya struggled to shut out the chaos.

Every storefront displayed flashy signs and crowded windows crammed with products. A vendor yelled from a doorway. "The best vodka in the Republic on sale today only!"

The sickly sweet scent of perfume wafted from a tall blond woman holding an extravagant bottle. "Try the scent men can't resist!"

Pedestrians jostled one another, their nervous energy pouring into Maya. As she continued to follow Jacob up the sidewalk, the unfamiliar sights and sounds merged into a thunderous monster bearing down on her. Too many sounds, too many smells, too many people. Maybe Jacob was right about the city being no place for uncured Fragiles.

After a few more blocks, a black concrete structure with enormous glass windows towered above them. An elegant gold sign above the revolving glass door read, *"Modern Republic Broadcasting Service - The Only Network You Need."* Maya took a deep breath and glanced at Jacob before opening the door. Once inside, they headed straight for the elevator.

When the elevator doors opened on the twentieth floor, a spacious reception area with a view of the city greeted them. Fresh flowers on the table perfumed the waiting area which was furnished with dark leather chairs and an exquisite rug. The receptionist sat alone at a sleek angular desk which also displayed a vase of fresh flowers, the stems cut short. She appeared to be in her early thirties, her chestnut hair pulled back in a bun accentuating her perfectly made-up face and strong jawline.

"If you're here to audition, the casting call is on the twelfth floor." The receptionist glanced up with a tight-lipped smile before going back to typing.

"Excuse me, but we're here to see Mr. Fitzgerald Doyle, please." Jacob approached the woman and Maya followed, her mouth too dry to speak.

"I'm sorry, but Mr. Doyle is not available at the moment. He's a very busy man."

"It will only take a minute. Can you at least ask him? It looks like he's in his office." Jacob gestured toward the door which was ajar. "You can tell him we're Tully's friends."

"One moment." The receptionist picked up the phone and spoke into it. "I'm sorry to disturb you, but there are some *children* here who say they are friends of Tully?" The receptionist paused and then spoke into the phone again. "Thank you." She hung up and gave Jacob a curt smile. "Mr. Doyle says he doesn't know anyone named Tully."

Tully lied? Maya's heart sank.

"It's important that we talk to him." Jacob's voice gained strength. "We have information about questionable matters occurring at the reconditioning center."

"If you'd like, I'd be happy to call security to escort you out." The receptionist picked up the phone but set it down when Mr. Doyle came out of the office.

Mr. Doyle placed his hand on her shoulder and smiled, softening her expression. "That's okay, Miranda. I have a minute to speak with them." He offered Jacob a smile. "Please take a seat in my office." Jacob walked past Maya, beads of sweat forming on the side of his face.

Mr. Doyle's expansive office was as elegant as the building. On his desk near the phone, sat a framed photo of him standing next to a beautiful woman with long red hair and a young girl who unmistakably resembled Tully. Mr. Doyle had the same blue eyes as Tully, but they were missing the spark. Maya guessed he was in his mid-forties, but his receding hairline and tired eyes made him appear older.

As Mr. Doyle took a seat behind his desk, Maya pointed to the photo. "Is that your family?"

"Yes. That's my late wife Rose and my daughter Petulah." He picked up the photo. "Petulah is about your age now."

Maya sunk into her chair, weighed down by his grief. "You must really care about her."

"Yes." He gazed wistfully at the photo. "She's my world."

Jacob elbowed Maya. No doubt Tully would be mortified if people knew her real name was Petulah.

"Anyways, you say you wanted to speak about the reconditioning center?" He placed the photo back on his desk. "I'm actually in the middle of reviewing our marketing campaign to promote the center. A personal request from Commander Abigor. It's quite incredible."

Mr. Doyle handed them a glossy poster. "It's housed in the new Apex Enterprises building. Isn't it beautiful?"

Maya glanced at the poster. The spectacular building had an eerie familiarity. Before she averted her eyes, the words "Apex Building Company" caught her attention. The name rang a bell, but she couldn't remember why.

"Yes, it's a nice building," said Jacob. "But do you know what they do there?"

"Well, yes. They are helping rehabilitate Fragiles." Mr. Doyle set the poster aside. "What exactly did you mean when you said 'questionable activities' are going on there?"

Jacob wrung his hands in his lap, but kept his voice steady. "We have knowledge of a memo. A memo that says children are being harmed by the reconditioning process."

"Harmed?" He wrinkled his brows. "Where did you see this memo?"

"I'm afraid I can't tell you that. But it's true. We both saw it." Jacob swallowed before looking him in the eye. "It says the process can cause irreparable psychological and physical harm. They plan to send Fragiles from the Arc there."

Mr. Doyle frowned and ran his hand through his graying hair. Maya caught a glimpse of despair before he straightened his posture.

He met Jacob's stare. "Well, I can't broadcast a report without some kind of proof. I didn't come this far with shoddy journalism. Did you know I was able to crush the competition and become the sole media conglomerate in the Republic in only two years? It took Durkheim seven to control manufacturing." He smiled at Jacob. "But how about I ask my best reporter to investigate it?"

"We would appreciate you looking into it as soon as possible." Jacob wiped his palms on his pants and rose to shake his hand. "We don't have much time."

Mr. Doyle got up and shook his hand. "You have my word." As he walked them to the door, he eyed Maya. "Shouldn't the two of you be in school?"

Her eyes darted to Jacob who stared back at her. She cleared her throat, but the statement still squeaked out like a question. "We have a free period?"

"Yes, we should really get back to school. Thanks again." Jacob ushered her out the door.

Maya waited to speak until they were safely inside the elevator. "He sounded like he might really try to help. I could sense his concern. What do you think?"

"Yeah, maybe. I hope so." Jacob shrugged and dropped his eyes.

She beamed at him. "You were amazing! I was so nervous, but you acted so confident. If it wasn't for you, we would never have even made it past the receptionist."

"Thanks." He let out a heavy sigh.

"What's wrong?"

He faced her, posture stiff. "Yesterday you called me a wuss and today you say I'm brave? You should really make up your mind."

"What are you talking about? I never called you a wuss."

"You said you wished I could be strong like Tully instead of weak like me. You obviously think something is wrong with me."

"I didn't mean it like that. I meant—"

"I thought you of all people would understand." When the elevator door opened, Jacob stormed out. He might as well have punched her in the gut. Fighting the tears burning her eyes, she made her way out of the lobby and onto the street.

During the walk back to the hotel, she stayed a few paces behind him. At least he glanced over his shoulder a couple of times to make sure she was still there. The crowded and noisy streets pounded in her head by the time they got back to the hotel. When Tully unlocked the door for them, Jacob headed straight to his room, calling out over his shoulder. "Hey Maya. Tell Petulah how it went."

Chapter 21

AFTER CONVINCING TULLY NOT to beat up Jacob, Maya recounted their visit with Mr. Doyle. "Your dad seemed nice. He said he would ask one of his best reporters to investigate the center."

"Seeming nice and being nice isn't the same thing. Did he mention he locked away his unwanted daughter?"

"He showed us your photo and called you 'his world'."

"What a lying sack of shit."

"I don't know, Tully. He seemed to really care. I could sense it."

Tully scoffed. "Let's see if he actually helps. Do you still think the center is where they're torturing that girl?"

"I think so. And probably other kids, too. I hope we're not too late."

"Yeah, and let's hope your faith in Fitzgerald Doyle isn't as misguided as I think it is."

The throbbing in Maya's head intensified, so she went to take a shower. She let the water run over her body, trying to wash away the stress of the city and her argument with Jacob. When she felt better, she knocked on Jacob's door to apologize, but he didn't answer.

Jacob stayed in his room until Alastair brought up lunch. While they were eating, Tully put on the television to watch cartoons and a commercial came on that caught Maya's attention. The ABC jingle sparked a memory from her childhood. ABC. Apex Building Companies. Humming along with the tune under her breath, she remembered waiting in her living room for her mom to come home from work. Her mother had worked for Apex. "My mom worked there," she said to no one in particular.

Jacob put down his sandwich. "Apex? That's the company where the reconditioning center is. I saw it on the poster next to the address."

"Yeah, I saw that, too, but couldn't remember why it was familiar." At least Jacob was talking to her again. "I wonder if my mom might be able to help us." Her heart leaped at the possibility of seeing her parents again. "Maybe I could go see her."

Jacob frowned. "Let's wait to see what happens with the investigation first. We don't even know if your mom still works there or if she was even involved in the project. And didn't we agree none of us would see our parents until we knew it was safe? It was risky enough we visited Tully's dad."

"Sorry, Maya, but I gotta agree with him on this one," said Tully. "Besides, Apex builds everything. Odds are your mom wasn't even a part of it."

Tully's cartoon came back on and the three of them finished their lunch in silence. As Maya stared at the screen, her mind remained on her parents. She dreamed of the day she would see them again. When she arrived at Arc, she assumed she would return home after a few weeks. Just long enough for her to be cured. But the weeks turned into months and the months into years. Would they even recognize her? Her thoughts were interrupted by a knock at the door. Jacob checked the peephole and paused for a moment before opening it for Ren.

"Sorry, I didn't make it back last night. By the time I finished delivering all the flowers, I crashed at my cousin's place." Ren glanced at the empty cans of O'Malley's in the trash by the door and raised his eyebrows. "Looks like you all are adapting to Republic life." He gave Maya a wry smile and sat down in one of the chairs by the television. "So how goes the plan to overthrow the government?"

Jacob glanced at Maya, drawing her gaze away from Ren. "We went to the Modern Republic Broadcasting Service today and they'll be investigating the center for us."

Maya beamed at Jacob. "Yes, Jacob was great. He convinced him to do it."

"Shhh!" Tully turned up the volume on the television. "Look."

On the television, a cheerful news reporter sat in front of a photo of Tully's dad shaking hands with Commander Abigor. "We interrupt this program to announce our daily citizen spotlight," said the reporter. "Mr. Fitzgerald Doyle, founder and CEO of our very own Modern Republic Broadcast Service, has invested one million dollars into the expansion of the new reconditioning center to cure Fragiles. The Republic thanks Mr. Doyle for his investment and asks what have YOU done for the economy today?"

Tully cut the silence. "My dad is such an asshole."

"Fitzgerald Doyle is your dad?" Ren turned to Tully. "My cousin Jonah's in prison because of him."

Tully's eyes widened. "Seriously? What happened?"

"Doyle gave him a package full of money to deliver one night. On his way there, a Republic Guard stopped and searched him. They arrested him for possession of unapproved monetary funds. Jonah told them he was delivering it for Doyle, but Doyle denied everything. Jonah's been in prison ever since."

"That's awful," said Maya. "And so unfair. Isn't there any way to prove he is innocent?"

Ren scoffed. "They don't care if he's innocent. They'll use any excuse to screw us over. The Republic is run by a bunch of rich pricks who don't give a shit about him, or you, or any of us." Ren's face tightened as his eyes locked on hers. "You need to remember that."

She swallowed hard and nodded.

Tully turned off the television. "I hate to state the obvious, but if my dad just gave a million to the center, you know there's no way he is investigating it, right?"

As a heavy silence filled the room, Maya turned to Jacob. "Maybe we could investigate it ourselves. You remember the address from the poster, right?"

"Yes, but I'm not sure that is a good idea. We could easily get caught."

"Not that I want to encourage this plan," said Ren. "But the word from the Arc is that you drowned in the lake. They kept it out of the media, but my cousin knows one of their food delivery guys."

Maya looked at Ren. "So, they're not searching for us anymore?"

Did her parents think she died?

"Maybe. It's hard to say for sure." Ren got up and headed for the door. "Anyway, the bad news is we need to move you. Alastair needs every room for a last-minute event tomorrow. You can stay at the warehouse we use for storing goods just outside the city. It should be safe. I'll be back in an hour, so be ready."

Chapter 22

By the time they arrived at the warehouse, the late afternoon sun hung in the sky. Because they had driven beyond the outskirts of the city, the air no longer burned with a smoggy haze. Maya filled her lungs, happy to be away from the capital.

As Ren led them toward the entrance, he grabbed Jacob and stopped in his tracks. "Hold up."

Jacob struggled to free himself. "Let go of me."

"Heads up!" A man called from the roof as a large paint can crash to the ground where Jacob was about to walk. Ren released Jacob and continued into the building without saying anything.

Jacob shot Maya a look of surprise. "How did he—"

"Let's just get inside." Maya followed Ren into the warehouse.

Inside the warehouse, stacks of empty flower crates covered the cement floor. Beams of sunlight burst through the high windows, warming the damp interior. While smoggy haze and skyscrapers obscured the sun in the city, here it shone brightly.

Ren led them through the warehouse. "It's not much, but there's a living space in the back with a couple of beds, a bathroom, and a small kitchen."

Jacob glanced around. "Is it safe?"

"The warehouse isn't on the Republic Guard's inspection list since the building is condemned. You should be fine."

Jacob's eyes widened. "Condemned?"

"Only according to their records. The Chief of Inspections is one of my best customers."

When they reached the living space near the back, Tully threw her backpack on one of the two twin beds.

Jacob set his backpack on the other bed and then glanced at Maya. "Unless you want this one?"

"It's okay, I'll sleep on the couch." Maya placed her backpack on the coffee table in front of the worn upholstered couch. Its cushions looked like they were squeezed into old scratchy sweaters.

Ren pointed to a door in the corner. "The bathroom's in there." He walked toward an open space with a counter and a fridge. "Don't put anything down the kitchen sink. Help yourself to what's in the fridge, but I won't be able to restock it for a while. I'll be staying with my cousin Trey not far from here, but will check in on you. Any questions?"

Tully walked over to the old box television with an antenna across from the couch. "Does the TV work?"

"Yeah, but no cable, so it's mostly commercials." Ren grabbed a water bottle from the fridge. "I'm going outside to talk to Trey. I'll be back in a minute."

Ren returned to the warehouse with the young man from the roof. "Hey, this is my cousin, Trey."

Shorter and stockier than Ren, Trey appeared to be in his twenties and had light brown skin, a buzz cut, and elaborate tattoos covering both arms. Trey ran his eyes over Tully. "So this is Doyle's kid?"

Tully crossed her arms and thrust out her chin. "My name's Tully. I'm nothing like my father."

"Easy, Trey. I told you she's cool," said Ren.

"My bad, your dad's just a dick." Trey took a seat on the couch.

Tully rolled her eyes. "Tell me something I don't know."

"I'm sorry about your mom though." Trey leaned back on the couch and spread his arms out across the top of it. "The hit, I mean."

Tully's face tightened. "Hit? My mom died in an accident."

"That's what they told you?" Trey shook his head "It was a hit. Your dad is involved in some serious shit. The same shit that landed my brother in jail." His voice softened. "Your mom was murdered."

As Tully stared through Trey, an immense pain struck Maya in her gut. Maya reached out to Tully. "Tully, I—"

"Don't." Tully scanned the room until her eyes rested on the back door. She turned and stormed out, slamming the door behind her.

Trey turned to Ren "Hey, man, I didn't mean to set her off. You know how I feel about Doyle, right?"

"It's cool. We can talk to her on the way out." Ren turned toward Maya. "Trey and I are going to go pick up some supplies for Huruma, but we'll check on her, okay? There is not much out there but a dried-up field."

Sunset approached, and Tully hadn't come back inside. Jacob lay napping on one of the cots, so Maya went out the back door to search for her. The large barren field surrounded by an old wood fence lay empty in the evening glow. If anyone could take care of herself, it was Tully, yet Maya couldn't shake the queasy feeling in her gut.

The sound of tires on gravel called Maya to the front of the warehouse. She hurried toward Ren who was already outside the truck. The passenger door flung open, and

Trey climbed down followed by Tully. Tully shoved Trey on the way out as they both dissolved into laughter. There was a lightness about her. Emotions always rolled right off Tully.

Tully grinned at Maya. "Trey is going to teach me how to fire a gun. You wanna try?"

"It's okay. Maybe later."

Once Trey and Tully disappeared around the side of the warehouse, Maya looked questioningly at Ren.

"We picked her up on the side of the road on our way out. She's fine. They bonded over their mutual hate for her dad."

Her shoulders slumped forward. "That's good, I guess."

"I have one more pick-up to make. I'll come back for Trey later." He approached her, studying her eyes. "You ok?"

"I'm fine."

"If you say so." He gave her a half smile before dropping his stare and heading toward the truck.

As gunshots and laughter exploded behind the warehouse, a pang of loneliness struck Maya. She should have been happy Tully was okay, but her chest recoiled with a spark of envy. It didn't seem fair that emotions clung to her while Tully's cares vanished into the night on a cloud of gun smoke. At least with the emotions bottled inside her, they couldn't hurt people. Tully didn't seem to care who her emotions landed on. In fact, she and Trey probably hadn't even considered the damage a stray bullet could do.

Ashamed of her thoughts, Maya shuddered and headed into the warehouse. The irony of being filled with emotions while still feeling hollow inside made her soul ache. Despite his warm smiles, Ren only wanted to take care of her. Tully didn't need her, and Jacob had been distant since their argument at Mr. Doyle's office. And Jacob was the one person who always felt like home. Maybe she missed Jacob.

Jacob had just come away from the window, no doubt investigating the thundering bursts of gunshots that echoed from behind the warehouse. His eyes met hers. She returned his gaze and tried to pretend she was seeing him for the first time, noticing the flecks of gold in his eyes and the way his dark wavy hair fell on his forehead. Taller than her now, he was no longer the skinny little boy from their childhood. She waited for her pulse to race or to feel a warm flush to her skin.

Jacob walked over to the television set he had been watching and shut it off. "I was checking to see if there was any news on the reconditioning center. In case they decide to investigate."

Her pulse remained unmoved, and there were definitely no tingles. She slumped down on the couch. "I think we're going to have to do that ourselves."

He frowned, "And how do you propose we do that?"

"We could go there or talk to people who work there. Or sneak in or something. Tully's good at that."

"I'm good at what?" Tully and Trey had come in the back door. Tully's cheeks were flushed from the cold or the excitement of firing a gun.

"I was telling Jacob that maybe you could help us sneak into the reconditioning center so we could get proof about what is happening there."

"Depends on the security. The Arc's basically my bitch, but the Republic Guard is a lot more hardcore. So I'd have to check it out first." Tully dropped down onto the couch, while Trey grabbed a bottle from the fridge.

"Maybe we can go tomorrow. I'll ask Ren," said Maya.

Trey sat down next to Tully on the couch and used his teeth to remove the bottle cap. "Nope, tomorrow's no good. We got some business to take care of, right Tull?"

"Yeah, sorry Maya. We're gonna go see some guys who have dirt on my dad. Maybe another time." Tully grabbed the bottle from Trey and took a swig before handing it back to him.

"I just think it's important that we do it as soon as possible." Maya turned to Jacob for reassurance. "Remember the kids are in danger."

Tully leaned back on the couch. "We don't even know those kids. Not really my problem."

"Not your problem? Don't you care about their suffering?" Maya's voice shook as anger rose in her chest.

"It must be so easy to only care about yourself. To be so selfish."

Tully got up from the couch. "Hey Trey, it sounds like Ren hasn't left yet. Can I crash at your place with Ren tonight?" Trey nodded and got up from the couch.

Maya followed Tully and Trey to the door. "I'm so sorry, Tully. I didn't mean it that way."

"I know exactly what you meant." Tully opened the door. "See ya around."

Chapter 23

LATER THAT NIGHT, MAYA lay awake in bed along the back wall of the warehouse. She had started out on the couch in case Tully came back, but as the hours ticked by, the lumpy couch became unbearable. She shifted on the thin mattress atop the squeaky bed frame. She hadn't meant to upset Tully, but how could she be so unfeeling? Kids were being tortured and all she cared about was some vendetta against her dad. Had Tully just used her and Jacob to escape the Arc?

When she turned to her side, the frame creaked, and Jacob let out a loud sigh from his bed. "Can you not be so loud?" He pulled his scarf over his eyes to block the moonlight that had found its way in through the windows.

"Sorry," she whispered. She pulled up her blanket inch by inch, making only a slight shifting noise.

"Maya—"

"I barely moved. Are you serious?"

"Yes, it's loud to me."

She sat up and looked at him. "Is something wrong?"

"We're in the middle of nowhere in a creepy warehouse. What could be wrong?"

"I know, I just mean we haven't talked much since we got here and now Tully's gone and I..."

He sat up straight. "I'm not still mad about what happened in the elevator if that's what you mean."

"Ok. I'm really sorry for saying what I did. For saying you should be like Tully or whatever. I shouldn't have said that. Tully doesn't even care about people. I'm glad you're not like her."

"It's okay." He pulled his scarf around his neck and lay down. "Goodnight."

Although the conversation felt far from over, she lay back down and whispered, "Good night." She tried to stay as still as possible so Jacob could get some sleep. Unable to quiet her mind, she was thankful that at least the nightmares with the blue-eyed girl had stopped.

The next morning, Maya waited until Jacob had finished his cereal before joining him at the table. "I was thinking we could try to find my parents today. Now that Tully is gone, we could really use their help." He didn't respond, so she continued. "My mom might have worked on the building or know someone on the inside."

He dropped his spoon into the bowl. "We talked about this already."

"The Arc thinks we are dead. We have to do something." She noticed his haggard eyes and slouched shoulders, but couldn't stop herself from adding, "Why do you always have to worry so much about everything?"

"Because I'm not stupid enough to take unnecessary risks." He got up and took his bowl to the sink.

Her shoulders tensed. "Or maybe it's because you are so hypersensitive to everything that you make up risks that aren't there."

"Think what you want, but it's a bad idea." His eyes panned the room. "This was all a bad idea."

Her voice rose in anger. "What are we supposed to do? We can't go back to the Arc."

"I know you feel guilty about Tully leaving, but don't take it out on me."

"I'm not. And it's not my fault she doesn't give a crap about anyone. I thought at least you would care." Trembling with anger, she headed out the back door before she said something she would regret.

She crossed the field and pulled herself up to sit on the wooden fence. The harsh edges of the splintered fence cut into her, but she didn't move. She fought the tears burning in her eyes. Even if Jacob wouldn't help, she had to do something.

The sound of Ren's truck approaching caught her attention. He parked on the side of the road and started across the field. She checked the passenger side for Tully, but it was empty. After using one arm to hop over the fence, he walked toward her with a smile. She returned her gaze to the field.

Leaning against the fence, he waited a moment before speaking. "Tully and Trey went into the city. I'm not sure when they'll be back."

She continued to stare straight ahead at the expanse of dried yellowish-brown weeds decaying in the sun.

Ren nudged her. "Nice view, huh?"

She glanced up at him from the corner of her eye. "If I gave you an address, could you take me there?"

"Depends where. What's the address?"

"16 Wrights Borough. I think it's in the commuter belt."

"The commuter belt is about thirty minutes from here. I can take you. Can I ask where we're going?"

"To see my parents."

Chapter 24

MAYA'S STOMACH DROPPED AS soon as they turned into Wrights Borough. She didn't remember the houses being so close together or the streets being so empty. As they pulled up across the street from her house, she rubbed her palms on her jeans. Though she had memories of playing on their front lawn, gravel now surrounded the walkway that led to the door. The house appeared smaller and frailer than she remembered.

Ren turned toward her. "Is that it?"

"Yes, but what if they don't live there anymore?"

"Only one way to find out, right?" He gave her a reassuring smile.

Maya put her hand on the door handle, but her legs were like jello. Maybe she should have told Jacob she was going to see her parents, so he could have stopped her.

Ren placed his hand on her shoulder. "I'll be right here. If it's not them, just tell them you were looking for someone else and leave."

"What if they had another child and don't want—"

Ren turned off the engine and walked around to the passenger door to help her out. "You can do this."

Maya swallowed the lump in her throat and got out of the car. Heedful of her weak knees, she moved cautiously toward the house. When she reached the door, she paused before knocking lightly. No one answered. She stepped back from the door and glanced at Ren who nodded toward the door. She pressed the doorbell and was about to leave when the door opened.

A woman stood in the doorway. Although her hair was styled shorter and her eyes showed signs of age, Maya recognized her in an instant. Maya gazed into her mother's eyes as her heart threatened to explode.

"Can I help you?" Maya's mother searched her face. Her eyes got wide and welled up with tears. She let out a small gasp. "Maya?"

Maya nodded.

Her mother took her in her arms and began to sob. Maya collapsed into her mother's embrace as tears streamed down her own face.

When her mother finally released her grip, she gazed at her. "But how?"

"I left the Arc."

Her mother ushered her inside and closed the door. "They let you go? Why didn't they tell me?" She gestured for her to take a seat on the sofa. The living room was just as she remembered—the picture of the three of them on the mantle, the ocean blue throw rug where she built castles with her blocks, the faint smell of pine wood polish—but it felt different. An unfamiliar emptiness filled the room.

Her mother stared at her in disbelief. "I missed you every day."

"Me, too, Mommy."

Mommy? She was seventeen. Should she call her mom?

"Tell me everything. I've missed so much." Her mother dabbed her eyes with a handkerchief.

"I'm not sure where to start. We had teachers at the Arc, and I made friends. Jacob's my best friend. And um..." She struggled to continue, unsure how to convey the enormity of emotions colliding within her.

Her mother beamed at her, her love enveloping her, making her whole.

She was finally home.

As the surreal nature of the moment sank in, Maya's heart soared.

Leaning toward her with a loving smile, her mother gazed at her. "Tell me more."

"Well, they tried to teach us to be strong and uh—" Her voice broke as tears formed. "I missed you and Dad so much." As the memories flooded back, her eyes rested on her dad's empty reading chair. She turned back to her mom. "Where's Dad?" When her mother dropped her eyes, panic rose in Maya's chest. "Mom?"

"They took him away." Her mother choked on the words. "About a year ago. He was at school, and they arrested him. I haven't been allowed to see him."

No, not Dad.

Maya struggled to speak. "I don't—I don't understand."

"They called him a traitor to the values of the Republic."

"Where is he? Will they let him out?"

"I don't know." Her mother smoothed her hair and arranged her house dress before smiling at her. "But I'm so happy that they released you from the Arc. It's been so long. I was afraid you were never coming home. Were you cured by the new procedure?"

Maya paused, considering her words. "Do you mean the treatments they're doing at the reconditioning center?"

"Yes, it's a beautiful facility. My company designed it. Have you been there?"

"No, I haven't." Maya shifted on the sofa. "But I heard that sometimes the procedures can harm kids."

"Oh dear! Did they hurt you? There are people I can call—"

"No, I'm okay, but I think there are kids at the center that need our help." She searched her mother's eyes for a reaction.

"Well, I could make some calls." She sprung up from her chair. "But let's do that later. Let me show you your room. I've kept it the same since the day you left. Do you have a suitcase or something?"

"I'm sorry, but I can't stay." Maya glanced away before her mother could react. "I have a friend waiting for me outside. But I can come back tomorrow to find out how the calls went if that's okay?"

"But Maya, you just got here. How can you—"

"I promise I'll explain later. Please just make the calls and I'll be back tomorrow morning. If you could get the building plans for the new Apex building, that would be great, too." Her mother's crushed expression was too much for her to bear. Maya hugged her and whispered, "It's not safe for me here."

Tears burned her cheeks as she ran across the street toward Ren's truck.

When Ren dropped Maya back at the warehouse, Jacob sat on the couch engrossed in a documentary. The March of the Republic droned on in the background, as waves of soldiers marched in unison. They must have seen this documentary at least half a dozen times at the Arc. Jacob glanced up at Maya while she grabbed the last yogurt from the fridge and then went back to watching.

"Did you know that one Republic bomber can destroy a whole city?" His eyes remained glued to the screen.

"Yeah." She sat down on the opposite end of the couch from him and turned toward him. "I'm sorry for leaving without telling you this morning."

"It's okay, I heard Ren's truck."

"And I'm really sorry about what I said this morning. I know this has been hard on you, and that you were just worried."

"Did you and Ren have a good time?" Jacob continued to watch the television.

"Uh yeah. We went for a drive. We—"

"That's nice." His tone was flat. "Do you know why it was so easy for the Republic to end the insurrection? Because they didn't care how they did it. They destroyed cities full of innocent people. They have no conscience. There's no way to beat that." He got up and turned off the television. "Don't worry about earlier. It's fine. I'm going to go outside and get some fresh air."

While she poked at her half-eaten yogurt, Jacob went out the back door, shoulders slumped forward. His indifference clung to her. She tried to bring a spoonful to her mouth, but couldn't stomach it. She set down her yogurt on the coffee table. Something was wrong.

Outside, Jacob sat on the wooden fence with his head down. Maya sat beside him giving him a few feet of space. They sat in silence, but she sensed his despair.

After a few minutes, he raised his head and turned toward her. His stare passed through her, almost as if she didn't exist.

"Are you okay?" she asked.

"I'm fine. I'm just tired." He rubbed his temples.

"Okay." She looked out across the field and cleared her throat. "So, earlier, when I went for a drive with Ren, we—"

"It's okay. You don't have to tell me."

"But—"

Jacob got up and shoved his hands in his pockets and started walking back toward the warehouse. She caught up to him. Maybe it was better he didn't know that she went to see her mom until she found out if her mom could help them. Nudging him with her shoulder, she asked, "Are you sure you're okay?"

"Yeah, I'm fine." He stopped walking and turned toward her. "We'll always be friends, right?"

"Of course."

"That's good to know. Thanks." He dropped his head and continued into the warehouse.

Chapter 25

The next morning, Maya woke early. Jacob's blanket covered his entire head, so she pulled on her sweatshirt and shoes, careful not to wake him. She slipped outside into the brisk morning air to wait for Ren. While she listened for his truck, an old sedan came up the drive. Before she could retreat to the warehouse, the car parked and Alastair got out.

"Good morning. I hope I didn't startle you." He went around to the passenger side of the car. "Ren had something urgent to attend to. He asked me to pick you up."

Maya walked toward the car. "Is everything okay?"

"He didn't have time to talk. He seemed worried, but I'm sure he'll fix whatever it is. He always does. Good kid, that one." He opened the car for her. "Is Jacob alright?"

She took a seat. "Jacob? Why?"

"I saw him walking on the side of the road a couple miles back. He asked me how to get to the nearest transit hub."

How could he have seen Jacob? He was asleep. Unless the lump below the blanket wasn't Jacob. Her stomach dropped. "Did he say where he was going?"

"No, I'm sorry I didn't ask. I would've offered to drive him, but I didn't want to keep you waiting."

The knot in Maya's stomach clenched. What hadn't Jacob told her he was going out? Maybe she should wait for him to get back. But her mom was expecting her. The anguish consuming her mother's face when she left yesterday still haunted her.

Just as she began to spiral, Alastair placed his hand on her shoulder. "Are you ready to go?"

"Yes, thank you." She glanced back at the warehouse and then settled into the leather seat.

Alastair closed the door and returned to the driver's seat.

As they drove toward the commuter belt, Alastair hummed along to a jazz tune on the radio. When the song finished, he turned off the radio. "You like jazz?"

"We learned music at the Arc but didn't get to listen to it outside of class. I don't really know what I like."

"Ren loves jazz. When he was little, he wanted to play the saxophone. Poor kid could barely hold the thing up. One time he decided to have a concert for his aunt and me. Simply awful." He gave a hearty laugh. "Luckily he moved on to piano, which was easier on the ears."

Maya smiled. It was hard to stay worried with Alastair around. The twinkle in his eye and the warmth of his smile were contagious.

During the remainder of the drive, his calm presence kept her anxiety at bay. When they reached her old street, she turned to him. "You can drop me here. Can you or Ren pick me up at noon?"

"Sure, whatever you need."

"Thank you." She got out of the car and waved as he turned the sedan around and drove off. Her old house sat a few houses from the corner, so she took a deep breath and headed down the cracked sidewalk.

As Maya approached the house, she tried to ignore the sinking feeling in her stomach. Before she could even knock, her mother opened the door. Something was wrong.

Very wrong.

"I'm sorry, sweetheart. I just want you to be safe." Concern gripped her face.

"Mom? What's wrong?" Someone yanked her arms behind her. She spun around trying to break free, but the grip was too strong. There were two of them. Republic Guards.

Her mother clutched her stomach and steadied herself in the doorway. "Don't be afraid. They're just taking you back to the Arc. Everything will be okay." Her voice broke. "I love you so much."

"Mom!" Maya screamed as the guards dragged her out onto the street.

One of the guards shoved her against a vehicle while the other one opened the door. She steadied herself with her breath and willed the anguish she had absorbed from her mother to travel to her fingertips. The pain seared through her arm as she reached for the guard. It was then that she realized her hands were bound too tightly to reach him. The last thing she remembered was her head hitting the pavement.

Maya regained consciousness when the guard pulled her out of the vehicle. As he led her toward a large building, her blurred vision could barely make out the sign on the glass doors: *Modern Republic Holding Facility.* Inside the building, he dragged her past several rows of desks where officers milled about. Her head throbbed with every step, so she kept it down to avoid the bright lights.

"Maya?"

It sounded like Jacob. She must be hearing things.

"Maya!"

She raised her head to where Jacob sat at a desk with an officer. He attempted to get up, but the officer shoved him back into his chair. Had they arrested him, too?

The guard nudged Maya to keep walking and led her down a narrow corridor lined with doors. Outside one of the doors, he paused to unlock it. He released her hand restraints and shoved her into the cell before locking the door behind her. Bile rose in her throat as she stumbled across the cell to a rusted bucket in the corner. With one hand braced against the concrete wall, she leaned over to vomit into the bucket. She crawled across the cold stone floor to the cot and curled into the fetal position without the strength to cry.

A pounding on the door jarred her awake. "Hey Fragile, you have a visitor. Put your back to the door." She rose from the cot and did as instructed. The guard slid open a small window in the door and placed her hands in restraints before opening the cell door. The new guard was younger than the first one. "I'm sorry about the restraints. Facility protocol." He grinned at Maya. "I know you're just a girl."

The young guard led her down the corridor and through a door into a small room. Once inside, she struggled to keep her eyes open against the bright fluorescent lights. The guard sat her down at the metal table and attached her restraints to latches on the table. "I'll be right outside. Your visitor will be here shortly." He smiled at her again before leaving.

A visitor. Had her mother come to visit her? Even if she apologized, she wasn't ready to forgive her. In fact, she couldn't bear to see her. She called out to the guard. "Uh, guard?" She raised her voice. "I'm not sure if you can hear me, but I don't want to see her. Can you take me back to my cell, please? Guard?" When the door opened, Maya's jaw dropped.

"Why, Maya, I thought you'd be happy to see me." Commander Abigor curled his lips into a smile and walked toward her. "I was devastated when I thought you'd drowned."

Maya's chest tightened.

"If it wasn't for your mother we might never have found you. You're lucky she loves you so much."

Lucky my mother turned me in?

She shifted her body away from him.

He strolled behind her and placed his hands on her shoulders. As he leaned in close to her ear, his hot breath scalded her neck. "You must be embarrassed for causing so much trouble."

The words seared through her, filling the pit of her stomach with shame. Jacob would never have left the Arc if it wasn't for her.

Abigor returned to the other side of the table and took a seat. "But perhaps it's not all your fault. Fragiles are so sensitive that they often succumb to excessive worry and paranoia. It's no wonder you created a fantasy in your mind about our prestigious center harming children. You poor girl." He reached out to place his hand on hers, but drew it back at the last minute.

He removed a pocket knife from his inner coat pocket and began to polish its surface with his handkerchief. Its elaborate handle engraved with the Republic seal glistened under the bright lights. "Do you know why I keep this in my pocket? It reminds me of where I came from. Trained in hand-to-hand combat as a mere soldier, I rose through the ranks to become one of the most powerful men in the Republic, commanding armies and bombers with the raise of a finger." He returned the knife to his pocket. "I tell you this to remind you that we all have the ability to become stronger, to become better, to take what is rightfully ours. Your mother wants what is best for you, and so do I. Your rehabilitation. Don't you want that, too?"

Maya stared at him, unsure what to say.

As he continued speaking, his expression softened. "You know, neurotic hypersensitivity is such an unfortunate condition. In fact, my very own mother suffered from it.

She became deluded into thinking she could feel other people's suffering and gave away a large portion of my father's fortune. Pity back then there was no cure."

She forced out the words, "What did you do to Jacob?"

"Jacob's fine. He's staying in the barracks. He turned himself into a transit guard this morning so that he could go back to the Arc. Poor boy got caught up in your delusion."

"Jacob turned himself in?"

Abigor nodded. "You must feel awful. Especially with him finally passing his review."

He passed his review? Why didn't he tell me?

As she squirmed against her hand restraints, her voice rose to a frantic yell. "What are you going to do to us?"

"Calm down. I'm not here to hurt you. I'm here to help you to return safely to the Arc. The capitol is no place for unrehabilitated Fragiles."

"And what about the kids at the reconditioning center?" Despite her pulse pounding in her throat, she added, "I saw the memo."

His face twitched before relaxing into a self-assured smile. "I don't know anything about a memo, but the center is rehabilitating children. Don't you want to be cured? You must be tired of experiencing so much unnecessary pain."

His words shot through her. What she would give to be free of the pain. "I don't know...but the kids..."

"Oh, you poor thing. How about you accompany me to the center tomorrow to see for yourself?" Without waiting for an answer, he smiled and stood to leave. Once he had knocked on the door to be let out, he turned back toward her. "Oh, I thought you should know that your friend Tully is about to be arrested for her role in the murder of her father. I'm sorry as I know how difficult it must be to be deceived by someone you trust."

Chapter 26

Dressed in a baby blue dress with white ruffles, Maya squirmed in the back seat of the Republic guard vehicle. What was she? Six? She should have thrown the dress in the waste bucket when it was delivered to her cell, but Abigor's note was clear— she needed to look "presentable" for her visit to the center.

As they waited in the holding facility parking lot, the guard in the driver's seat glanced at her in the rearview mirror. She turned to head to the window just as an officer dragged a man in handcuffs to the facility entrance. Was Tully going to be arrested? Maybe Abigor was just trying to scare her. Neither Tully nor Trey seemed capable of murder.

At least she didn't think so.

Once a shiny black sedan pulled out in front of their vehicle, the guard put the car in gear and followed the sedan out of the parking lot. After they had been driving for a while, the tall shiny buildings of the city transformed into squat warehouses surrounded by chain link fences and dirt yards. Tattered billboards sprouted from the terrain like overgrown weeds. A cheerful woman holding a can of O'Malley's smiled from a billboard, her faded face peeling in the sun. She held the pristine can of O'Malley's high like a beacon of hope, oblivious to the decay surrounding her.

For miles, discarded appliances and garbage littered stretches of barren earth on both sides of the highway. Every few minutes, clusters of tiny dwellings with sheet metal roofs appeared out of nowhere. The clotheslines and occasional rusted tricycle out front were the only signs of life. While the scene mirrored her history book's depiction of the wasteland, the mile markers and highway signs confirmed they were still in the Republic. How many more lies had they been taught?

When they reached their destination, lush shrubs, and soaring pine trees lined the entryway to the parking lot. For a moment, the beauty of the trees took her attention away from the apprehension building in her gut. Rivaling its image from the poster, the spectacular Apex Enterprise building spanned multiple levels and boasted a beige stone facade with huge, mirrored windows.

The guard pulled Maya out of the vehicle. When he removed her handcuffs, he gestured to the gun at his side. As he led her toward the building glinting in the sun, a wave of dread flowed through her.

Commander Abigor joined them at the building entrance. "I hope you understand what a special occasion this is for you." He ran his eyes over Maya. "The media will be joining us shortly. Maybe you should try to do something with that hair of yours." She ran her hand down her braid and tried to smooth the frizz surrounding her face.

They entered the front lobby. A tall slim woman in a lab coat approached and took the Commander's hand in both her hands. "Hello, Commander. What an honor to have you here today." Her sandy blonde hair was graying at the temples and cut short to accentuate her angular features. The stroke of blush applied to her cheeks failed to bring the least bit of warmth to her face.

"Thank you, Barbara. Always a pleasure to see the great work you are doing here at the center." The Commander motioned to Maya who was standing behind him with the guard. "I've brought a Fragile who hopes to be rehabilitated. Say hello to Dr. Schader, Maya."

Maya offered a weak hello and pulled the scratchy dress ruffles away from her neck.

Dr. Schader gave her a curt nod and turned back to Abigor. "I'm happy to let you know that we're making excellent progress. We're working on several cutting-edge procedures and may one day be able to eradicate the Fragile gene completely."

Abigor beamed at Maya. "Isn't that exciting?"

A chill ran up her spine. "Yes, Commander."

Dr. Schader motioned for them to follow her and used a pass card with a yellow triangle to unlock the door at the far end of the lobby. "Because our work is so important, Apex has allowed us to use this entire wing of the ground floor." Abigor nodded his approval and ushered Maya through the door.

As Dr. Schader led them through the center, she pointed out the various therapy rooms and explained how they gently expose children to stimuli to desensitize them. Most of the rooms were empty, but a few of them displayed toys and stuffed animals.

Maya stopped walking. "Would it be possible to meet any of the kids?"

Dr. Schader's look of annoyance twisted into a semblance of a smile. "The children are in their rooms for quiet time." She turned to Abigor. "But if the Commander would like you to meet one of the subjects, I can arrange it."

Abigor's eyes lit up. "Why yes, that would be wonderful. Always great to see our progress firsthand."

Dr. Schader stepped away and made a call from her earpiece. A moment later, a door opened and a little girl of about five or six walked out accompanied by an orderly wearing scrubs. The girl's dark hair was styled in a tight ponytail, and she wore a white shirt and pants. Maya's heart leaped for a moment, but the girl had brown eyes. The icy blue stare of the girl in her dream had permanently stained her memory.

Dr. Schader dismissed the orderly and turned to Abigor. "This is K. One of our most promising subjects. We assign each child a letter of the alphabet as their new name to help them overcome their painful past. Once they are rehabilitated, they can choose a full name that starts with their assigned letter. I came up with it myself."

Commander Abigor bent down and smiled at K. "Why don't you tell us what you think about living here at the center?"

K looked up at Dr. Schader and then back at the Commander. She rubbed her arm and studied her shoes. "I like it a lot. We get to play with toys and I'm learning to be strong." She glanced up at Dr. Schader who nodded.

Maya reached out to shake K's hand. "Hi K, my name is Maya. It's nice to meet you." The terror radiating from K cut into Maya. She met K's eyes and tried to convey how much she wanted to help her.

Dr. Schader stepped in, causing K to release Maya's hand. "Thank you, K. It's time to get back to your room now. I'll send for the orderly." As the orderly took her away, K glanced over her shoulder at Maya. When she disappeared behind the heavy door, a deep pain settled in Maya's chest.

Dr. Schader turned to Commander Abigor. "Now that that's done, shall we meet the media outside for our photo opportunity?"

"Yes. We've seen more than enough." He turned toward Maya with a smile. "We've already begun incorporating these new treatments at the Arc. I'm confident that you can be fully rehabilitated upon your return."

As Dr. Schader led the way back to the entrance, Maya focused on K's trauma burning through her body and tried not to collapse. She forced the wave of painful emotions toward her hand and glanced at the guard beside her, his hand inches from his weapon. Her eyes panned to Commander Abigor and Dr. Schader, but it was no use. She was outnumbered.

Chapter 27

AFTER SPENDING ANOTHER RESTLESS night and most of the next day in her cell, a guard took Maya to the meeting room at the end of the corridor. Thankfully, he hadn't bothered with the hand restraints. Inside the room, a young man sat at the table with his head in his hands. She would have recognized that mop of brown hair anywhere. When the guard slammed the door on his way out, Jacob lifted his head. As his eyes met hers, a wave of relief passed over his face. He had dark circles under his eyes but otherwise appeared okay.

He looked her over. "You look awful."

She ran her hands over her frizzy hair that still smelled like vomit and glanced at her tear-stained sweatshirt. She gave him a weak smile. "Thanks."

"Did they...uh...hurt you?" His eyes dropped.

She touched the bruise on her forehead and could still feel a bump from where she had hit the concrete. "I'm okay."

"That's good. I'm so—"

"Why did you—" Maya turned when the door opened.

The guard entered followed by Commander Abigor, Director Williams, and an Arc campus security officer. The Commander squared himself in front of Maya and Jacob. "Director Williams has assured me that security measures have increased at the Arc. You'll be transported there immediately under her watch. Director Williams knows that if you should somehow leave the Arc again, she will be held directly responsible." He turned to Director Williams, "Isn't that right, Natasha?"

"Yes, of course, Commander." Her voice cracked, mirroring the unease in her tight-lipped smile.

He turned his attention to Maya. "You will receive intensive reconditioning treatment upon arrival to the Arc and, if unsuccessful, you will be transferred directly to the adult ward. Do you understand?"

Adult Ward.

Intensive reconditioning.

Maya struggled to nod as the blood rushed from her head.

While the holding facility guard led them toward the building exit, Maya focused on the door to keep her head from spinning. For a moment, a flash of red hair caught her eye, but the turn of the woman's head revealed a middle-aged face. Jacob kept his head down until they reached the Arc vehicle outside. When the guard shoved them in the back seat and slammed the door, Director Williams got in the front seat as the Arc CSO started the engine.

Maya rested her head against the thick reinforced window and glanced at the interior of the door which had no handles. If the reconditioning process was anything like the pain she had shared with the girl, she might not be able to bear it. At least Jacob had passed his review. Maybe they would give him a chance to be free. It was her fault he had left. As they drove off, she let out a heavy breath and gazed out the window. The sun would be setting soon, and by the time they reached the Arc, they would be surrounded by darkness.

They had been driving for about twenty minutes when Director Williams pointed out the window. "Pull over to that convenience store."

The CSO slowed the vehicle and turned into the parking lot.

She turned to him. "Please go in and get me an aspirin. I have a headache."

Once he was inside the store, Director Williams looked at Maya through the bars dividing the front seat from the back. "I'm afraid you're right about the reconditioning process."

Maya's eyes widened. "You mean about permanent damage?"

"I expressed my concerns to the Commander, but it's no longer safe for me to disagree. One of the children was killed not too long ago. Meg. Such a sweet girl. I still have her photo." Her voice broke as the CSO opened the vehicle door.

The girl in the photo.

That's why the dreams stopped.

A surge of anguish tore through Maya. She doubled over in pain, struggling to breathe.

The CSO handed the aspirin to Director Williams. He was about to start the vehicle when Jacob spoke. "I think Maya is sick. Can you let her out for a minute please?"

The CSO glanced at them in his rearview window. "She'll be fine."

Jacob watched Maya as she groaned in pain. "I think she's going to throw up."

"Tell her to hold it." He started the engine.

"Harvey, I don't want the stench of vomit in my vehicle." Director Williams glared at the guard. "And I'm sure you don't want to be the one to clean it off the seat."

Shaking his head, he shut off the engine and exited the vehicle. He opened the door closest to him. When Jacob got out, Harvey gripped his shoulder. "No funny business. You stay right here." He motioned to the nightstick in the holster at his waist.

The grief that Maya shared with Director Williams constricted her lungs. As she inched toward the door, she strained to draw the pain away from her chest and into her arm. She crawled out of the vehicle and placed her hand on Harvey to steady herself. She whispered, "I'm sorry," and lurched forward. A piercing pain scorched through her body and into him. When he dropped to the ground, she turned to Jacob, her arm still reeling with pain. "Come on! We need to run."

Jacob glanced at Maya and then to Harvey trembling on the ground.

Unable to wait for his decision, she stumbled toward the nearest alleyway without looking back.

Chapter 28

IN THE SHADOWY TWILIGHT, Maya and Jacob kept in the darkness as they ran through the maze of alleys. They moved in silence, but she was glad he had chosen to come. She was also glad that he had grabbed the keys to the vehicle on his way out and discarded them in a nearby dumpster. When they had gotten far enough away, they stopped to rest down an embankment below a small overpass. Night had fallen, but the lone streetlight offered some relief from the darkness.

Jacob bent over to catch his breath. "I don't think they followed us."

"Yeah, I hope not." Maya dropped down to the ground, exhausted.

"We should probably try to head to the warehouse."

All the questions she had suppressed bubbled to the surface. "Are you sure that's what you want to do? I mean you turned yourself in, but you followed me, and now I don't know what you want. Don't you want to go back to the Arc?"

"We can't go back to the Arc now. It isn't safe."

She took a deep breath. "Abigor took me to the reconditioning center. Just to see it, I mean. He made me wear this stupid dress and there was a little girl K and it was so awful and I couldn't help her and they arrested me and I hit my head on the concrete and my mom, my mom she..." Her body shook.

"Whoa. Slow down. It's okay." Jacob sat beside her and put his hand on her shoulder. "Your mom?"

"I went to see her. It was a mistake."

"Okay, don't worry. We can talk about this later. Let's just get to the warehouse."

"And Tully..." her lips trembled.

"What about her?"

"Abigor said they're going to arrest her for killing her father." Her whole body began to shake as the tears streamed down her face.

"Shit! Are you serious?"

She stared at Jacob through her tears and a giggle escaped her lips. "I've never heard you curse before." In between her tears, the giggle grew to a hearty laugh. She doubled over, sobbing with laughter, and couldn't stop.

Despite his scowl, her laughter only increased.

Eventually, his expression softened, and he yelled "Shit!" into the sky before dissolving into laughter beside her.

Tears streamed down their faces, and she laughed until her belly ached. When their laughter finally subsided, it was as if a weight had been lifted from her. She wiped the last tears from her eyes and smiled softly at him. He returned her smile, and a warm tenderness filled her soul.

"Did you know you passed your review?" she asked.

He hung his head. "Yeah."

"Why didn't you tell me? If I knew, I never would have asked you to risk coming with us."

"I passed, but I told them I wasn't ready to leave. I guess I was afraid."

"Afraid of what?"

He took a deep breath before glancing at her. "I was afraid you wouldn't pass, and I didn't want to leave you."

"Oh."

"It's like you're a part of me."

For a moment, she connected with the feeling as if it was her own. Overwhelmed by the warm rush of emotions, she stood up. "Well, I'm glad you're here with me now." She peered down the road. "So how do we get back to the warehouse?"

He rummaged around in his pocket and pulled out a folded piece of paper and some bills. "This is the transit schedule. I remember the hub closest to the warehouse. This should be enough for tickets" He spread out the bills.

She beamed at him. "You're amazing!"

"We just have to find the hub closest to us." His face fell, "And not get caught."

Maya hid in the shadows outside the tiny transit hub kiosk while Jacob used the machine to buy tickets with his remaining cash. Joining Maya in the darkness, he gave her his scarf to tie around her head. She covered her hair completely and wrapped it around her chin hiding as much of her face as possible without drawing attention to herself. Once they passed through the automated ticket-reader, they used the elevator to descend to the platform level.

Weary commuters packed the hub floor, jostling one another as they vied for positions closest to the track. While scanning the floor for guards, Maya locked eyes with a frail woman gripping the hand of a little boy, just as the woman was shoved to the floor by a man in a suit plowing across the hub. The woman gathered the child beneath her as the herd of commuters barreled against her body, not one of them bothering to look down. Maya crouched beside the woman and held out her hand. "Here, let me help you."

The baffled expression on the woman's face softened into gratitude as Maya helped her to her feet. Once the woman was up, someone yanked Maya's hand from behind her.

A transit officer gripped her wrist. He studied her face and then glanced at the jumbo screen suspended from the hub ceiling. She followed his gaze to the screen which displayed photos of her and Jacob with "Missing Persons" stamped across them. Her body became rigid and her breathing heavy, as if the world had come to a halt.

When he reached for his radio, the woman Maya had helped threw her body against his arm that held Maya.

The woman wailed. "Help me! My child. I can't find him." She beat her fists against the officer's chest with hysterical sobs as her child hid behind her.

While the woman accosted the officer, Maya squirmed from his grip and broke free. She pushed her way through the crowd searching for Jacob.

Jacob caught her eye. "Come on!" He grabbed her hand and pulled her deeper into the crowd toward the tracks.

As Maya followed Jacob, she checked over her shoulder for the transit officer. Several feet behind them, he struggled to push his way through the crowd of commuters who were oblivious to the sound of his whistle and his commands to "move aside."

When Maya and Jacob neared the tracks, the blaring of the incoming train's horn echoed through the hub. The train came to a stop, and the crowd of people advanced as one giant mob toward the door. Maya and Jacob forced their way to the center of the horde and allowed themselves to be carried by the ocean of bodies surging into the train.

Inside the already full train, the new passengers crammed in shoulder-to-shoulder until the very last person squeezed in and the doors slid shut. With all the commotion, Maya had lost sight of the transit officer. Her chest constricted as they forced their way through the blur of bodies deeper into the crowd.

The poorly ventilated compartment reeked of cigarettes, cheap perfume, and body odor. Maya fought the urge to collapse and glanced at Jacob. Sweat dripped down his face, his short shallow breaths becoming even more rapid. Taking his head in her hands, she turned his face toward her. "Look at me. Just breathe." He met her eyes and nodded, matching her deep breaths. Although the crippling anxiety that radiated from him threatened to overwhelm her, she focused on her own breathing and tried to remain calm enough for both of them. As the train barreled forward, she kept his face close to hers and continued to breathe deeply, shutting out the world around them—hoping they hadn't been followed onto the train.

By the time the train arrived at their stop, the crowd had thinned with no sign of the transit officer. But a thinned crowd meant more visibility. Maya readjusted the scarf over her head and prepared to exit. When the train doors opened, her heart began to pound. Jacob motioned toward an elderly couple who were exiting the train, engaged in an argument. Maya nodded and they stuck close to the couple as they stepped off the train. The couple's argument echoed through the empty hub as they approached the exit officer.

The elderly woman became flustered and dropped her bag just as they were passing the exit officer. Jacob quickly picked it up. "I got it, Mom." Maya kept her head down and hurried the woman past the guard before she could turn around to look at Jacob. Once they were out of earshot, Jacob handed the bag to the woman. "Here you go, ma'am."

"Oh. I thought you called me mom," she laughed. "What a nice young man you are." The man stood waiting for her several feet away.

"No problem." Jacob smiled. "Have a nice evening."

The bright lights of the city shone from one direction and a dimly lit road headed the opposite way. Jacob pointed down the shadowy road. "If I remember correctly, the warehouse should be a few miles that way."

Chapter 29

AFTER APPROACHING THE WAREHOUSE from behind, Maya and Jacob peered in the dusty windows. The light inside illuminated Tully who got up from the couch to turn off the television. She walked back toward the couch, tying her hair into a knot atop her head. Maya hurried to the backdoor and tried the lock. Unable to open it, she knocked. "Tully, it's us. Let us in."

The lock turned and the door opened a few inches. Tully peered through the crack. "Oh, it's you." She opened the door for them to enter. "Where have you been?"

Maya hugged Tully. "I'm so glad you're okay."

Tully checked outside the door and then locked it behind them. "What the hell happened to you guys?"

After Maya and Jacob collapsed on the couch, Maya explained everything that had happened as if they had been apart for weeks instead of days. When she mentioned Commander Abigor saying Tully was going to be arrested, Tully stopped her.

"I did not kill my father." Her clenched jaw began to quiver.

"What happened?" asked Maya.

Tully checked the lock on the door before sitting across from them. "I took Trey and a couple of his friends to my dad's house. Trey wanted to get him to admit he set up his cousin. Nothing too serious." She wrung her hands together. "When we got there, the door was wide open. Dad was lying on the floor bleeding. Shot in the chest." Her face tightened and tears burned in her eyes. "Of course, Trey's asshole friends took off."

Despite Tully's steady tone, her pain knotted in Maya's chest. "What did you do?"

She cleared her throat. "He was still alive. He told me to call emergency services, to tell them a man in army fatigues and a ski mask broke in and shot him, but the phone line was dead. I tried to stop the bleeding." She let out a shaky breath. "There was too much."

Tully wiped her eyes and straightened her posture. She walked over to her backpack and retrieved a small black pouch. "He had me take this from his safe and asked me to promise that I would never go back to the Arc. He told me he sent me there to protect me from the people who killed my mom, but that it wasn't safe anymore."

"So he didn't want to get rid of you after all. He just wanted to protect you," said Maya.

"Yeah." A faraway look softened her face. "Anyway, right before he died, he mumbled something about the reconditioning center. He was choking on blood, so I couldn't really hear." She winced as her nails dug into her hands. "I ran when I heard the sirens. Lucky for Trey, he was waiting for me outside."

She tossed the pouch on the sofa between Maya and Jacob. Jacob flinched when it landed beside him.

Her eyes narrowed. "Don't worry. I got the blood off it."

Jacob picked up the pouch and opened it. He unfolded the thin piece of paper. "These look like security plans for a building." He spread out the paper onto the couch.

Maya studied the plans. "I think they're for the reconditioning center. I recognize the layout from when I was there."

"I was wondering if that's what it was," said Tully.

"Do you think maybe he found out the truth about the reconditioning center?" asked Maya.

"Maybe that's why they killed him. I need to find out who did it."

Jacob folded up the plans. "If he sent you to the Arc, why would he tell you not to go back there? Was he afraid of you being reconditioned?"

Tully shrugged. "I don't know. He died before I could find out. He died before I could—" She swallowed. "Anyway, I was thinking Ren could take us to the center to get some intel."

"Have you seen him?" Maya bit her lip as she waited for Tully to answer.

"Trey dropped me here yesterday. He's going to lay low for a while. Apparently, they have security footage of us entering the house. He said Ren should be here by tomorrow to load up the truck to take supplies back to Huruma."

"Okay, so maybe we can ask him when he gets here." Maya got up. "I'm going to take a shower."

"Good idea. I didn't want to say anything, but you reek. Both of you."

Chapter 30

MAYA HAD NEVER BEEN so happy to take a shower in all her life. She washed the residual vomit from her hair and scrubbed away every trace of the holding facility from her body. No matter how long she ran the hot water down her back, she couldn't remove the sting of Commander Abigor's breath against her neck. Shuddering beneath the stream of warm water, she finally turned it off.

Jacob and Tully were eating pre-made sandwiches when Maya came out of the bathroom. Maya's stomach growled so she grabbed one and tore through the packaging stamped with a Gino's logo. "Hey, Tully, is this the same guy who makes your favorite pizza?"

Tully laughed as bits of sandwich spewed from her mouth. "Gino's makes everything. You didn't know that? You know Gino's food conglomerate? Unless you make it at home or eat it at that putrid Arc Commons, Gino makes it." Regardless of who made it, Maya was so hungry that it tasted divine.

While they ate, a truck pulled up out front. It was hard to miss the rumbling of Ren's engine. Maya put down her sandwich and went to the front of the warehouse. She stood in the half-opened doorway and waited for Ren to get out of the truck.

Instead of hopping down from the front seat like usual, Ren hesitated before easing himself down. Without noticing Maya in the doorway, he headed toward the warehouse with his shoulders slumped forward and his head down. When he approached the door, he raised his gaze. His eyes brightened and his lips curved into a smile. "Hey, Fragile." Maya resisted the urge to throw her arms around him and offered a smile.

"Alastair told me you never came out when he went to pick you up. He tried knocking on a couple of houses, but no one answered. He thought maybe you decided to stay with your mom. I was hoping you were okay."

"I'm okay now." She sighed. "A lot has happened."

He noticed the bruise on her forehead and gently moved her hair away from it. "Who did this to you?" His hand lingered for a moment, the tenderness of his touch sending a rush of warmth through her. She let out a soft breath.

As he continued to stare at her, she stepped back and cleared her throat. "It's okay. I got arrested when I went to see my mom and I hurt my head, but I'm fine now."

"Arrested? What happened?"

"My mom turned me in. But it's okay. Abigor took me to visit the reconditioning center, so at least I've seen it. Jacob and I escaped when they tried to take us back to the Arc."

"I'm sorry. I should have been there." His shoulders drooped. "I would have been there, but—"

"What's wrong?" Something was terribly wrong.

He took a deep breath and exhaled. "It's Evie. She's at the reconditioning center."

Maya's heart sank. "What?"

"June reconciled with her ex-husband, and they went to stay with him on the outskirts of the Republic. The morning when I was supposed to pick you up, she called me at Trey's apartment. She was sobbing and begged me to come because he was taking Evie to be assessed." Ren swallowed. "By the time I got there, it was too late."

No. No. No. Not Evie.

"They kept her?"

"Yes, she's at the new center. I was hoping we could scope out the place tomorrow."

"The process killed Meg. One of the girls there." Her voice began to tremble. "We have to save Evie before it's too late."

"Killed her?" He clutched his head and let out a heavy breath. "Don't worry. We'll get her back." The quiver in his voice betrayed a lack of his usual confidence—the confidence she desperately needed from him at that moment.

Her insides collapsed.

The next night, as they drove to the reconditioning center, a chill ran up Maya's spine. She hadn't anticipated all the gut-wrenching emotions of her previous visit rushing back, but at least she was with her friends this time. When Ren parked the truck on a narrow turnout not far from the center entrance, she wiped her sweaty palms on her jeans.

Tully took out a pair of binoculars.

Jacob studied them. "How'd you get those?"

"Ren got 'em for me. Luckily you didn't steal all my stash to buy your train, or should I say, traitor ticket."

Jacob scowled. "If you hide money under your mattress, you're kind of asking to have it taken." He took out the security plans and spread them on his lap. "Remember the shift change is at ten, which should be soon."

Tully peered through the binoculars at the side entrance of the building. "I see a keypad by the door. There's a security camera above it."

Ren checked his watch. "It's ten."

They exited the truck and hid behind the thick shrubbery to get a better look. Ren turned to Tully. "He's coming now. I just saw it. The code is 5-9-7-4-2-3."

"What do you mean you saw it? He is not even here yet." Tully returned her focus to the binoculars. A moment later, a stocky guard in uniform walked around the side of the building and put a code in the keypad. Tully whispered, "5-9-7-4-2-3. Someone remember that." She glanced at Ren. "How did you—"

"Shh." Ren pointed to the door.

When the door opened, a taller guard from inside handed the first guard his weapon belt and a lanyard from around his neck. The first guard took the items, went into the building, and secured the door, while the taller guard rounded the building toward the back parking lot.

Tully put down the binoculars. "I think there's a passcard on the lanyard."

"Does it have a yellow triangle?" said Maya. "The doctor used one to get into all the rooms."

"Yeah. We need to get our hands on one of those."

Once the guard had driven off, the four of them snuck around the back of the building and hid in the shadows behind a row of humming generators. A sole vehicle remained in the lot. Everyone else must have gone home for the night.

Tully started toward the back of the building. "Let's get closer. I don't see any security cameras along the back wall."

Jacob rubbed the back of his neck. "I think we should head back. We're too exposed out here. Someone could see us, and the breeze is really cold."

"Seriously? The breeze is too cold? And there's no one even out here to see us."

As the wind whipped up from behind the building, Jacob's teeth chatted. "I'm freezing. Let's head back." He pulled his scarf around his chin.

Tully's eyes narrowed at Jacob. "Quit making excuses. We need to see if we can get in the windows."

"I'm not making excuses. I need to move. Feel my hands." He placed his hand on Tully's wrist.

She winced and batted his hand away. "Ow! Shit! What the hell, Jacob?"

Ren clamped his hand over her mouth before she could yell any more expletives, as a light came on in one of the windows. He forced a whisper through his clenched jaw. "Back to the truck everyone. Now."

As soon as Ren released her, Tully shook out her wrist. She glared at Jacob and then sprinted back to the truck.

When they were safely in the truck, Tully broke the silence. "What the hell happened back there?" She shoved her discolored wrist in Jacob's face. "I think you gave me frostbite."

Jacob rocked back and forth, his hands clasped tightly in his lap. "I'm sorry. I don't know what happened. I was really cold and..." He glanced at Maya.

"It's okay, Jacob. You didn't mean to do it." Maya looked at Tully. "You'll be okay, right?"

Tully rubbed her wrist. "Yeah, I'm fine."

As Ren started the truck, Tully turned toward him. "And maybe you can tell me how you saw the code before it happened. Am I seriously the only one here without a superpower?"

Ren grinned. "You are a superpower."

Chapter 31

By the time they returned to the warehouse, it was almost midnight. Ren stayed outside to load his truck with the clothes and household items he had collected to take back to Huruma. The rest of them went inside. Tully sprawled out on one of the beds. Maya took a seat on the couch, watching Jacob pace back and forth. He was still bent out of shape over what happened in the parking lot. Maybe she could help.

She went to the fridge and removed the ice tray. She dumped the ice in a bowl and filled it with water. "Jacob, come put your hand in this."

He furrowed his brow. "Are you serious?"

"Yes." She brought the bowl over to where he stood by the table and set it down. "It's an experiment. I know how scientific-minded you are."

He glanced at her and then the bowl. Wincing, he inched his hand into the bowl until it submerged. "It's really cold."

"Good. Tell me when it's unbearable."

"It's already unbearable."

Of course, it is.

"Just keep it in as long as you can." She walked back to the sink and filled another bowl with water.

Jacob's teeth started chattering. "Is this really necessary? My fingers are getting numb."

By this time, Tully had sprung up from bed to watch. "I bet I could keep my hand in there for an hour." She hovered over Jacob with a smug smile.

Jacob's voice rose. "It's too cold. I'm taking it out now."

Maya brought the other bowl of water to the table. "Okay, you can take your hand out. Put your finger in here." As soon as he placed his finger in the water, the surface crackled and froze in one continuous wave.

"What the?" Jacob stared at his finger.

Tully leaned over to get a better look, eyes wide. "Cool!"

Maya put down the bowl. "When I saw the frost on the cup you touched in Huruma it made me wonder. And then when you touched Tully's wrist tonight, it clicked."

"I wonder if it works with heat." Tully scanned the kitchen. "I think I saw some matches—"

"I'm not a party trick, Tully." Jacob rubbed his hands together and then held them in front of him. "So, I can intensify temperatures or something?"

"It seems like it. Do you have any idea how you do it?" asked Maya.

"I'm not sure. In the parking lot, I just got really cold and really annoyed."

Tully scoffed. "He gets powerful when he's annoyed? That might be my actual hell loop."

"You better watch out or I'll give you more than a little frostbite." With a smirk, he reached for Tully.

She batted his hand away and held up her fists. "I got all the power I need right here."

The next morning, Tully and Jacob were fast asleep when Maya got up. Ren had spent the night and was already outside getting ready to head back to Huruma. Maya put on a hoodie and went out front to say goodbye.

Ren glanced up from loading boxes into the truck. "Hey, you're up early."

"I wanted to say goodbye. When will you be back?" She walked over to the truck.

"I'll try to be back early tomorrow. I hate leaving knowing they still have Evie." He placed the last box into the truck and let out a heavy breath. "If only I could have stopped them from taking her."

She sat on the edge of the truck bed. "You know it's not your fault, right?"

"I tried so many times to talk sense into June. I would see the bruises, but she kept going back to him. She's a grown woman, but Evie..." He shook his head and leaned up against the truck beside her.

"That must have been hard for you to see June back with him, especially since, uh, because of your relationship I mean." She glanced away.

"Relationship? Nah, I mean, one time we almost—but you know it was just—" He cleared his throat. "Well, you know what I mean."

She let out a small cough. "But I'm sure you still wanted to protect her, right?"

"Yeah." He shrugged. "I just don't get why women put up with it. Like my mom..."

"Your mom?"

"Yeah after my dad was killed—"

"Your dad was killed? I'm so sorry."

"Yeah, he was from Huruma. He used to deliver flowers to the Republic, that's how he met my mom. He got shot by a Republic guard making a delivery when I was five. Case of mistaken identity or some bullshit. After he died, my mom moved us to the Republic and got caught up with a guy. Some prick from her job. He used to hit her."

"That must have been awful."

"One time when he was beating her real bad, I tried to stop him. He threw me against the table. I was seven." He touched the scar on his forehead. "I remember it was the day of my assessment. I was so numb I must have shocked the poor mouse a dozen times before they made me stop."

Her heart broke for that seven-year-old boy. She wiped the tear from her cheek before he could see it.

"Sorry, I shouldn't have told you all that. You have enough to deal with."

"It's okay." She met his eyes. "I'm glad you did."

He broke her gaze. "I should go."

"Okay." Maya hopped down from the back of the truck. "Give my best to Celia."

"Will do. Hey, I almost forgot." He went around to the front of the truck and pulled out a stack of newspapers. "Can you give these to Tully for me? She asked for them—all the newspapers from the last week or so. Alastair gets them for his hotel guests, but they rarely read them, so he was happy to get rid of them."

"Sure." As she took the stack, a rush of emotions flowed through her. The heaviness of his past, uncertainty over the future, and the flutter in her chest that seemed to happen whenever he was around.

He turned and got into the truck. Before starting the engine, he met her eyes one last time. "When I get back, we'll rescue Evie. I promise."

When Maya went back inside, Tully sat on the couch watching cartoons. "In case you're curious where Wonder Boy is, he's outside. I think he's 'practicing'."

Maya glanced out the window at Jacob pacing back and forth making dramatic movements. She set the newspapers on the coffee table by the couch. "Ren told me to give you these."

"Thanks. I wanted to find out if there was any news on my dad's murder." She sifted through them.

Maya sat on the couch and stared at the television while Tully searched the newspapers. Her mind drifted to Ren. He'd been through so much. At least with her dad, she could hold on to hope that he was okay. She couldn't imagine what it would be like to never see him again. She wiped the tears from her eyes and started to help Tully search through the papers.

When Maya spotted an article with Mr. Doyle's name, she offered it to Tully. "Here, look at this one."

Tully snatched it from her hands. "Let me see that." She began to read silently and then blurted out, "What the hell?" She shoved the paper in Maya's face and pointed to the page. "Read this."

Maya read, "MRBS print media would like to pay tribute to our founder, Mr. Doyle, who died by suicide earlier this week. Although there were initial reports of a break-in, further investigations have confirmed this was not the case. Funeral Services will be held this Saturday morning at nine at Eternal Estates. Because Doyle's sole heir is ineligible to inherit the company, the transfer of ownership will be determined by the Council later this month. Apex Enterprises and Giovanni Industries are under consideration, and if either company gains control, they will exceed the 20% ownership of the nation's industries needed to earn an automatic seat on the Council."

As soon as Maya finished reading, Jacob burst in through the backdoor, his grin disappearing when he saw their faces. "What'd I miss?"

Tully paced back and forth as Maya and Jacob watched her from the couch. She paused and opened her mouth and then shook her head and resumed pacing. Finally, she stopped in front of them. "No way my dad killed himself. He was shot in the chest. I saw it with my own eyes. And he'd never let his company be taken like that. It's gotta be a setup." She narrowed her eyes on them. "Do either of you remember *anything* from your visit to his office that seemed off?"

Jacob shrugged. "Not really. I mean he was working on a marketing campaign for the reconditioning center. He seemed pretty proud of his company."

Maya chimed in. "I am not sure if this matters, but it seemed like he had a close relationship with his receptionist. Or that she had feelings for him?" At least all the feelings she absorbed weren't bad ones.

"You mean horse face?"

"Uh, maybe? She had a strong jawline."

"That's Miranda. I wonder if she knows anything." Tully began to pace again. "I need to talk to her."

Maya glanced at Jacob. "Wouldn't that be dangerous?"

"That's right," said Jacob. "Even though the media is calling it a suicide, Abigor knows you were there. And the authorities are definitely looking for Maya and me. It might be best to let it go."

Tully froze and planted her hands on her hips. "Let it go?" Her eyes narrowed. "Unless you know what it's like to have both your parents murdered, I suggest you shut the eff up. Whoever killed him needs to pay."

Maya tried to clear the tightness in her throat. "I understand but—"

"I'll ask Ren to set it up." She glared at Jacob. "I'm not gonna let this go."

Maya sighed. "But we need to focus on getting Evie back. What if they try to recondition her?"

"I was trying to do that last night when captain sensitivity screwed it up."

"Tully, you know that's not fair. Jacob was just–"

"It's okay, Maya. Let her think what she wants." Jacob went out the back door, slamming it behind him.

Maya found Jacob sitting on the concrete with his back against the building. She slid down next to him. "You know she's just upset about her dad, right?"

"Yeah." He rubbed his head and ran his fingers through his hair. "I know I'm more sensitive than normal people, but I can't help it."

"Believe me, I know."

"I just wish people would understand. Like I'm just wired differently."

"It's ok to be different."

"You know, Dr. Barrow once showed me a scan of my brain compared to a normal one. It was actually different. He called it scientific proof of the overactive Fragile brain. All that rehabilitation at the Arc didn't change a thing."

"He never showed me mine, but I'm sure it was worse." She stared across the field. "Have you ever thought that maybe we aren't meant to be rehabilitated?"

He turned toward her, brows furrowed. "What do you mean?"

"I just mean, maybe we were made this way for a reason. Like what if the problem is with the world, not us?" She lowered her head and sighed. "I'm tired of hating who I am."

"Hey," Jacob nudged her. "Don't hate yourself, okay?"

"I know." She straightened her shoulders and turned toward him. "You either, okay?"

"I don't. At least not usually." He let out a deep breath and then smiled. "Next time Tully opens her mouth, I'll just use my power on her."

Maya laughed. "About your ability—"

"Which I don't understand. It defies the laws of physics. How could I possibly intensify temperatures with my hands?"

"And how do I put feelings in people? I know it's weird." She rested her head against the building. "So our brains really are different?"

He shrugged. "Apparently so."

"Celia said something about how we're capable of things beyond what we know. She calls them abilities, not powers. She thinks my ability is just an extreme version of empathy. Like I take in so many emotions that it becomes powerful energy in my body that needs to be released. I didn't completely understand. But maybe yours is similar?"

"I don't know. None of this really makes logical sense."

"Didn't you once tell me that we're still learning things about how things work? When you were reading that book on quantum whatever."

"Yeah, but—"

"Well, couldn't it be possible that there's a scientific explanation that just hasn't been discovered yet?"

"I guess that's possible." He was silent for a moment and then his eyes lit up. "Like maybe we don't completely understand how energy moves and intensifies. And how it interacts with our bodies?" He turned toward her. "It's an interesting theory. But why us?"

"Maybe because we are so sensitive, our bodies react differently? Our brains are different after all." She shrugged. "So like you're so sensitive to the environment that your body is able to manipulate it or something? I mean temperatures at least. Or maybe more?"

"Whoa. I'm still getting used to the whole temperature thing, okay?" He smiled at her. "I've been feeling different since I stopped taking my medicine, though. Like clearer or something. I wonder if it's related."

"You stopped taking your medicine?"

"They confiscated it when I turned myself in. They didn't believe it was prescribed."

"Hmm. And I stopped taking mine way before you. Maybe it *is* related. If only Celia was here. She seems to understand this stuff."

"Yeah, it's a lot to think about."

She rested her head against his shoulder. "I'm just glad I'm not the only one."

Chapter 32

THE NEXT MORNING, MAYA had just come out of the bathroom when the warehouse door slammed open. Ren's voice echoed across the room. "Everybody up. Now!"

While Tully continued to snore, Maya sped toward Jacob who was already out of bed. Ren rushed to the couch and shoved it across the floor. "I just saw it. The Republic Guard will be here in minutes. They've been doing searches all over the Republic for you."

Maya shook Tully awake. Ren pulled open a trapdoor that had been hidden by the couch. "Grab your stuff and get down there. Do NOT come out until I come and get you, okay?" Maya grabbed her belongings and shoved them in her backpack. She ran to the trapdoor and hurried down the creaking wooden stairs into the darkness. Once they were all inside, Ren closed the trapdoor behind them. A scraping noise rumbled from above them as he dragged the couch back in place.

Lost in the darkness, she felt her way to the nearest wall and slid down into a seated position, her back against the cold concrete. Jacob started hyperventilating, his breath shallow and much too fast. Maya reached out to him, but her fingers met only the space between them. Tully cracked her knuckles from across the hiding space. Exhaling slowly, Maya tried to control the jackhammer in her chest.

After a few minutes, footsteps and muffled voices sounded from above. When stomps thundered across the ceiling, Maya gripped her knees close to her body. She clutched her arms across her chest, convinced the guards could hear her every heartbeat. Digging her fingers into her arms, she strained to discern the words echoing overhead.

They must be shouting.

Or be right above them.

The minutes crawled on like hours as she sat paralyzed with fear. At one point, the volume increased, but then faded away into silence. Not even a footstep. Moments later, the screech of the couch being moved jarred Maya's frozen limbs.

A beam of light cut through the darkness as the trap door opened. Shielding her eyes while they adjusted to the light, Maya held her breath.

"It's okay to come out. They're gone." Ren peered down at them.

After Tully and Jacob started up the stairs, Maya exhaled and pushed herself to her feet. Once she had climbed out, Ren secured the trapdoor in place.

Tully turned to Ren. "So they were looking for us?"

"Yeah. They tried to give me a hard time, but they eventually gave up." Ren slid the couch back. "They had no idea you were here." He scanned the room. "I have to finish my flower deliveries, but should be back in a few hours so we can work out the details of getting Evie out of the center."

Maya leaned against the couch to support her legs that still shook. Ren caught her eye. "Are you okay?"

She straightened and forced a smile. "Yes, I'm fine."

When Ren turned to leave, Tully rushed to her backpack and retrieved a folded piece of paper. "If you are going to see Alastair, can you give this to him please?"

"Sure." Ren shoved the paper in his pocket before heading out the door.

Tully walked over to the television and put it on. "From now on, the TV stays on. I need to make sure I don't miss news related to my dad. Anyone have a problem with that?" She glanced at Jacob who was back in bed staring at the ceiling. At least his breathing had returned to normal.

Maya poured herself a glass of water and joined Tully on the couch. "So they probably won't come looking for us here again anytime soon, right?"

Tully leaned back into the couch. "Yeah. We should be safe here for a while. But I'm gonna head back to the hotel tomorrow. Ren's taking my note to Alastair, so hopefully, he'll set up the meeting with Miranda for tomorrow night. I just hope horse-face shows."

Maya glanced across the room to where Jacob lay in bed and kept her voice low. "But what if she turns you in?"

"She won't. I'll tell her I was released from the Arc to attend my dad's funeral. It's perfect."

"So, Ren will take you to the hotel? We really need to focus on rescuing Evie."

"I still have to ask him, but I'm sure he will. Miranda probably knows stuff about the center, too. It could help save Evie."

"Maybe." She set her glass on the table. Or maybe it was too late.

Later that afternoon after Ren had returned, Jacob called out from where he was sitting by the television. "Hey, it's one of those commercials for the reconditioning center." Joyful music played in the background as the camera panned the inside of the center. Children played with toys while onlookers in white coats gestured and nodded with self-satisfied grins and their chins held high. The camera came to rest on a man in full military attire with a girl on his lap. Maya let out a gasp.

Commander Abigor smiled at the camera, his long fingers stroking Evie's hair. K stood beside him, her face vacant and pale. Although Evie strained to smile, her lips trembled, and her eyes were wet. Abigor spoke to the camera. "I'm having a special event at the center tomorrow at 8 pm. It is a private event for certain misguided Fragiles who might want to witness first-hand the final rehabilitation of these sweet little girls."

Silence permeated the room. Maya's insides numbed and the world came to a halt. Ren rose in slow motion, his body stiff and his jaw clenched. Maya's mouth fell open, her voice lost inside her. Tully stood in front of the television with her back to it and her arms folded. "You know it's a trap, right?"

A trap.

The words echoed in her head. Evie. K. She had to save them. Everything went black.

When she opened her eyes, Ren stared down at her. "Maya?"

She pulled herself up from the cot and rubbed her face with her hands. "What happened?"

Jacob sat across from her. "You blacked out."

Blacked out. Like with the mouse. Crushed to death when she tried to save him.

Ren put his hand on her shoulder. "You okay?"

She would never be okay. Not until they got Evie back.

"Yeah, just give me a minute." Her knees were weak, but the back door wasn't far. "Maybe I'll go outside and get some air." She pushed herself up and stumbled out the back door into the sunlight.

The parched yellow field spread out before her like a blanket of death. Even the sun seared her skin. She staggered across the field and pulled herself over the decaying wood fence, collapsing on the other side. The image of Abigor holding Evie burned in her mind. Her tears began to flow. What if he hurt her?

At first, she barely noticed the crackling of the dry grass behind her. Ren climbed over the fence and sat beside her. She sat motionless as they both stared off into the distance.

Wiping her eyes, she turned toward him. "We need to save her before Abigor—"

"I know. We'll go tonight. He's not expecting us until tomorrow so it's our best chance." The deep resolve in his voice gave her a sliver of hope.

Chapter 33

TULLY AND REN SET up the back of the warehouse like a tiny war room. On the coffee table, the open security plans spread out next to a large piece of cardboard which Tully had found by the dumpster. Ren provided markers that he used for labeling flower crates as well as some packing supplies like duct tape and scissors.

Jacob knelt on the floor near the coffee table and began to draw a map of the Apex compound that housed the reconditioning center on the cardboard. Maya sat cross-legged next to him while Tully and Ren sat on the couch. In his drawing, Jacob included the turnout before the entrance and started to draw detailed shrubs and trees lining the turnout.

Tully grabbed the marker and scribbled the rest of them. "We don't have all day."

He scowled and took back the marker. "Okay, I get it." He continued drawing the outline of the parking lot, the building and the entrance where they had seen the guard go in.

Tully picked up the plans and showed Jacob. "So it looks like the whole south wing of the ground floor is the reconditioning center."

Jacob marked off the southside of the building. "Like this?"

"Yeah. We can refer to the plans for the rest of the details. Looks like the dorms are in the back through a few locked doors. Hopefully we can get the passcard from the guard."

Jacob put down his marker and sat back on the floor. "So what's the plan?"

Ren leaned and pointed to the turnout on the drawing. "I say we park the truck in the turn out like last time and wait for the guard change. That's the best way in. There was only one car in the back, so maybe there's only one guard on shift at a time."

"But we don't know for sure," said Jacob. "And there's a security camera by the exit, remember?"

"So we wear disguises." Tully turned to Ren. "Can you get us ski masks? I still have cash left."

Ren nodded. "There's a sporting goods store back towards the business district."

"Speaking of disguises," said Maya. "What if we stop the guard on the way in and take his uniform? Then someone could put it on and use the code to open the door."

Ren nodded his head. "That could work. We have the code."

"But what about when the other guard comes out?" asked Jacob.

Ren made eye contact with Maya. "We debilitate him and take his passcard. Remember he wears it around his neck. And we debilitate the first guard to get his uniform."

"Debilate." Tully rubbed her palms together. "I like that. What kind of weapons they got at that sporting goods place?"

"We already have a weapon. Remember how Maya took down Evie's dad?" Ren nodded at Maya. "You could do it again, right?"

"I don't know. Doing it once kind of drains me. I'm not sure if I could do two in a row."

Tully stood up. "So let's try. Get up."

"What do you mean by try?" Maya pushed herself up from the ground. "You want me to hurt you?"

"Not hurt me. Put some feeling into me and then try Ren. I'm sure Jacob has enough feelings in him already."

"Very funny." Jacob took Tully's seat on the couch.

Ren joined Tully and Maya. "Okay let's try."

Maya searched her body for an emotion, but didn't pick up anything. "I have to take in an emotion from someone first. Or at least recall one."

"Think of my grief about my dad," said Tully.

"You want to feel that? It magnifies."

"I know. Remember what you did to me before we jumped off the cliff? Don't worry. I can take it."

Maya let out a heavy breath. "Ok."

She recalled Tully telling them how she struggled to stop her dad's bleeding. How she tried to hide her pain beneath a measured account of what happened. The ache in her heart as she described his last breath. As the grief flowed through Maya, she placed her hand on Tully's arm.

The color drained from Tully's face and she dropped to her knees. She buried her face in her hands and started to sob.

Maya knelt beside her. "I'm so sorry."

Tully curled into the fetal position as her sobs transformed to guttural groans.

Maya got up. "What do we do?"

Jacob helped Tully onto the couch. "She'll be okay. I'll get her a glass of water. You try Ren now."

Ren stood in front of her. "Maybe not grief, okay?"

"Okay." Maya shook out her arm which still stung with residual emotion.

"Like maybe a positive feeling."

Searching for a happy emotion, her mind returned to Huruma. To Evie skipping through the greenhouse, the flowering plant she gave Jacob, Evie's pure heart filled with love. As the love flowed through Maya, she touched Ren. The warmth in her arm radiated to her hand, causing her fingertips to tingle.

Ren's lips parted and he gazed into her eyes.

The intensity of his stare made her drop her hand. She took a step back to catch her breath. "Are you okay?"

He grinned. "Yeah. That was quite an emotion."

Her cheeks burned. Maybe she should have chosen a different emotion.

Tully groaned from the couch. "How come he's not on the floor?"

"Did it work?" Jacob set Tully's water on the table and turned to Maya. "The two in a row. Do you think you can do it?"

Ren smiled at her. "She can do it."

That night, the four of them rode to the Apex building in silence. When Ren parked the car in the turnout, they got out and huddled by the back of the truck. Tully handed Jacob a roll of duct tape.

Ren checked his watch. "It's five to ten. Remember, if anything happens and we get separated we meet back at the hotel. Alastair's expecting us tonight. They searched the hotel a couple of days ago so we should be fine. We get in, get Evie and any other kids and get out. Everyone ready?"

Maya nodded along with Tully and Jacob. They donned their ski masks and slipped through the darkness to wait by the side entrance.

Maya crouched behind the bushes closest to the building with adrenaline coursing through her veins. She focused on Evie. Her terror. Abigor's hands running down her back. The scream that threatened to explode from her insides.

As soon as the guard rounded the corner from the parking lot, Maya sprung from the bushes and grabbed his arm, releasing the terror that tore through her. His eyes got wide and he let out a horrific groan. She held on until he collapsed to the ground motionless.

Ren and Tully slipped off his uniform, leaving him in an undershirt and boxers. As soon as his clothes were off, he started to stir, so Tully and Ren held him in place while Jacob secured a piece of duct tape over his mouth. Jacob then bound the guard's wrist together and ankles together with duct tape.

Maya's arm reeled with pain, so she shook it out as she watched them. Her eyes caught the guard's, and her stomach sank. Lying on the cold hard ground in his underwear, he looked so vulnerable. Tied up like a tortured animal.

Her breath hitched and she took a step back. What had they done?

Once Ren was dressed in the guard's uniform, he motioned for Maya to move towards the entrance door like they had planned. Time to attack the next guard. She felt sick to her stomach. The guards hadn't done anything to deserve this.

While Ren approached the entrance door with the beret pulled low over his mask, she inched along the wall next to the door out of the security camera's view. Ren entered the security code with his head down to hide his face from the camera directly above the door.

Maya steadied herself against the wall, racked with guilt and anguish. When the door opened, she reached for the guard's arm but pulled it back at the last minute. She couldn't do it.

"Hey! What are you doing here?" The guard turned to Maya and reached for his weapon.

Ren tackled him from behind. With the force of the tackle, the gun flew from his hand. While Ren and the guard struggled, Maya backed up against the wall.

Ren pinned the guard face to the ground, but the guard flipped him over. The guard jumped on top of Ren and drew back his fist.

Tully scrambled for the gun. She pointed it at the guard. "Freeze."

The guard released Ren, but pulled up Ren's ski mask half-way before backing up into a seated position with his hands up. Ren quickly lowered his mask and got up. He stood above the guard as Tully brought the gun close to the guard's head.

The guard kept his eyes on Ren. "I'll remember you."

Tully knocked the gun barrel to the guard's head and he collapsed to the ground. She holstered the gun in the waist of her jeans.

Ren grabbed the lanyard with the passcard from around the guard's neck and handed it to Maya. Then, he un-hooked the handcuffs from the guard's weapons belt. "Come on, help me move him. We can cuff him to the fence near the generators."

The four of them carried him to the chain link fence and Tully handcuffed him to one of the bars. When Jacob put duct tape across his mouth, Maya turned away.

Tully nudged Maya. "What happened back there?"

"I couldn't do it." Her voice started to shake. "I mean, I wanted to but..." She was a Fragile. She was weak. And now the guard had seen Ren's face.

Ren removed the guard uniform and tossed it by the fence. "It's okay. Let's get inside."

By the time they got back to the building entrance, the door had swung shut. Ren put in the code and led them into the dimly lit lobby flanked by Tully who held the gun in her hands. An eerie silence filled the room, the air heavy and stale as if the HVAC system had cut off.

Tully scanned the perimeter of the room which appeared to be empty, still clutching the gun.

Jacob pointed to a closed door. "According to the plans, the therapy rooms should be behind that door and the dorms behind that." He turned to Maya. "Is that the door you went through?"

She nodded and led them towards it, gripping the guard's passcard in her hand.

When she approached the door, she held the passcard against the panel with the red light and held her breath. After a moment, the light turned green and the lock clicked open. As they passed the empty therapy rooms, beads of sweat collected behind Maya's mask.

Tully put her gun back in her waistband. "Remember the plans showed there's no cameras in here and I don't see any. We should be fine." She peeled off her mask. "It's hot as hell in here."

Maya kept her mask on while Jacob and Ren removed theirs. Seeing Ren's face reminded her of the guard's words. *I'll remember you.* She shuddered and inched off her mask.

When they reached the door where the orderly had brought out the girl, Maya held the pass card in front of the panel, but the light remained red.

"Try it again," whispered Ren.

She tried again, but the light wouldn't change. Her hand started to shake.

Tully approached Maya. "Here, let me try." After wiping the card on her jeans, she held it by the sensor. The panel beeped and turned green. Tully entered and led them into a stuffy room with three doors along the far wall.

Once inside, Tully took off her sweater and tied it around her waist. Next to the two bathrooms, stood a door labeled "dormitory." While Ren and Jacob checked the bathrooms, Tully tried the pass card on the dormitory entrance, but it remained locked. The long narrow window along the side of the door was too dark to see through.

Ren pulled his hoodie sleeve over his hand and struck the window with the side of his forearm. It held firm.

Jacob approached Ren. "Can I use your jacket?"

Ren shot him a quizzical look, but unzipped his hoodie and handed it to him.

Jacob put it on and zipped it all the way up before tightening his scarf around his neck. Bouncing up and down, he rubbed the sides of his arms. It had to be at least eighty degrees. How can he possibly be cold?

Jacob approached the door. He placed his hand near the center of the window, his eyes wide. As he held his hand in place, the window splintered and cracked. He stumbled backwards and threw off his scarf and jacket, gasping for air.

Maya rushed to his side to keep him from collapsing.

"Man, how'd you do that?" Ren picked up his hoodie.

Jacob mustered a weak smile. "Thermodynamics."

Tully leaned into the window with her covered shoulder, and it fell to pieces against her weight. She used her sweater to clear the jagged shards and squeezed through the opening with the others close behind her.

Although the air seemed cooler inside, a heaviness wrapped itself around Maya. As they continued down the narrow hallway, they approached a row of doors. A colorful sign with a smiling monkey and the letters A-D hung on the first door. Placing her hand on the doorknob, Maya glanced at Tully before turning it. She opened the door to a small room with a bunk bed on either side. Although the beds were made up with blankets and pillows, they were empty.

The four of them spread out down the hallway to check the other rooms. Maya rushed towards "I-L" with the smiling elephant to look for K, unsure of what letter Evie would have been assigned. But it was empty.

They were all empty.

Every. Last. One.

Chapter 34

MAYA GAZED OUT THE hotel room window overlooking the city. So many buildings. Evie could be anywhere. Her heart ached. When they arrived last night, Alastair had assured them that the Republic guard had searched the hotel earlier that week, but she was still on edge and barely slept. Tully lay sprawled across her bed snoring.

Evie could be anywhere, but Maya knew where Commander Abigor would be that night. It was her only hope. She stepped back from the window and glanced at the clock. After tiptoeing across the hallway, she tapped on Ren and Jacob's door. She was about to turn back when Ren opened the door. Standing in the doorway with only a white towel wrapped around his waist, his smooth brown skin glistened with drops of water that accentuated his toned chest. He tilted his head to tap water out of his ear. "What's up?"

Maya's mouth opened, but nothing came out. She stammered, "Um. I can come back."

"You sure? Jacob's still in bed but—" He motioned for her to enter.

"Yeah, it's okay." She focused on his eyes. "Just come to our room once Jacob's up." She stepped back, stumbling over her own feet.

He leaned against the doorway. "Sure." He watched her with a grin as she backed away and then closed the door.

By the time Ren and Jacob joined them, Maya and Tully were halfway through the breakfast Alastair had sent up. While Tully devoured her eggs and pancakes, Maya picked at her muffin. Tully took a gulp of juice and wiped off her mouth with the back of her hand. "Miranda should be here around six. I'm gonna meet her in one of the rooms downstairs."

Jacob sat down on the bed. "Do you trust her?"

Tully rolled her eyes. "I don't trust anyone."

"I just mean, what if she alerts the authorities?"

"If she was as into my dad as I think, she won't. Besides, I have insurance." She sat back with a gleam in her eyes. "It never hurts to have a little dirt on someone."

Maya got up and went to the window. She stared across the cold gray backdrop of the city, her voice a faint murmur. "What about Evie?"

Ren approached her. "What did you say?"

She turned around. "How are we going to get Evie back?"

Tully got up. "If Miranda knows about my dad's involvement with the center, she might be able to help us. Let's wait to decide until I talk to her."

"Wait?" Her voice shook. "What if he hurts her?" She turned back around to the window.

"He might have already done that." Tully's words sliced through her.

Maya spun around. "No. We're not going to let him. He'll be there tonight. And so will we."

Tully glared at her and placed her hands on her hips. "And do what? Get arrested? I told you it's a trap."

Maya's eyes narrowed. "Don't you even care?"

"I care, but I'm not stupid."

Ren positioned himself between the two of them. "How 'bout we just finish breakfast?"

Maya let out a sharp exhale before nodding. Arguing with Tully wouldn't get Evie back. She'd have to do that herself.

Later that evening, after Tully had gone to meet Miranda, Maya sat at the table watching Ren and Jacob play cards with the hotel deck. She took a deep breath. "So I know it might be dangerous to go to the center, but I was thinking that we could at least drive over there." She glanced at Jacob. "We wouldn't have to go in. We could just watch from the truck. You know with the binoculars. If we go early enough—"

"You're serious?" Jacob put down his cards.

She looked at Ren. "Yes, we can just wait for him to arrive and see if he has Evie or maybe even follow him once he leaves."

Ren nodded. "That's actually not a bad idea."

"Not a bad idea?" Jacob pushed himself back from the table. "It's a trap."

"Not if he doesn't see us," said Maya. "If we leave now, we can get there before he does and just watch. We don't have to do anything unsafe."

"The whole thing is unsafe."

"I know, but Evie—" Her voice broke.

"I want to help her as much as you do, but we need a better plan." Jacob turned to Ren with a frown. "You know this is dangerous, right?"

Ren put his cards down. "Yeah, man, I know, but we're running out of options. And it beats sitting around here." He got up from the table. "Besides, we're just going to check things out." Ren turned to Maya, his tone as serious as his stare. "Right?"

Avoiding his eyes, she nodded. She would do whatever it took to save Evie.

Night had fallen when they reached the turnoff before the center. Ren parked as far back as he could alongside the row of shrubbery and turned off the lights.

Maya turned to Jacob. "I think Tully put the binoculars in the glove box."

Jacob opened the glove compartment. "Looks like she put something else in there, too." Next to the binoculars lay the gun Tully had taken from the guard. Jacob took out the binoculars and closed the compartment. Already half past seven, the front parking lot of the center remained empty.

Soon, the lights of an approaching vehicle cut through the darkness. The vehicle passed the turnoff and pulled into the parking lot. As it drove around towards the front entrance, Ren peered through the binoculars. "I see a driver and someone in the back seat. I think it's Abigor."

The vehicle came to a stop and shut off its headlights. She turned to Ren. "I need to get closer."

He put down the binoculars and stared at her. "I want to rescue Evie just as much as you do, but if Abigor catches me, that's it for me and my family. It could even put Huruma at risk."

"I know."

"It's bad enough the guard got a glimpse of me last night."

She winced at his words. "I just think we could get a better look from behind the bushes. Jacob and I can go check while you stay here ready to start the truck, okay?"

Ren shook his head and let out a deep breath. "Just be careful, okay."

"I will." She nudged Jacob who sat by the door. "Let's go."

When they reached the end of the bushes, only a short embankment separated them from the parking lot. Jacob grabbed her arm. "This is as close as we get."

Maya nodded and peered into the vehicle trying to get a glimpse of Evie. The back car door opened and Abigor exited, dragging Evie out with him. A shot of adrenaline surged through Maya and she took off down the embankment towards the vehicle.

She froze at the edge of the parking lot.

Abigor stood on the walkway leading into the building with Evie by his side. The guard who had been driving leaned against the vehicle.

"My-yah."

Maya's skin crawled as Abigor called out her name.

He pivoted in place. "My-yah." As she walked towards him, his eyes rested on her. "Don't be afraid. I only want to help you."

Evie tugged toward Maya, but Abigor tightened his grip on her wrist.

Forcing the words up from her diaphragm, Maya yelled, "Let her go."

Abigor twisted his face into a pout. "I'm afraid I can't do that."

"She's just a kid." Maya drew closer to Abigor, now within a few feet of him.

The guard locked eyes with Abigor who replied with a slight shake of his head.

"She's a Fragile. You of all people should know how unsafe the world is for Fragiles." He motioned to Evie. "And her rehabilitation is going beautifully."

Maya glanced into the back of the vehicle. "Where's K?"

"She wasn't feeling up for the drive."

Maya met Evie's eyes, inviting her terror to flow through her. As the pain surged through her, she lunged for the guard's arm. He reached for his gun, but she shot pain through him until he dropped to his knees. When he collapsed flat on the ground, her stare returned to Abigor. Her arm still burned with terror.

Abigor took a step back with Evie, but then straightened his collar and smiled at Maya. "Poor child. You're even more defective than I thought. When the Arc guard told

me you were one of them, I thought perhaps he was lying.
But here we are."

Maya took a step forward. "I said let her go."

Evie glanced up at her and then back at Abigor. She took
a deep breath and bit down on Abigor's hand. When he
flinched, Maya lunged at him, knocking Evie free.

While Maya grasped for Abigor's arm, she yelled, "Evie,
run!"

Evie sprinted across the parking lot.

Before Maya could send pain through Abigor, he
yanked her towards him and whipped out his pocket knife.
He pinned her arms behind her. As he held her body
tightly against his, the blade rested against the flesh of her
exposed neck.

"You forget that I trained in the military. Now be a nice
girl and get in the car." He walked her towards the vehicle
as the guard on the ground began to stir.

"Let her go."

Abigor spun around, still holding Maya to his chest.
Jacob gripped Tully's gun with two hands, pointing it at
Abigor.

"Oh. It's only you," Abigor chuckled. "For a moment,
I thought I was about to get shot." He laughed to himself,
loosening his grip.

Seizing the moment, she ripped her right arm from
his grasp just as his knife pierced her skin. She grabbed
Abigor's arm with her free hand and forced terror into

him. Despite the weakness in her limbs, she forced him to stumble back enough to let go.

Once free, she raced towards the embankment, her chest constricting as her feet pounded the pavement. When she reached the edge of the parking lot, she turned to look at Jacob. But he hadn't run.

Her hand rose to her mouth. Jacob stood by the vehicle with his hands behind his head. No longer quivering on the ground, the guard had a gun to Jacob's head. He shoved Jacob into the car and slammed the door behind him.

Before her knees buckled under her, she ran towards the thick shrubbery up the embankment. She dove into the bushes and crawled with her belly close to the ground. As she peered through the tangled branches, the car pulled out of the parking lot. It slowed as it passed the turnoff, but then sped off. She wriggled through the rest of the shrubbery and pulled herself up when she reached the edge.

Not sure which way to go, she turned and slammed into Ren.

"It's okay. I got you." Ren held her tight.

Her lungs threatened to collapse, so she shoved his body away from hers. She struggled for air. "They... took... Jacob," she managed between breaths. She glanced at Ren's shirt, smeared with blood. Her lips quivered as she raised her arm to point at his chest. "What happened?" Blood ran down the side of her arm.

"Maya, you're bleeding." He slipped off his hoodie and held it to her neck, then lifted her hand to hold it in place. "Keep the pressure on. Let's get you to the truck." Dizziness overtook her as he guided her to the truck. When they approached the back of the truck, he called out to Evie who got up from a nearby bush. Ren slid open the back door and lifted Maya into the truck bed.

As she held the hoodie in place with one hand, she lifted the other towards her neck. Her fingers moved across the fabric until they reached the side of her neck that was sticky with blood. She ran her hand down her sweatshirt. It was soaked through. Ren climbed in beside her with a lantern while Evie sat on her other side, slipping her hand into hers.

Although Maya could barely make out his frown and furrowed brow, the severity of his concern barreled through her.

How bad is it?

He made eye contact. "I have a first aid kit in the truck, but I want to check the wound first. Ok?" She nodded and closed her eyes while he exposed her wound. Once he replaced the hoodie, he let out a shaky breath. "I'll be right back."

She opened her eyes and swallowed as the pain burned across her neck.

Ren hopped down from the truck. "Keep the pressure on."

Evie pushed herself up onto her knees and leaned over Maya. Maya gave her a faint smile before she closed her eyes again. Darkness closed in on her. Her breathing became shallow and her muscles dissolved into uncontrollable trembling.

Evie inhaled.

She slid her hands under the hoodie and placed them lightly on Maya's neck.

Evie exhaled.

Maya relaxed into the comfort that spread throughout her body. A peaceful love washed over her. Evie took another deep breath and exhaled slowly. A warmth radiated from Evie's fingers that stopped Maya from shivering. Within minutes, Maya's breathing normalized, and she opened her eyes.

When Ren hopped into the back of the truck, Evie placed her hands on the top of the hoodie. "Sorry, it took me so long. Damn thing was under the seat." He sat down next to Maya with a lantern and the first aid kit. "I'm going to move this again so I can bandage it, okay?"

She nodded and Evie moved her hands.

Ren clenched his jaw as he removed the hoodie. His facial muscles relaxed as he examined her wound. "Huh. It's not as bad as I thought. I think the bleeding has slowed."

He searched through the kit and pulled out a small packet. "This might sting."

Maya winced as he cleaned the cut.

He placed gauze on her neck and secured it in place with tape. "Do you think you can make it to the front seat?"

Maya nodded and pulled herself up to a sitting position. After Ren helped her down, he led her to the open passenger door of the truck. There on the seat, lay Jacob's scarf. She reached for it and pulled it towards her as she collapsed onto the seat.

Chapter 35

Maya sat in the hotel bathtub, her warped reflection staring back at her from the shiny faucet. As she ran her hands under the tap, the blood-tinged water spiraled down the drain. She dug her fingers into the bar of soap and scraped the dried blood from beneath her nails. Finally, the water ran clear. She rose and wrapped herself in one of the fluffy white robes.

As she stood in front of the mirror, her fingers explored the edge of the bandage. The steam from the bath softened the tape, so she peeled up one corner. Little by little, she pulled up the bandage. She had to see it. Although the gash ran diagonally several inches across her throat, the blood had begun to dry. She removed the bandage and threw it in the trash.

Her forefinger traced the edge of where the blade had pierced her skin. Abigor's knife. His hot breath on her neck. Her hands pinned. Shuddering, she dropped her hand to her side. She tightened the bathrobe around her body.

When Maya came out of the bathroom, Evie lay sleeping on the bed with her head resting on Ren's lap. Ren inched out from under her and placed her head on a pillow before he got up. He put his hand to his lips and motioned for Maya to follow him across the hall to the room where he and Jacob had stayed. Once they reached the doorway, she steadied herself against the frame to fight the wave of dizziness that overtook her.

As soon as they entered the room, Tully got up from one of the beds and approached Maya. "You don't look as bad as I thought you would." She studied Maya's cut. "In fact, it kinda makes you look like a badass."

"Thanks." Maya eased herself down onto the other bed. Jacob's bed. Her eyes panned the room to Jacob's backpack on the table.

Ren glanced at Maya. "I told Tully about Jacob."

Her eyes burned. "Okay." She fidgeted with the edge of the bedspread.

Tully sat across from her. "I think they might be taking him to the Arc. I spoke to Miranda."

"The Arc?" Maya sat up straight. "What did she say?"

"She said Abigor and Apex cut a deal to use the reconditioning center as a front to get funding for Apex's new building. The plan all along was to transfer any remaining kids to the Arc and use the procedure there instead. My dad found out they were hurting kids, so he backed out of funding the center." Her face tightened. "Apparently, he was worried about me. Anyway, he got paranoid near the end and started recording all his phone conversations. Miranda has one where Abigor threatened him, so she thinks either Apex or Abigor put a hit on him."

Beneath Tully's matter-of-fact tone, Maya sensed her pain. "I'm so sorry, Tully."

"The person who's going to be sorry is Abigor when I destroy him."

"Are you sure it was him? Apex could have arranged it, too, right? Aren't they trying to take over your dad's company?"

"That's what I'm going to try to find out. Tomorrow I'm—"

"Tomorrow? We need to rescue Jacob from the Arc before it's too late." She turned to Ren. "Can you take us? We have to save him and the other kids. If it wasn't for him..." It should have been her.

Ren shook his head. "I get it, but I need to take Evie back to Huruma. It's not safe for her here." He let out a heavy sigh and sat next to her. "It's not safe for you either, Maya.

We need to leave tonight. Then we can talk to Trey's friend who does food deliveries to the Arc and figure a way in."

"But is Huruma safe?" asked Maya. "After having to leave in such a hurry last time?"

"They've already searched there for you." Ren's face dropped.

She felt his pain in her gut. "What happened?"

"Once June's ex got her and Evie to come stay with him in the Republic, he reported you being there to the authorities. They ransacked the place looking for you. "

Tears burned her eyes. It was all her fault. Everything. Huruma. Jacob. She started to shake.

Ren placed his hand on her knee. "It's okay. Hardly any permanent damage. But that's probably how Abigor knew he could use Evie to get to you."

She wiped her eyes with the edge of her sweatshirt.

Tully got up. "You all do what you want, but I'm stay-ing. I'll crash at Trey's."

Maya glanced up at Tully. "I think you should come with us."

"Why? I can take care of myself." She scoffed. "The Republic doesn't scare me. And if I have to put a bullet in the head of every last person responsible for killing my parents, I will."

"I don't think we can do it without you. Jacob needs you—I need you." She averted her gaze before Tully could react.

Instead of responding, Tully walked to the window. She continued staring out the window until she turned to Maya. "I'll go back for a day. Just one. We rescue Jacob and the kids and then I'm coming back here. Got it?"

A wave of relief passed through Maya as she got up from the bed. "Yes, I got it. Thank you."

"That's good because staying here with Trey is not an option. He gave up his place and went to Huruma." Ren rose and opened the door. "Let's all try to get a couple hours of sleep. We'll head out at 2 am when the streets are empty and make it to Huruma by sunrise."

After returning to her room, Maya crawled into bed and curled up next to Evie who was fast asleep. Although her body ached from exhaustion, her mind replayed the image of Jacob with a gun to his head. Was he on his way to the Arc now? Did they hurt him? Maybe they were taking him to jail. Or the adult ward. She smothered her tears in the pillow.

At some point, she must have succumbed to her fatigue because a thump on the door startled her awake. Glancing at Evie's wide-open eyes, Maya whispered, "It's just Ren," and pulled herself up from bed. Tully's rumpled bed lay empty, the sound of her showering coming from behind the bathroom door. Still lightheaded, Maya stumbled across the room and peered through the peephole into the empty hallway. As soon as she turned from the door, another loud thump drew her eyes back to the peephole. Again, her eyes met a vacant corridor.

She cracked the door and peeked out just as the door pushed into her, knocking her backward. Panic struck her until her eyes dropped to Jacob lying at her feet.

Evie sat glued to Jacob's side, holding the glass of water she had gotten him from the bathroom. Maya sat across from him, studying his face, her heart filled with gratitude and her mind filled with questions. Still a bit groggy, he struggled to answer the questions that Tully fired at him from across the room.

"Tell me again what happened."

He rubbed the back of his neck. "I was in the car with Abigor, and he said he needed to find Maya and asked where she would be going, but I said I didn't know. Then he injected me with something. When I woke up, I was in a room, like a cell or something. It was dark and my vision was blurred so I don't really know. I thought maybe they were outside, but it was so quiet, and they just left me there." He took a sip of water and handed the glass back to Evie. "Anyways, once I could stand, I broke the lock on the window and climbed through it. I was in the business district, so I made my way back here."

"I'm so glad you got away. I was so worried when I saw you at gunpoint. I thought—" She raised her fingers to her neck and blinked back the tears. "Thank you for saving me."

He shrugged. "I'm sure you would've done the same for me. And maybe we should thank Tully for being careless enough to leave the gun in the glove box. I guess Abigor knew I had no idea how to shoot it."

Tully's face twisted into a smirk. "If it wasn't for that gun, you might all be locked up, so you're welcome." She leaned forward. "But I don't get it, there were no bars on the window or anything and they just left you there?"

"Maybe they didn't think the drug would wear off so quickly? I don't know."

"I hate to interrupt, but the truck's ready." Ren stood in the doorway. "We need to head out."

Although the Republic had no border check on the way out, they huddled in the back of the truck behind rows of empty flower crates. Instead of the sweet smell of jasmine, they had inhaled on the way into the Republic, only the musty scent of the empty crates remained. Evie shifted in the darkness and moved close to Maya. "Do you think K and the other kids from the center are at the Arc?"

"We think they might have moved them there."

"I hope K is there. I told her you were my friend. She was really sick, so I helped her, but then they took her away. Just like the other kids."

"You helped her feel better?" Maya's fingers traced the cut on her neck.

"Yes. She's my friend." She yawned and rested her head against Maya.

Sometime later, the truck slowed down and pulled over. The back of the truck opened, flooding the interior with moonlight. Ren climbed into the back of the truck. "There's a checkpoint just around the bend. They must have just set it up."

Maya shook Evie awake as Tully and Jacob got up.

"You need to walk about a hundred feet across that field and then follow the ravine until you go under a bridge. I will pick you up on the other side of the bridge. Okay?"

Maya nodded and tried to get up, but her knees buckled.

Ren offered his hand. "You've lost a lot of blood. Can you walk?"

She grasped his hand and pulled herself up. "I think so."

Brows furrowed with concern, he turned to Jacob. "Keep an eye on her, okay?"

They made their way to the steep slope of the ravine in the moonlight. Clutching Evie's hand, Maya inched her way down the hill behind Tully, with Jacob right behind them. After only a few steps, her foot slid into a loose patch of soil. She lost her footing and stumbled several feet, dragging Evie behind her. When they finally reached the bottom, she stopped to catch her breath. Although Evie had skinned both knees, she smiled sweetly at Maya.

A tiny stream of water flowed through the center of the ravine surrounded by dry, parched ground. They had been walking for a couple of minutes when Tully froze in her tracks. She held her hand out in front of them and then pointed up the embankment at lights from what must be the checkpoint. She continued forward with deliberate footsteps not making a sound with Evie close behind her.

Could they see them from the ravine? The heaviness in Maya's legs made it impossible for her to step forward. Her heart beat pounded in her ears. What would Abigor do when he caught them? The heat in her chest rose up her neck. It burned like Abigor's hot breath on her skin. The stars in the night sky swirled above her.

Just as she lost her balance, Jacob grabbed her. "Are you okay?"

"Yeah, I'm just light headed."

Tully looked her over. "It's the blood loss. Can you walk?"

Maya nodded.

"Good. They can't see us down here, so if we're quiet, we'll be fine."

Jacob stood by Maya's side. "I'm right here. I'll help you if you need it."

Staring straight ahead, Maya put one foot in front of the other until they passed the checkpoint. After the checkpoint, the ravine began to incline and soon the bridge appeared in the distance. Despite the lightness in her head and the weakness in her muscles, Maya willed herself to keep walking. If only she could make it to the bridge, everything would be okay.

Once they passed under the bridge, Tully led them up a short embankment where they huddled in the shadows. Ren should have been there by now, but the desolate road lay empty in the still night air. Tully motioned for them to stay put before inching her way closer to the road. She froze as two Republic Guards vehicles flew by with their lights flashing.

Panic rose in Maya's chest. Had they caught Ren?

Once the vehicles disappeared down the road, Tully joined them where they sat in silence.

With every minute that passed, Maya's dread grew. Unable to wait any longer, she nudged Tully. "If Ren doesn't come, we need to—"

"Don't worry. He'll come." Her eyes remained glued to the road.

Maya frowned. "But what if they caught him? If they somehow knew—"

"Shh!" Tully stood up. "You hear that?"

Maya heard it. The truck's engine rumbled in the distance. Once Ren pulled over to the side of the road, they emerged from the shadows.

Ren hopped down from the driver's seat and opened the back of the truck. "Sorry about that. They were searching every vehicle so it took a while. We should be okay the rest of the way."

Maya climbed into the back of the truck and collapsed. She hoped he was right.

When Ren opened the back of the truck again, the sun had begun to illuminate the Huruma sky. Maya stretched her cramped limbs and stepped down from the truck. As soon as her feet came to rest on the solid earth below her, she felt a deep connection with the land. Her lungs welcomed the fresh air and her soul embraced the peace of Huruma.

As they walked towards the front of the truck, Celia greeted them. Evie sprinted towards her. "Miss Celia!" Celia wrapped her in a warm embrace.

When Evie finally let go, Celia smiled at her. "Your mother is here. She's in my tent. She'll be so happy to see you."

Evie's grin widened and she ran off towards the tent.

Celia turned to Maya, her eyes sparkling with kindness. "Ren told me what happened. You are all welcome to stay here as long as you need."

"Thank you. That's very kind of you."

In the distance, the poles around the dining area stood barren without the delicate strings of lights. The side of the greenhouse was sealed with garbage bags and duct tape. Maya lowered her head. "Ren told me what happened, how they came searching for us. I'm so sorry."

Celia placed her hand on her shoulder. "We knew the risk. Why don't you all get some rest? You must be exhausted. We can talk more later."

Chapter 36

THE AFTERNOON SUN HEATED the tent when Maya awoke. She turned over to go back to sleep, but the thick, warm air made it difficult to get comfortable. As she rose from her cot, Evie peeked inside the tent and motioned for her to come out. Tully was searching through the box of clothes in the corner, but Jacob was still out cold.

When Maya met Evie outside the door, Evie handed her a glass of a pungent dark liquid. "Miss Celia told me to tell you to drink this."

Maya eyed the dark green liquid and swirled it around, getting a whiff of its earthy scent.

"She says it will help you get your strength back."

After a few hesitant sips, Maya gulped it down. Despite its earthy taste, it wasn't that bad. She handed the glass back to Evie whose eyes lit up. "Now we just need to get you some clothes."

Maya glanced down at her dirty sweatshirt. "Thanks, that'd be nice."

Evie grinned and led her down the path towards her tent. When they reached the tent, Maya paused outside. The canvas door had been torn off completely and rehung with duct tape. She ran her fingers over the tape.

Evie grabbed her hand. "It's okay. Let's go inside."

Once inside, Evie sat on the bed and spread out a pile of brightly colored clothing. "I think these should fit you. Which one do you like?"

Maya joined Evie on the bed and sifted through the clothes. "Are there any tee-shirts?"

"No, you need something pretty." Evie giggled and held up a blue sundress. "How about this one?"

Except for the dress Abigor made her wear, Maya hadn't worn a dress since she was a child. Perspiring beneath her sweatshirt, she took the dress and slipped it on. It was a little snug, but she liked the feel of the soft fabric against her skin. Evie led her to the mirror. Although Maya's curls were all over the place, and she couldn't help but cringe at the gash across her neck, she didn't mind what she saw.

"You look beautiful!" squealed Evie. Maya turned to examine her profile. She wasn't tall and built like Tully, but at least her awkward angles had finally softened into curves. Maya began to tie her hair into a braid. "Your hair's so pretty. I love all the curls. How come you always braid it?"

"I don't know. Habit, I guess." She let the braid unwind in her fingers. Evie beamed.

"Miss Celia asked me to go to the oasis to get some senna root for your scar. I'm not supposed to go by myself, so Ren and Trey are taking me. Can you believe Ren's from here and he doesn't even know how to find senna?" Evie giggled. "Do you want to come? We can swim."

Whatever it was that she drank had given her a spark of energy. "Sure, that sounds nice. Let's see if Tully wants to come. Jacob's still asleep, but she's up.

While Tully, Trey, and Ren walked ahead on the trail, Maya and Evie followed behind, enjoying the scenery. Although the path was hot and dry, the farther they walked, the lusher the surroundings became. Wild greenery twisted in unique patterns and every now and then, a vibrant flower burst forth. Maya imagined this must have been what it looked like centuries ago when plant life spread unfettered around the planet.

As they continued to walk, the trail sloped upwards towards the sound of rushing water. Moments later, it opened into a clearing with a large crystal pool of water surrounded by palm trees and flowers. Tully followed Trey to explore the waterfall flowing from a rocky incline at the far edge of the pool.

Evie took Maya's hand. "Come on. I'll show you where we can find the roots."

Ren removed his shirt and tossed it onto one of the rocks surrounding the pool. He smiled at Maya as Evie yanked her towards a large flat rock jutting out from the water, surrounded by broad green leaves. Evie waded into the shallow water by the rock and lifted one of the leaves. Beneath the leaves, light pink roots grew into the water. Evie broke off a few of the roots and handed them to Maya. Maya took the roots, but her eyes remained on Ren who waded out into the water.

Evie broke off a few more roots and cradled them in her skirt. "That should be enough. Let's put them in the sun to dry."

Evie and Maya climbed up onto the rock and laid the roots out in the sun.

"I'm gonna go look for flowers." Evie smiled and climbed down from the rock.

Maya sat on the rock with her bare legs dangling in the cool water below. The sound of the waterfall soothed her soul, and her face relaxed into a smile. Ren swam towards her and pulled himself up in the shallow water. Standing waist deep in the water, his eyes met her eyes. Almost forgetting to breathe, she returned his gaze, twisting a curl around her finger.

His eyes narrowed on her. "Huruma suits you." He continued staring at her so intently that it sent tingles through her body. "Hell, it suits you more than it does me and I was born here." The warmth in his eyes matched the smile that spread across his face.

"Look out below!" Trey flew from the top of the waterfall and plunged into the pool below, sending ripples across the water.

Tully stood at the top of the waterfall, wriggling out of her clothes. Once she was down to her bra and underwear, she jumped off the ledge. She swam towards Maya. "That was amazing. You got to try it." She stood up and squeezed the water out of her hair.

Trey came up behind her and kicked a spray of water over her. Tully spun around and lunged towards him, throwing him back into the water. As he swam away, she went after him and dunked him under the water. They both exploded in a fit of laughter.

Ren held out his hand to Maya. "I'm gonna jump. You coming?"

Maya smiled and took his hand to climb down from the rock. As soon as he helped her down, she dropped her hand from his. She followed Ren around the side of the pool towards the waterfall. He stopped when they got to the rocky face that led to the top.

"We climb up here. It looks harder than it is." He placed his hand on her waist and guided her in front of him.

"I'll be right behind you in case you need me." His hand lingered on her waist for a moment, so she paused to catch her breath.

Focused on the climb, she pulled herself up to position her feet on the first set of rocks. The path to the top was well worn making it easy to see which ones to grab and balance on. She climbed as fast as she could, avoiding the stones that were slippery with moss. Maybe Ren would see that he didn't always have to take care of her.

When she pulled herself up to the ledge, he was right behind her. The flat rock above the waterfall where they stood had barely enough room for the two of them. Now that she peered down from the top, it seemed so much higher. As she backed away from the edge, she stumbled into him.

He clasped her waist to keep her from falling. When she turned to face him, his warm hands remained on her waist. He lowered his head towards hers and gently brushed a curl from her face, his hand lingering on her cheek. Drawn to the heat of his body next to hers, she couldn't help but focus on his soft lips.

He gazed into her eyes and lowered his voice. "If you're scared, you don't have to."

She met his stare despite the butterflies in her stomach. "I'm not scared."

"Are you sure?"

The smoothness in his voice sent tingles through her body. She nodded and let out a soft breath. His lips were now inches from hers. As his hand slid from her waist to her back, she closed her eyes. His lips met hers and a wave of warmth rushed through her body. Their lips had barely touched when he pulled away.

"Shit. I'm sorry." He dropped his hands and stepped back. "I shouldn't have done that."

As heat rose to her face, her chest constricted. "It's okay." Glancing over the edge, she stammered, "I think, uh, I think I'm ready to jump." She fumbled with her hair and twisted it in a knot behind her head.

He reached for her. "Wait, let me—"

She flung herself off the top of the waterfall in her dress and braced for the impact of the cold water below.

Chapter 37

By the time they returned from the oasis, the sun had set. Maya had kept up a steady stream of conversation with Evie during the walk back until Ren walked on ahead with Trey and Tully. She wasn't ready to talk to him any time soon.

When Maya got back to the tent, Tully sat on her cot drying her hair with a towel. "I was wondering when you would make it back. Jacob's at dinner. I'm about to head over."

Maya dropped down onto her cot. "Thanks."

"And speaking of Ren." Tully put down the towel. "What's up with you two?"

"I should ask the same about you and Trey."

"Oh, that's nothing. He just gets me. You didn't answer my question."

Maya let out a heavy sigh. "There's absolutely nothing going on."

"Come on. I saw the way he checked you out in that dress. Who knew you had boobs under all those baggy clothes?" Tully laughed. "And it looked like something up on the waterfall."

Maya got up and searched through the box of clothes that Evie had given her. She pulled out a hoodie and slipped it over her dress that hadn't quite dried during the walk back. "Maybe it was something, but now it's nothing." Nothing for him at least. She could still feel the spark of his lips on hers. "I'll walk with you to dinner."

When Maya and Tully reached the outdoor eating area, most everyone had already finished eating. Jacob, Evie and some of the other kids sat at the end of one of the tables talking and laughing, but the rest of the tables were empty. Tully joined the group and began filling her plate with food from the serving platters. Maya scooped out a small piece of vegetable casserole and sat on the other side of Tully.

Maya had just finished eating when Ren sat down across from her. He leaned towards her. "Hey, I've been wanting to talk to you."

To make what happened even more awkward? No thanks. She stared through him. "I was about to go get something from Celia, but did you find out if Trey talked to his delivery friend about getting us into the Arc? We need to save those kids. That's the only reason I came here."

"Uh, okay." He sat back. "Well, Trey just left to see his friend, so hopefully he'll agree to help. But I—"

"Okay. Let me know what he says." She picked up her plate and left before he could say another word.

When she got to Celia's tent, a small box sat outside the door with a note that read. "Apply the cream twice per day. Celia." She picked up the box and carried it back to her tent. Once she was situated on her cot, she removed the cover from the box. Inside, a small jar had been wrapped in a white cloth. As she lifted the jar from the box, the fabric unfolded, revealing an embroidered pattern in the corner. It was the same symbol of the uprising Celia had shown her that matched the one on her handkerchief.

Her mother's handkerchief.

She dumped out the contents of her backpack until she found the crumpled handkerchief. With a lump in her throat, she spread it out next to the one from the box. She hadn't thought about it since the day she had gone to see her mother. Tears pooled in her eyes. Was it as easy for her grandmother to abandon her mom as it was for her mom to abandon her?

She let out a deep sigh and opened the jar of cream, releasing the scent of rancid pond water. She dabbed her finger into the cream and smoothed it across her cut. At least Tully and Jacob weren't there to tell her how bad she reeked.

Ren poked his head in the doorway. "Hey, can I come in?"

Of course, he showed up now.

She shoved the handkerchief under her pillow and used the cloth to wipe off the cream. "Ah, it's not the best time."

He stepped into the tent. "I just need a minute."

She sighed, "Whatever."

He walked in and sat down on the cot across from her. "Whoa. I see you got the cream from Celia. It doesn't smell the best, but it works."

"Doesn't smell the best is a nice way of putting it." She got up and walked across the tent to sit at the table. "What did you want to talk about?"

He followed her to the table and sat across from her. "I wanted to apologize for what happened at the oasis."

"It's fine. You don't have to apologize for not liking me or whatever. I get it." Her shoulders dropped as she forced a smile. "Can we talk about something else now?"

"It's not that. It's just that I tend to screw up relationships. And I don't want it to be just a hook-up so–"

"Hook-up?"

"Yeah, you know, like when people get together, but it's physical. I know that's not what you want."

She crossed her arms. "How do you know what I want?"

He leaned towards her with an intense gaze that shot through her. "Is that what you want?" The warmth in his low voice sent tingles across her skin.

She met his gaze, his deep brown eyes and perfect lips releasing the butterflies in her stomach. What *did* she want?

She let out a sharp breath and pushed her chair away from the table before getting up. "I don't know, but it's not up to you to decide what's best for me all the time."

"I know. I just care about you and respect you and would never want to do anything to hurt you."

She sat back down and studied his face. He seemed to be telling the truth. "So, are you kind of like a player?"

His brows furrowed. "What?"

"You know. Like someone who only does casual relationships? I grew up in the Arc, but I'm not that naive."

He shook his head. "How about we just say I have issues?"

"You and me both."

Chapter 38

LATER THAT NIGHT, MAYA crawled into bed exhausted. As her body relaxed into her cot, her mind drifted. Just as she was about to fall asleep, an image of a young woman sharing features with her mother invaded her thoughts. The frantic woman clutched a basket, her feet pounding on the pavement below her. As the woman ran, Maya's chest constricted, and she struggled to breathe. She could feel the rough wood of the basket in her clenched fist and the cold night air as it chilled her lungs. Was she dreaming?

Footsteps echoed on the pavement and tears streamed down Maya's face. Together with the woman, grief consumed Maya as the footsteps ceased. Her fist released the basket. Another sprint forward and a violent pain tore through her. Maya shot up in bed gasping for breath. She grasped the handkerchief from below her pillow and held it to her chest.

Grandma?

At first light, Maya headed to Celia's tent. If anyone could help her understand her vision or dream or whatever it was, it was Celia. When she arrived at the tent, Celia was on her way out. "Good morning, Maya. I was about to tend to the garden. Care to join me?'

"Sure."

She followed Celia around the back of her tent and down a small dirt path lined with wild shrubbery. The path led to a garden with an assortment of plants and flowers. Celia walked across to a rusted metal pump and began to pump water into a watering can. After filling a second can, she handed one to Maya and motioned across the garden. "We'll start over there."

Maya nodded and followed her.

Celia watered the flowers. "So how are you?"

"I'm fine." Maya mustered a smile and tried her best to water the flowers like Celia.

Celia stopped watering and faced her. "How are you really?"

The words cut into her. She was trying to hold it together, but she hadn't been fine for a long time. She sighed. "Maybe not so fine."

Celia nodded. "Go on."

"I couldn't save Meg, the girl from my dreams. They killed her. And then I put Jacob's life at risk when I ran from Abigor. I saved myself." She bit her lip as the tears formed in her eyes. "I thought I was strong enough to fight Abigor but...and what about K and the other kids? What if they don't survive?" She put down the watering can.

Celia placed her hand on Maya's arm. "You saved Evie, didn't you?"

"I know, but—"

"Losing a battle doesn't mean you're not strong. What you decide to do afterward is what's important." She handed the watering can to Maya. "Let's water the flowers over there." She pointed to a patch of purple flowers that resembled the galeas from the greenhouse.

Maya wiped her tears with her sleeve and approached the flowers. "Aren't those the really fragile ones? What if I water them wrong?"

"Fragile?" Celia let out a warm laugh. "Their sensitivity protects the entire garden. That sounds like strength to me."

Maya wasn't so sure, but Celia seemed convinced. "Is that why it's the symbol on my handkerchief? Of the uprising, I mean?"

"I imagine it is." Celia took the watering can from her and set it down. "Have you thought any more about how your mother ended up with it?"

"I'm not sure, but I had a dream last night. About my grandmother, I think." Maya glanced at Celia. "I think she gave my mom up because she was in danger."

"I suspected the same thing. Your grandmother must have been related to Leonora or deeply connected to the uprising. Abigor's men hunted them down and executed them. That may have been why she abandoned your mother. To save your mother's life."

A heaviness gripped her core. "So, Abigor hates us?"

"People often hate what they fear. Abigor views the most sensitive and empathic as threats to the Republic."

"Because of Leonora?"

Celia knelt next to the gaeleas. "Do you know how these flowers hold us accountable for protecting the whole garden? They notice the slightest pollutant in the soil, so we can make the necessary adjustments. Without the galeas, the garden could be mismanaged for years. The damage would be so gradual that it might not be detected until it was too late to save the garden."

"So, if someone wanted to pollute a garden without being caught, they would get rid of the galeas first?"

Celia rose and picked up the watering can. "Precisely."

"So Abigor wants to get rid of the Fragiles—"

Celia cut her off. "Fragiles? That's just a word created to oppress you. It's not who you are. Try again."

If she wasn't a Fragile, who was she?

She tried again. "So Abigor wants to get rid of, uh, sensitive people because he is afraid of another uprising? Because we care about the bad things the government does and might fight back?" She glanced at Celia for approval before continuing. "But I don't get it. We don't have any power."

"That's what he's made you believe." Celia set down the watering can and placed her hand on Maya's arm. "Look around you. There's power in Huruma. The power of community. The power to sustain our environment and nurture life. Look at Evie. She's only eight and is one of the strongest souls I know and one of the most sensitive. She uses her ability effortlessly because she was nurtured to accept it. You've been taught a lie."

Maybe if she had grown up in Huruma, things would have been different. Maybe she would feel strong like Celia. But she was a Fragile, and Abigor wanted to destroy her. Her knees buckled. "Is it okay if I head back? I'm feeling a little queasy."

"Sure." Celia's brows knitted together in concern. "I can finish without you."

"Thanks. I probably just need breakfast." She turned to go before Celia could see the pain in her eyes.

Celia stopped her, taking her hands in hers. Her bony, withered hands were gentle, yet strong. "You are more powerful than you think. You just need to accept your power." Celia gently squeezed her hands before letting go.

"But why me? What if I don't have the strength to—"

"I know you didn't choose it, but it's who you are. You're one of us."

"You mean you're..."

Celia nodded. "Yes. You, me, Evie, Ren. And Ren told me about Jacob. For whatever reason, we have special abilities unique to our sensitivities. As do others. More and more children are being born this way." She picked up the watering can and began watering the galeas.

"So that's why they send them places like the Arc?"

"Yes. To drug them, torture them, all in the name of rehabilitation." A shadow passed over her face. "Not all sensitive children develop these abilities, but I believe Abigor views all children with heightened empathy as a threat."

Somehow knowing the truth helped. "Can I ask what your ability is?"

Celia smiled. "I can often read people's thoughts."

Maya scrambled to remember any embarrassing thoughts she might have had in Celia's presence. Ren. She had thoughts about Ren. Her cheeks burned.

"Don't worry, I don't share them with others." She handed Maya the other watering can. "But you might want to tell him yourself."

Maya took the can. "It's complicated." She began to water the flowers. "So, like Ren feels responsible for everything so he sees the future? And Evie is sensitive to other's physical pain so she heals?"

"Yes, and Jacob is sensitive to the environment, so he manipulates it. And you experience other's emotional pain and can manifest it in others."

It was a lot to take in, but she felt lighter. Like a weight had been lifted from her shoulders. "Thank you for sharing this with me."

"You're welcome. Why don't you head to breakfast? I can finish up here."

"Thanks." She handed Celia the watering can and headed to the eating area.

When Maya joined the others at breakfast, she tried not to fixate on the way Ren's t-shirt hugged his biceps and focused on his eyes instead. His warm brown eyes with perfect dark lashes and a spark that melted her insides. Shifting her gaze to her juice, she picked it up and took a sip.

Tully glanced from Ren to Maya with a sly grin. "So Maya, what happened up there after you kissed Ren at the waterfall?"

Maya spit her juice across the table.

"What?" Jacob stared at Maya, his eyes wide.

"It's nothing." Maya glared at Tully, her cheeks burning. She cautioned a glance at Ren, but his relaxed posture and playful grin only fueled her anger.

"It doesn't sound like nothing." Jacob's stare remained fixed on her.

"It was a mistake, barely a kiss, nothing, okay?" Maybe that would wipe the smile off Ren's face.

It didn't.

"Can we please just change the subject?" Maya fiddled with her fork. "Aren't we supposed to be trying to figure out a way to save the kids at the Arc?"

"About that." Ren leaned forward. "Trey's friend says there's a wing behind the east wall or something. He said that's where he delivers food to the dining commons."

Tully sat back in her chair. "I knew there had to be another entrance. If I had known, we could've avoided the whole crawling through a pit of human waste thing."

Ren chuckled. "I wondered why you all smelled so bad when I met you." His smile faded as his forehead pinched with concern. "Seriously, though, about the Arc, Trey's friend said they ramped up the security. Like Republic guard officers with guns. Trying to save those kids could be dangerous."

"But we need to save them." Maya's stomach clenched. "What about K? Evie said there are others. What if the treatments kill them?"

"I know." Ren's expression softened. "We'll think of something. But we need time to plan."

Jacob rose and grabbed his plate. "I told Evie I'd help her with something in the greenhouse. I'll see you all later."

"Oh, Jacob, before you go, I wanted to—" Maya rose from her chair. With all that had happened, she had forgotten to give him back his scarf.

Avoiding her eyes, he turned to go. "I'll see you back at the tent later."

After Jacob left, Tully rolled her eyes. "What's with him?"

Of course, he was upset about the kiss, but Tully didn't need to know that. Maya had been denying how Jacob felt about her for so long, that she might as well avoid it a little longer. She got up to clear her plate. "He'll be fine." She would talk to him that evening.

After heading back to their empty tent, Maya took a deep breath and scanned the room. Tully's clothes were strewn across her disheveled bed, while Jacob's bed resembled the neatly made-up ones in Alastair's hotel. His Arc sneakers were tucked under the bed, so he must have found a new pair in one of the boxes. Maya glanced down at her own sneakers and then eyed the box. It would be nice to have a pair without the "property of the Arc" label on the back. When she glanced back at Jacob's shoes, she noticed the label protruded as if concealing something underneath. She reached for his shoe when a voice from behind her startled her.

"So, a mistake, huh?"

Instead of picking up the shoe, she turned to face Ren who was standing in the doorway. She offered him a wry smile. "I believe your exact words were 'I shouldn't have done that' preceded by some profanity."

Returning her smile with a genuine one, he stepped into the tent. "Not my finest moment. But you did call me a player. And I want to clear that up because I'm not."

"But don't you—"

"No, I don't. I just find it hard to trust people or let them in, so my relationships haven't lasted long. I wanted to—"

His voice dissolved into the blare of sirens.

Chapter 39

As Maya sprinted behind Ren, the heaviness inside her left little room to breathe. By the time they approached the front gate, she was gasping for breath. A swarm of Republic guard vehicles with flashing lights littered the area just outside the gate. Sean stood by the entrance arguing with an officer flanked by two armed guards.

Ren locked eyes with Maya, his jaw clenched. "Stay here." Before she could reply, he joined the men at the gate. Maya inched forward to get close enough to hear.

Ren glared at the officer and turned to Sean. "What's going on?"

"He said they're here for the Fragiles. He has a list of names." He gestured to the officer who held a paper in his hand.

The officer handed Ren the paper. "Yes, I have the authority to take these Fragiles back to the Arc. They escaped. It's for their own protection."

As Ren scanned the paper, his face tightened. He glanced at Maya before shoving the paper back at the guard. Chest thrust forward, he stepped into the guard's face, his penetrating stare filled with fury. "Authority from who?"

The door of the vehicle closest to the officer swung open. "That would be me." Commander Abigor exited the vehicle and joined the officer.

Maya stepped back, only now noticing the crowd that had gathered behind where she stood. As she searched the crowd, she found Tully near some of the kickball players and Jacob and Evie near the back of the crowd. She returned her attention to Abigor.

Abigor caught her gaze. "Oh. I see Maya is anxious to come home. How about you come through the gate now, so I don't have to send my guards in? I would hate to see anyone get hurt."

Her body urged her to flee, but she started towards the gate. When she joined Ren, his panic surged through her. She took a deep breath, forcing his torrent of emotions through her. Abigor stood within reach, but there were too many guards. Too many guns.

I would hate to see anyone get hurt.

Maya swallowed the bile burning the back of her throat and turned to Ren. "Who's on the list?"

He shook his head. "All of you."

"Evie?"

His pained expression gave her the answer.

She turned to Abigor, "Evie's from Huruma. She was never at the Arc. You can't—"

Abigor scoffed. "But I can. Her father signed her over to the Arc after her assessment. In fact, I have the paperwork right here." He offered it to her.

A familiar hand rested on Maya's shoulder. "Let me speak with them." She turned to where Celia stood beside her. Celia approached Abigor. "May I see that, please?" Abigor handed her the paper. She read it and handed it back. "I wonder if we could come to some sort of agreement?"

Abigor raised his eyebrows in amusement. "Agreement? How about the Fragiles come with us and we don't bomb Huruma off the map? I'm sure the council would be very concerned to learn that your settlement is harboring fugitives." He nodded at a guard.

When the guard approached Maya with handcuffs, Ren lunged at him. A second guard drew his weapon and pointed it at Ren. Ren froze, lowered his head and put his arms up.

Another guard exited a vehicle with his gun drawn—the guard from the center who had glimpsed Ren's face.

Maya stepped in front of Ren and held out her hands to be cuffed. Under her breath, she whispered. "You need to go. It's the guard."

Ren kept his head down and backed up.

The guard from the center watched Maya get hand-cuffed and then eyed Ren. He holstered his gun. "So this one thinks he's tough, huh?"

Maya pivoted to glance at Ren who kept his chin to his chest.

The guard took a step closer to Ren.

Tully emerged from the crowd. "Not as tough as me, asshole." She held out her wrists. "Aren't you supposed to cuff me?"

"My pleasure." He whipped out his cuffs and slammed them onto her wrists.

She winced, but kept her eyes on him while Ren backed up into the crowd.

By this time, Jacob had made it to the gate. He stood next to Tully and held out his hands to be cuffed.

Abigor beamed, "It's so nice to see you again, Jacob. If it wasn't for you, we might never have found you all."

Tully looked at Jacob with her eyes wide and lips pursed, her words like venom. "You sold us out?"

As the color drained from Jacob's face, his eyes widened. "I have no idea what he's talking about."

An anguished scream bellowed from the crowd. "No! Evie, no!" June gripped Evie, holding her back from joining them by the gate. Tears streamed down June's face, her dark eyes wild with panic. Several of the other residents had gathered around them, some attempting to comfort June, others forming a protective barrier around Evie.

Celia's calm voice brought Maya's focus back to the gate as she pleaded with Abigor. "Would you consider just leaving the child? She's been through so much already. Perhaps we could pay you for your trouble?"

Abigor shook his head. "She's a Fragile. We can consider returning her once she's fully rehabilitated. Guards?" He motioned for the guards to pass through the gate and retrieve Evie.

The guards pushed through the crowd with their assault weapons drawn. June flung her body in front of Evie behind the wall of residents that had surrounded her. When the guards reached the wall, they raised their weapons, ready to fire. One of the young kickball players stepped forward, bringing his head just inches from the barrel of the gun. His eyes were wet, yet filled with determination.

"Awaiting your instructions, Commander," barked the guard.

Abigor turned to Celia and clicked his tongue against his teeth. "Did I mention the council has authorized the use of deadly force?"

Celia faced the crowd. "Let Evie through."

The lips of the boy with the gun to his head quivered as he took a step back. Two of the other residents peeled June's arms away from Evie as she desperately fought to hang on. Once Evie slipped from her grasp, June collapsed to her knees sobbing. As Evie made her way towards the gate, she fixed her gaze on Maya. When she made it to the gate, she gave Maya a weak smile before holding out her hands to be cuffed.

Chapter 40

THE ROOM WAS ODDLY familiar. As Maya sat on the bed staring at the cold gray wall, she remembered. She had awakened in this room when she was seven. Like all Fragiles, she had spent her first three days in confinement to prepare to join the Arc community. In the upper corner of the room, a red light on the camera blinked. She used to count the blinks at night when she couldn't sleep, imagining her parents were watching over her. That was until she was taught it was the Arc—not her parents—that would keep her safe. And that her parents couldn't hear her cries.

She lay down on the bed and shut her eyes.

There was no way out.

The room had no windows and a sole light bulb that remained on, blurring night and day. After what might have been several hours, someone shoved a bowl of soup on a tray through the slot in the door. She sat on the floor by the door and sipped the lukewarm broth. Her stomach churned, so she returned the bowl to the tray and pushed it through the slot. She rested her back against the cold rough wall and let her head slump forward into her hands.

She pushed herself up off the floor and walked towards the bed, pausing by the wall. After glancing at the camera, she pounded on the wall. "Tully! Can you hear me? Jacob?" She beat her fists against the concrete until her knuckles were raw. "Evie! Where are you?" Tears streamed down her face as she fell to her knees and sobbed. She cried until her tears ran dry and then staggered to the bed, exhausted.

Maya awoke when someone pushed a tray through the slot at the base of the door. She nibbled on the toast before sliding the tray back through the opening. A few minutes later, the door opened. Two armed guards grabbed her and shoved her out into the corridor. Her legs could barely keep up with their strides as they led her down the hall. The guards brought her into a small room with stadium seating facing a large window overlooking a laboratory.

One of the guards took her to the front and sat her in the aisle seat. He gestured to his gun. "Don't even think about moving. The director's on her way." He positioned himself to the left of her chair while the other guard stationed himself by the door.

Director Williams had let them go once. Would she help them again? The door opened, interrupting Maya's thoughts. As she turned to the door, her jaw dropped.

Dr. Schader entered the room and walked over to the window. "You must admit it's quite beautiful. All state-of-the-art equipment. Our work is so important to the future of the Republic that our investors have been more than generous." She turned towards Maya. "Oh, you weren't expecting Natasha, were you? You must know that some people just aren't director material."

Abigor had said he would hold Director Williams accountable if they escaped, but Maya hadn't considered what he would do to her once they did. A knot formed in her stomach.

Schader returned her gaze to the window. "Commander Abigor requested that I give you a demonstration. That's why you have the privilege of being in our viewing room today."

Maya stared straight ahead. Inside the laboratory, two white egg shaped pods with bright yellow trim and black bench interiors faced the viewing window. Near the top of each pod, the words Apex shined in gold aside its yellow triangle logo. In between the pods, a monitor on a thick white stand displayed the Apex logo on its screen. A table with two computers and rows of binders lined the side wall next to a video camera on a tripod.

Dr. Schader turned from the window to Maya. "The process I created is quite ingenious. We expose subjects to images to elicit an empathy response and then scan their brains to determine the areas of activation. Once we have identified the empathy centers, we send an electrical current to destroy the offending brain matter. Our success rate is currently around seventy percent. Unfortunately, some subjects' brains have so many areas of activation that they lose significant brain matter in the process." Her lips twisted into a smirk. "But we're working on that."

Maya glared at Dr. Schader. What she would give to make her feel the terror she inflicted on innocent kids. On K. On Meg. Her arm buzzed with emotion and her fingers twitched. She eyed the guard to her left.

He placed his hand on his weapon and stared her down until she returned her eyes to the window.

A door opened into the lab and two men in white coats entered with Evie. Maya sprung towards the window and choked on a scream, but the guard shoved her back to her seat. As she struggled to grab his arm, the second guard drew his weapon and pointed it at her. She froze with her arms up and eased back into her chair.

One of the white coats took a seat by the video camera. The other led Evie to one of the pods and positioned her inside on the bench. He pressed a button on the side of the pod and a headset attached to a white cable lowered from the pod's dark interior. Once he had positioned the headset on Evie and adjusted a dial, he secured her wrists to the armrest with black straps. The goggle portion of the black head set began to glow with iridescent white light.

After checking her wrist straps, the white coat positioned himself in front of the monitor and gave a thumbs up sign to Dr. Schader through the window.

Schader nodded.

He touched a series of buttons on the monitor.

Evie shifted in her seat. Then her body stiffened.

"No!" Evie screamed. "No. No. No." Her little legs kicked against the interior of the pod.

A yellow light near the top of the pod came on and began to blink.

Evie fought against her wrist straps and let out a blood curdling wail. Her tiny body began to spasm.

Maya whipped her head toward Schader. "Shut it off! You're hurting her." She leapt towards the window and placed her palms against it. "Evie!"

The guard approached Maya. "Back to your seat."

Schader waved him off. "It's alright. Let her watch."

The light at the top of the pod turned red and blinked at a rapid pace. The man in the white coat looked up at Schader with concern, but she nodded at him to continue. He shrugged and pressed another button on the monitor.

Evie's whole body began to convulse. Her arms flailed against the restraints and her head whipped from side to side.

"Shut it off!" Maya screamed at Dr. Schader. "You'll kill her!" She lunged at Dr. Schader, but the guard grabbed her around the waist.

Evie let out a moan.

Maya returned her attention to the window, and the guard released his grip.

"Evie?" Maya pressed her face against the window. Instead of blinking, the light remained red. A continuous high pitched beep sounded from the chair. Evie didn't move.

Maya pounded on the glass. "Evie!"

The white coat nudged Evie's leg, but she didn't flinch. He pressed a button to raise the headset and Evie slumped forward. He lifted her from the pod and carried her lifeless body across the room to a gurney like she was nothing.

"Evie. No!" Maya pressed her body against the window and then collapsed to her knees. Her hands slid down the glass. She couldn't be gone. Not Evie. Her breathing became rapid. She rose and threw herself at Schader. "You killed her! You killed a child!"

She pummeled Schader with her fists until one of the guards pulled her off and slammed her facedown against the floor. He held her wrists together behind her back as she struggled against him.

Schader approached her with a syringe. "I was going to do this gently, but after your little outburst, I changed my mind." She raised the syringe and jabbed it into Maya's arm.

Maya winced as the warmth of the drug spread through her. An image of Evie's lifeless body haunted her from the edge of the darkness that overtook her. The world dissolved into nothing.

When Maya's eyelids fluttered open, she strained to focus on her surroundings. Although conscious of the chill of the metal chair and the tension of the leather straps that dug into her wrists, she remained detached from all sensations. A figure sat before her. Or was it two figures? The fuzzy cloud in her head made it hard to think. Where was she?

"It's a shame what happened to Evie. Such a sweet little girl." Abigor's voice. The figure in front of her. She focused on the medals on his jacket.

So shiny.

What did he say about Evie?

Evie's dead. Gone.

Darkness crept through her hollow insides. She felt nothing.

Abigor's face moved closer to hers. "As you can see, the reconditioning process has not yet been perfected. However, we are also working on a serum that is much more cost-effective. The injection you were given will only last a few hours, but Dr. Schader assures me that eventually it will have the ability for long-term success. Isn't that exciting? Someday we could completely eradicate the Fragile condition." His lips curled into a smile, as his words danced around her head.

"Unfortunately, your particular condition is especially dysfunctional because it seems that you're able to pass your weakness on to others. Imagine how much worse a flaw is when it can infect other people." The weight of his hand rested on her shoulder, but she didn't flinch. "We'll attempt to recondition you tomorrow, but I need to know more about your condition first. How do you pass your fragility on to others?"

She stared through him. The pain had been too much to bear, but now it was gone. "You mean why I'm 'one of them'?" Her head drooped forward as she mumbled. "Your guess is as good as mine."

His voice rose. "You must know something."

She spied the straps on her wrists. "Why are you afraid of me? I'm a Fragile."

I'm nothing.

He stood up. "Afraid of you?" he scoffed. "My poor child. I'm just trying to help you. Don't you want to be rehabilitated? You could return to your family."

Her family? Her dad was in prison, and her mother had her arrested. She struggled to focus on his face. "Where's my dad?"

He stared at her for a moment before speaking. "Your father was corrupting young minds and undermining their faith in the guiding light of our great economy, so he gave the council no choice but to incarcerate him."

Tilting her head, she squinted at him. She felt no pain, but also no fear. "Great economy? You mean like all the tall, ugly buildings and polluted air? Does that cost a lot?"

His face hardened. "You stupid, foolish girl. You have no idea what you are talking about. If you're not careful, you'll end up in Jamesville, like your father and all the wretched Fragiles who refuse to embrace the ideals of our great republic."

Jamesville. The underground prison. Her father was there?

Instead of the words ravaging through her, the cloud in her head absorbed them as soon as she tried to feel them. She lowered her head and mumbled, "The adult ward?"

Ignoring her, he approached the door. "Guards."

Two guards entered the room and unstrapped Maya before pulling her up from the chair. Her knees buckled, so she leaned into the body of the guard closest to her.

Abigor's eyes met hers. "Best of luck at your reconditioning tomorrow. I'll be rooting for you."

Chapter 41

BACK IN HER CELL, Maya fiddled with the note left on her nightstand with a syringe. She strained to focus on the words: *To be used once the initial dose wears off. Inject fully into the arm or thigh.* The note slipped from her limp fingers, and she flopped onto the bed. A thick haze spread through her, lulling her to sleep.

When she opened her eyes, the glare of the fluorescent bulb bore into her skull. She swallowed to moisten her parched throat and inched her stiff muscles into a seated position. Once she stretched her neck and shoulders, the feeling returned to her limbs. A sharp pain shot from her gut into her chest and wrapped itself around her lungs. Waves of grief thrashed her insides. Evie's lifeless body. Her father rotting to death in an underground cell. Her body heaved with thunderous sobs—her insides dark and cold.

Through her tears, she spied the syringe on the nightstand. Her trembling fingers fumbled for it, knocking it from the table. Gasping for air between sobs, she lowered herself to the floor.

She flailed her arms across the floor, sending the syringe beneath the bed. Flat on her stomach, she squirmed under the bed and grabbed the syringe. Once she steadied her back against the bed, she plunged the syringe into her arm. As the serum burned through her veins, she rested her head on the bed behind her. Her breathing returned to normal. The darkness lifted. She was at peace.

While Maya drifted in and out of consciousness, a noise caused her to stir from where she lay in bed. The fluffy clouds in her head cushioned any concern, so she slung her legs over the side of the bed to investigate. The slot at the bottom of the door opened, and a hand pushed a tray inside. This time, it was a grilled cheese sandwich and fries. Along with the tray came a forceful whisper. "Maya."

She rose to retrieve the food.

"Maya. It's me," the whisper said.

After slumping down by the door, she tried to peek through the slot. "Jacob?"

Why wasn't he locked up like her?

"Maya. Can you hear me? I only have a minute. I could get in trouble."

The warmth of the drug still coursed through her veins, numbing her insides. She shoved a handful of fries in her mouth. "I'm okay. They gave me some medicine to help cure me. So I won't feel things so much."

"Cure you? Nothing's wrong with you. They're going to recondition you tomorrow. You can't let them."

Did he know Evie was dead? Would she be dead tomorrow, too?

Dead. Dead. Dead. What a weird word.

She giggled.

"Maya?"

"It's okay. Everything will be fine." She picked up the sandwich. "They're just going to make me normal."

"But you aren't normal." His voice was so low that she could barely hear it.

Even Jacob knew she was a freak.

She bit into the sandwich, letting the greasy cheese cling to her chin.

Jacob put his face to the ground and peered at her through the slot. "You're not normal. You're special." Footsteps echoed down the hallway as Jacob slid the opening shut.

She set the sandwich on the tray and leaned her head against the wall. His words echoed through her mind, bouncing off the clouds as she struggled to think. Maybe she would at least survive the reconditioning process tomorrow.

The next morning, a pair of coveralls arrived with her breakfast tray. She searched the tray for a syringe, but found only a boiled egg, canned pears, and a cup of water. Stomach in knots, she pushed the food aside and sipped the water. As she changed into the coveralls, her mind drifted to Huruma—the beautiful flowers and the sun on her skin. Ren, Celia, and Evie. Sweet Evie. Evie was sensitive but not flawed; she was perfect. Her compassion was a gift. Maya's sensitivity was a weakness, a curse. She should've been the one to die.

A loud bang on the door signaled the guard had arrived.

Maybe she would be the one today.

The guard led Maya into the reconditioning room and sat her in a pod. The same pod where Evie had died. Maya's muscles twitched. Across the room, Jacob hunched over a computer next to the video camera. Was he there to watch her die?

Dr. Schader entered the room, followed by a new man in a white coat. Schader eyed Maya and then addressed the guard. "Stay just outside the door in case you're needed."

While the guard exited, the white coat approached Maya and placed her hands through the wrist restraints. Then, he pressed the button to lower the headset into the pod.

Dr. Schader loomed over his shoulder. "I've told you a hundred times the setting should be at four thousand, not three thousand. Are you really that incompetent?"

He dropped his gaze. "I'm sorry, ma'am. I just thought that after—"

"No excuses." She pushed him aside and fiddled with the headset above Maya's head.

"Do you at least want me to tighten her straps?"

"No, I'll do it myself. You may go."

As he headed for the door, his shame clung to Maya. Her instinct told her to comfort him, but it was too late. Too much pain existed in the world to have to experience everyone else's, let alone try to help them. She took a deep, shaky breath. Either way, it would be over soon.

Dr. Schader called out to Jacob. "Is the camera set up?"

"Yes, mam."

"Then come here. Program experience six while I strap her in."

"Uh, number six?" Jacob's voice cracked as he got up. "I think maybe number three would be—"

"You think? You're lucky you're not in the other pod. Abigor may think your environmental sensitivities are too valuable to risk, but you're just as much a freak as the rest of them."

The words cut through Maya. Jacob wasn't a freak. What would happen to him once she was gone?

Jacob pressed a series of buttons on the monitor and Schader placed the headset on Maya.

The dark interior of the goggles lit up revealing an image of the reconditioning room. A young girl was brought into the room—Evie—and placed in a pod. So close to Maya that she felt like she could reach out and touch her. Maya slid her right hand out of the strap and extended it towards Evie, but her fingers slipped through the air. She couldn't reach her. Couldn't help her. The man in the white coat placed a headset on Evie—the same scene that had haunted Maya since Evie's last breath. Maya let out a whimper.

"Did you start it already?" Dr. Schader huffed. "I still need to secure her straps." She tightened the restraint around Maya's left wrist.

A whisper escaped Maya's lips. "You killed Evie."

"What did you say?" Dr. Schader moved to her right side.

A lifetime of anger and pain surged through her veins causing the words to explode from her core. "I said you killed Evie!" Her right hand shot toward Schader's throat. A bolt of electrifying terror surged through Maya when her fingers made contact.

Schader screeched and stumbled away from Maya, her eyes wide. She crawled backwards towards the wall as she gasped for breath. "Guard!"

Using her free hand, Maya loosened the restraint around her left wrist so that she could slip out of the strap. She ripped off the headset with such force that its cable detached from the pod. Still holding the headset, she sprung from the pod just as the guard burst through the door.

Maya hurdled the headset at him. When he went to deflect it, she lunged at him and got ahold of his arm. She poured terror into him until he stumbled back towards the door. Jacob joined her as she shoved him out the door and closed it.

Jacob hit a red button on the wall.

"What did you do?" Maya glared at him between heaving breaths. "And why are you here—helping them?"

"It's a panic button. It locks down the room."

"So we're stuck here with her?" Maya turned to face Schader who had risen from the floor.

Schader braced herself against the wall, holding her throat, and glared at Maya.

Rage boiled within Maya. She grabbed the headset off the ground. A primal scream exploded from her chest as she hurled it at Schader. It crashed against the wall right above Schader as she ducked and covered her head. Maya pressed the button on the second pod to lower the headset and ripped it out. She pelted it at Schader. The headset slammed against the wall inches from Schader's head. She dodged the debris that showered down on her.

As the last remnant crashed to the ground, Schader scoffed. "You might want to work on your aim."

Breathing heavily, Maya approached her. "If I wanted to hit you, I would have."

"Of course, you're a Fragile." She braced herself against the wall in an attempt to rise. "An incurable Fragile. Just like Evie."

Maya bent over Schader. "Here, let me help you." She took Schader's arm, helped her up, and then slammed her against the wall. With all her strength, she grasped Schader's arms and shot bolts of torment through her. The thundering pain ripped at Maya's insides, but she held on until Schader convulsed and collapsed to the floor.

Jacob rushed to Maya. "We gotta get out of here." He knelt by Dr Schader and took a pass card from her pocket. "Eventually they'll override the lock down."

Maya scanned the room, her eyes resting on the video camera. "Grab the tapes. It's proof of what they're doing. Proof that they—"

Jacob took out a small cassette from the camera and put it in his pocket. He rifled through the binders and grabbed a clear pouch full of mini-cassettes and shoved it in his pants. "We need to leave now."

Maya headed towards the door, but Jacob stopped her. "Not that way. It's too dangerous." He pointed to the viewing window. "This way." As they approached the window, he turned to Maya. "If I could just get hot, I could melt the center to break it. Or maybe—"

Maya grabbed a chair. "Cover your ears." She swung the chair into the window, shattering it.

"Or that could work." Jacob climbed through the window. "Come on."

She followed him through the viewing room and out into the hallway.

Jacob turned down the corridor. "Tully's this way."

When they got to the door, Jacob used Dr. Schader's card to unlock it.

Tully leapt out of bed. "What the – how'd you get the key?"

Jacob motioned her toward the door. "We'll explain later. The guards will be here any minute."

Maya rushed to Tully. "Are you okay? Did they try to recondition you?"

"Me?" Tully scoffed. "You can't fix what ain't broke." She approached the door, but stopped and narrowed her eyes at Jacob. "How come you're not in coveralls? Didn't they lock you up?"

"No, but Abigor–"

"And now you have the key. What was that Abigor said about you leading them to us?" She stepped towards Jacob.

"I didn't tell them anything. They drugged me, remember?"

"Then how did they know we were in Huruma, huh?" She glared at him, her face inches from his.

Maya forced herself between them. "Tully, Jacob would never do that. Maybe they somehow followed us. Tracked us. When we were back at Huruma I saw something attached to Jacob's shoe."

"Tully, the door!" yelled Jacob.

Tully spun and jammed her elbow into the guard in the doorway. When he recoiled, Maya grabbed his arm, but he shook her off before she could get a solid grip.

The guard reached for his weapon. Tully jumped on his back and locked her bent elbow around his neck. The guard slammed his back against the wall, knocking her to the floor. Jacob scrambled to the corner and grabbed the trash can. With both hands, he wielded it at the guard's face, striking him across the jaw. Maya grabbed the guard's arm. She recalled Evie's terror during her reconditioning and forced waves of it through him.

He collapsed to the ground.

Once they dragged the guard farther into Tully's room, Jacob locked him in.

Tully checked the corridor and turned to Maya. "We got to move. Any idea where Evie's being held?"

Maya's eyes filled with tears. "Evie..." Her voice shook as she tried to form the words. "Evie's dead. They killed her."

Jacob shook his head in disbelief. "No."

"I'm sorry, but it's true," said Maya. "I saw them do it."

"No, I mean it's not true. They took her to the infirmary, but she's alive. I just saw her an hour ago."

Maya's mouth fell open. Was it true? Evie? Alive?

Chapter 42

When they reached the infirmary, Tully pushed open the double doors, and Jacob led the way through the rows of empty beds. By the time they made it to the last bed, Maya's heart pounded against her ribs. Her eyes met Evie's and then panned to Commander Abigor who sat beside her with a gun in his lap. Although Evie lay motionless in the bed, her eyes remained open.

Maya approached Abigor. "What did you do to her?"

"She's fine. Apparently, her entire brain lit up during the test which caused the machine to malfunction." He frowned. "It seems you caused a bit of a malfunction yourself."

Tully joined Maya. "Just give us Evie and no one has to get hurt."

Abigor threw back his head and laughed. "No one gets hurt? How about I put a bullet in this little girl's head?" Maya took a step towards Abigor. "I wouldn't come any closer if I were you."

Maya felt his power, but the same power now coursed through her veins. "Let her go. She didn't do anything."

"Maybe not. But you've done more than enough." He raised the gun and studied it. "Did you know that if it wasn't for me, the rebels and their vile leader would have destroyed the very heart of our Republic? I have tried to offer rehabilitation to those infected with her same disease, but you leave me no choice." He turned the gun on Maya. "I've always believed that the worst type of Fragile is the kind that refuses to accept their diagnosis." He cocked the gun. "And unfortunately, the only cure for that is elimination."

Tully lunged for the gun as Maya threw her body into Abigor. The gun went off and Maya scrambled to get a grip on him. She got a hold of his arm and summoned the pain from the depths of her soul to surface. It seared through her body and emptied into Abigor. Abigor grimaced in pain and shifted his weight to try to free his arm. Tightening her grip, she grabbed his free hand with her other hand. She stared into his eyes as the shock on his face turned to horror. His body convulsed, but she continued to force pain through him even after his body collapsed on the floor.

"Maya!" Jacob's panicked voice rang out.

She released Abigor and took a step back.

Jacob knelt beside Tully, holding a pillow to her wound as she bled from her side. "He shot her."

"How bad is it?" Tully's labored breathing crackled in her lungs as a pool of blood formed on the floor beside her. An alarm went off in the distance.

"Too bad for me to move." Tully winced. "You need to leave without me."

Maya crouched next to Tully. "No. Maybe we can help you walk."

"Not if you want to have a chance to make it out of here." Tully locked eyes with Maya. "You and Jacob need to take Evie and get out of here as fast as you can. I'll be okay."

"I'm not leaving you."

"Then you are even stupider than I thought. I would leave you in a heartbeat. Just take Evie and go, okay?"

Evie got out of bed and approached Tully. She knelt on the floor next to her. "Is it okay if I help you?"

Tully groaned. "Help me?"

Evie nodded and placed her hand under the pillow that Jacob had been holding against the wound. After taking a deep breath, Evie's lips formed into a peaceful smile. She breathed out deeply and closed her eyes. At first Tully grimaced, but then the muscles in her face relaxed and she closed her eyes. Evie continued to breathe in and out slowly and deeply.

As the alarm continued to blare, Jacob paced the room. "The guards will be here any second." He rubbed the back of his neck. "I am not sure what Evie is trying to do, but we need to leave."

Maya placed her hand on his shoulder imagining a sense of reassurance flowing into him. "Just give her a moment."

Jacob sighed. "Okay."

Evie removed the pillow from Tully's wound and wiped the blood from her hands on the bed sheet. She stood up and looked at Tully. Tully opened her eyes and ran her hand towards the wound, which was no longer spewing blood.

She pushed herself up and stared at Evie with a puzzled expression. "Thank you?"

Jacob opened his mouth, but no words came out.

Tully retrieved the gun from the floor, her other hand still holding her side. Using the gun, she pointed to Abigor who remained motionless on the floor. "Is he dead?"

Maya glanced at Abigor and shuddered. "I'm not sure."

Tully advanced towards Abigor, gun drawn. "Only one way to make sure."

"Wait!" said Maya.

Tully aimed at his head and cocked the gun.

Maya rushed to her side and pointed to the shallow rise and fall of Abigor's chest. "If you shoot him, it's murder. They'll throw you in jail or worse."

"Maya's right. They'd probably execute you." Jacob approached Tully's other side.

"I don't care." Fire burned in her eyes as she tightened her grip on the gun. "He deserves to die."

Maya wrapped her hand around the gun barrel. "The guards will be here any minute. We need to get the other kids." Her eyes pleaded with Tully.

Tully shook the gun loose and glared at Maya. "He killed my dad."

"I know. My dad's probably dead because of him, too. It's okay to be angry, but we have to go."

Tully's eyes locked on Abigor, but after a moment she exhaled and lowered the gun. She cursed under her breath and holstered the gun in the waist of her jeans.

Evie took her hand. "Come on. I'll show you where the other kids are."

Evie led them out the back door of the infirmary and into another corridor. They followed her through the winding hallways until they came to a door. Jacob unlocked the door that opened into a large room with rows of beds and a group of children gathered in the corner. When Evie ran towards the group of children, they looked up from where they were huddled around a young woman with a blonde bun.

"What are you doing here?" Bethany stood and stared at Maya. "What's going on out there? The alarm's scaring the children."

"We're here to rescue them. Where are the others?" Maya searched the group for K. "We don't have much time."

"Rescue them? We were in the middle of story time and the alarm went off. What have you done?" Bethany put her hands on her hips.

"Schader almost killed Evie. They've killed others. It's not safe for them here."

"Well, I am sure that is not true. Commander Abigor—"

Tully shot Bethany an icy glare. "Abigor's dead." She turned to Evie. "Get your friends."

Bethany's eyes got wide. "No, that's not possible."

Evie approached Maya holding K's hand. An older girl with a little boy with a shaved head and two more girls who must have been twins followed them.

Maya turned to Bethany. "You can come with us. We're going—"

"To the Republic." Tully narrowed her eyes on Maya.

Bethany scanned the children and began to tremble. "But how could I? I couldn't possibly."

Maya stepped towards Bethany. "You can. It'll be okay."

Bethany smoothed her bun and straightened her posture. "No. They don't belong outside the Arc. They haven't been rehabilitated. You can't take them." Bethany took off across the room to a red button on the wall.

Maya reached for her arm. "The reconditioning process is torture. This is what it feels like." She allowed a drop of the trauma she had absorbed from the children to release from her fingertips into Bethany.

Bethany froze as a wave of sorrow passed over her face. Her voice trembled. "I didn't know."

"It's okay. Just tell me where the other Arc kids are."

"There are no others. The rest were rehabilitated." Bethany brought her hands to her mouth.

"We have all the kids. We need to leave now," said Tully.

Maya glanced at Bethany. "Come with us."

She shook her head. "I'll throw off the guards when they get here. I passed my review earlier this month, so I'll be fine. Good luck."

Jacob darted to Maya and grabbed her hand. "Come on!"

Maya raced out the door behind Tully and the children without looking back.

As they ran down the hall, the alarm continued to blare. When they approached a branch in the corridor, Tully slowed down. "I think it should be to the right, but I am not sure. Once we get outside, we can find the delivery dock."

"I really don't remember." Maya glanced down the corridor to the right. "But that seems right."

The little boy pointed to the right. "The guards will come from that way."

"And you know this, how?"

"He just knows," said Evie, "And we should believe him."

Tully placed her hand on her wound. "Okay, to the left it is."

Tully led the way as they raced down the corridor. Within a few moments, the footsteps of the guards echoed behind them. Up ahead, a faint light signaled the emergency exit. Tully rushed to the door and pushed it open for Evie and the other children. Maya exited next and Jacob slammed the door behind them.

While Tully and the children ran around the side of the building, Jacob faced the door. Sweat beaded on his forehead as they stood in the sunlight. Pressing his hand against the rim of the door, Jacob grimaced as the metal melted into the steel door frame. He ran his hand along the edge until it was sealed. Maya beamed at him before they took off around the side of the building.

They caught up to Tully and the children outside a door marked "delivery bay." Tully tugged on the door as if brute strength and determination could get it open. As she battled the door, Jacob swiped the pass card to disengage the lock, and the door flung open throwing her backwards. Once she regained her balance, she smirked at Jacob. "I loosened it for you."

Jacob smiled. "I'm sure you did." He led the way as they rushed into the delivery bay.

Inside the bay, a man unloading food from a truck looked up at them.

Tully drew Abigor's gun and pointed it at him. "Hands up!"

He dropped the crate and raised his hands, cans of peas rolling across the floor.

Tully kept her laser focus on the man. "Where're the keys?"

Nodding towards the truck, the man kept his hands up. "In the ignition."

Without taking her eyes off him or lowering her gun, she tilted her head towards Maya. "Find something to tie him up."

Jacob glanced from the man to Tully. "Can you even drive?"

She scowled and stepped closer to the man. "How hard can it be?"

"It's a delivery truck. You can't be serious."

The determination on Tully's face led Maya to search the loading dock for something to restrain the man.

The man's eyes shifted beyond Tully. "Evie?"

Evie walked towards him and nodded.

Tully glanced at Evie and then returned her stare to the man, still pointing the gun at him. "You Trey's friend?"

He nodded. "Max."

"We need to get to Huruma, can you take us?"

"I need to unload first, if I leave with the food, they'll be suspicious."

"Okay, then let's unload. Everyone, come help. Hurry." She used the gun to gesture toward the back of the truck.

Max eyed Tully. "Can you at least put the gun down?"

Tully slipped the gun into the waist of her jeans and grabbed a box. While they unloaded the boxes, Jacob walked towards two Arc security vehicles parked just outside the delivery bay. Maya joined him just as he tried to open one of the car doors.

He tugged at the door. "I was thinking I could steal the keys or melt the ignition or something to buy us more time." He stepped back from the vehicle and surveyed it. "Or slash the tires?"

"Great idea." She ran back to Max, "You don't happen to have a pocket knife, do you?"

"I have a box cutter." He pulled it out of his pocket and offered it to her.

By the time Maya and Jacob finished slashing the tires, the others had finished unloading the boxes of food. Once everyone piled in the back of the truck, Max reached up to close the door behind them.

Tully drew her gun and narrowed her eyes on him. "I'm trusting you, Max. Okay?"

He nodded and slid the door shut behind them.

When the truck started down the winding road, Maya leaned her head against the metal interior and let out a deep breath. Once they had been driving for a few minutes, Maya glanced across at Tully. "Would you really have left me if I was the one who got shot?"

"What do you think?" Tully cracked a smile.

Maya returned her smile. "Are you still heading back to the Republic after this?"

"I don't know. I was thinking about hanging with you all in Huruma for a while, but after what you did to Abigor, I think we'll all need to hide out for a while."

"Do you think he really died?"

"No, but Bethany didn't need to know that."

"Tully's right," said Jacob. "We can't stay in Huruma for long. If they come after us, it'll be the first place they look."

"Maybe we can find another settlement. Ren or Celia might be able to help," said Maya.

Jacob frowned. "In the wasteland?"

Evie glanced up at Jacob. "Don't worry. There's other nice settlements where we can hide."

Maya had forgotten Evie was part of the "we" now, as were the five other children now in their care. She let out a deep breath.

Tully nudged the little boy beside her. "So little man, how did you know the guards were coming that way?"

Shrugging his shoulders, he grinned. "My name is Q, but you can call me little man." The other kids giggled. "Thank you for saving us. I knew you would."

Chapter 43

WHEN THE TRUCK CAME to a stop, Tully stood up and drew her gun. "Let's hope Max delivered on his promise." She made her way to the back of the truck and positioned her body by the edge of the door with the gun gripped in both hands. Following her lead, Maya positioned herself at the other side of the door, ready to draw on any painful emotions still trapped inside her. When the door opened, Tully spun forward and pointed her gun straight ahead, startling Max who stepped back with his hands up.

"Seriously, Tully?" Ren stepped into view with a wide grin. He noticed her bloody coveralls and his face dropped. "Are you okay?"

"Just a little gunshot wound. No biggie." She hopped down from the truck.

As soon as Maya jumped down from the truck, Ren grabbed her hand and pulled her toward him. "I knew you could do it." Their eyes locked and the warmth of his affection sent tingles through her.

She took a step back and smiled. "Thanks." She let go of his hand just as Evie bolted toward him and wrapped herself around his legs.

Maya approached Max. "Thanks so much for bringing us here. Can you do me one more favor?"

"Sure, as long as it doesn't involve that one pointing a gun at me." He rolled his eyes in Tully's direction.

Maya laughed. "Don't worry. It doesn't. I'll be right back." She rushed to the tent where they had stayed and pulled Jacob's Arc-issued sneakers from under his bed. Running her hand over the label, she discovered a small firm device below it. She grabbed the half-full box of clothes and emptied it on the bed before placing the sneakers in the box. When she returned to the truck, Max was alone getting ready to leave. She held out the box to him. "Where are you headed?"

"The capital."

"Perfect. Can you toss this box in the garbage on your way out there?"

He glanced in the box and raised his brows. "You must really hate those shoes."

"You have no idea."

He took the box and placed it in the front seat of the truck.

When he turned to go, Maya took his hand and looked into his eyes, sharing her joy of being back at Huruma with him. "Thank you for helping us, Max."

Happiness spread across his face with a bit of surprise. He beamed at Maya. "Glad I could help."

As she watched him drive off, Ren walked up beside her. "What was that about?"

"I think they put a tracking device in Jacob's shoe. I'm not sure if it's still transmitting, but if it is, hopefully, it'll lead them back to the Republic to buy us some time. We can't stay here."

"I know." He let out a heavy breath and turned to face her. Gazing into her eyes, he gently moved a piece of hair from her face. "We'll think of something."

She nodded. The warmth of his gaze threatened to swallow her. But she didn't need to be swallowed with emotions, she needed a plan. Breaking his gaze, she took a step back. "Where can we go? To hide, I mean. Evie mentioned other friendly settlements?"

Ren scratched his head. "Well, we have a sister settlement up in the hills. It's not an easy journey, but it's so remote that I doubt they'd search for you there. We should wait to leave until it's dark though."

"Ok. That sounds good. I'll let the others know." At least that gave her the rest of the day to shower and recharge after all that had happened.

As soon as she got the chance, Maya showered and changed out of her coveralls. She never wanted to see them nor the Arc again. As she inspected herself in the mirror, she ran her hand over the scar on her neck that had started to fade. Part of her wouldn't mind if it never completely disappeared. Maybe Tully was right about it making her look like a badass. Either way, it reminded her that she was stronger than she ever thought possible.

Her thoughts were interrupted by tapping on the tent door. "Maya?" June poked her head in the tent. "Can we come in?"

"Sure." Maya walked toward where June and Evie had entered the tent.

June wrapped Maya in a hug. "I didn't get a chance to thank you for saving Evie. I don't know what I would have done if—" Her voice cracked, and she released Maya to wipe her tears. "I can't tell you how much I appreciate what you did."

Maya smiled. "I'm just glad everyone's okay now."

"I wish I had half your strength when I was your age. Things would have been so different." June grasped Evie's hand. "I left him for good this time. He knows he's not welcome here."

"That's great. It must feel good to be back home."

"It does. But what...what–" She burst into tears as she collapsed onto a cot. "What if I lose her again? He signed the papers. They'll be back. We can hide in the hills but—" Her sorrow overflowed around her as she buried her face in her hands.

Evie sat beside her and patted her arm. "It'll be okay, Mommy."

Maya found the pouch full of cassettes on the table that Jacob had taken from the Arc and handed it to June. "This might help."

"What?" June wiped her tears and took the pouch.

"It's proof of what they are doing to kids at the Arc." She cleared the lump forming in her throat. "Proof of what they did to Evie. We can threaten to make it public if they try to take her or any of the kids. I was going to send it to someone Tully knows, but maybe we should keep it for now. At least until we know we're safe at the new settlement."

"What they did to Evie?" June's lips trembled as she dropped the cassettes.

Evie took her hand and smiled softly. "Don't worry. I'm okay now."

June pulled Evie into a hug. "I know. You always were the strong one."

Maya picked up the cassettes from the cot and studied them. Maybe there was more they could do. As she headed to the door, she called out, "Thanks for coming by, but I need to go find Tully."

Once she had gathered Tully and Jacob, Maya found Ren as he exited Celia's tent. "I just spoke to Celia," said Ren. "It should be fine to move you and the kids to the other settlement tonight. We'll leave as soon as it gets dark."

"Sounds good." Maya held up the pouch of cassettes. "Do you have anything we can play these on?"

He raised his brows. "Movies? We have a player but—"

"They're from the Arc. I think we might be able to use them."

"Use them?"

"I'll explain, but I need to be sure what's on it first."

"Okay. Cool. Follow me."

Ren led them down a path to a tent that stood away from the others. He paused outside the door. "I guess you could call this our tech room."

Inside the tent, two large tables held all sorts of electronics in various states of repair. While Jacob inspected one of the ancient devices, Ren dusted off the VCR and plugged it into the television.

Ren turned on the television. "Let's hope this works."

Maya found the cassette labeled *Subjects A-J* and handed it to him. "Meg was subject A. She had blue eyes and dark hair. They killed her."

Ren placed the small cassette into a larger one and slid it into the VCR.

The television monitor lit up with static. After a minute, a squiggly image broke across the screen, but it was too jumbled to make out. Maya dug her nails into her palms.

Ren slapped the top of the VCR. The image settled.

Reconditioning Subject A. Meg. Although the image displayed in black and white, Meg's icy blue gaze shot through Maya as if she was there in the flesh. Maya stared at the screen as Dr. Schader fitted the headset over Meg's head. Her tiny arms fidgeted against the wrist straps

Jacob placed his hand on Maya's shoulder, his concern flowing through her. "You don't have to watch. We can tell you what's on it."

She shook her head. "It's okay. I have to see it."

As Meg convulsed on the screen, tears formed in Maya's eyes. Was this when she died?

When Dr Schader removed the headset, Meg slumped forward and gripped her temples in agonizing pain. Her pain ripped through Maya like she was there beside her.

Tully's eyes widened. "What the actual hell?" She turned to Maya. "Is that what you were feeling?"

Wiping away a tear, Maya gave a slight nod before turn-
ing to Ren. "Can you fast-forward it? I want to see when
they...when she..."

Ren paused the tape when Meg's body lay motionless
on the floor. At least the lab attendant had tried to revive
her. As they watched him try in vain to get a heartbeat,
a heavy silence blanketed the room. Maya pointed at the
screen, unable to quell the trembling in her hand or the
quiver in her voice. "We have proof."

Although Evie was safe, Maya couldn't bear to watch the
scene that still haunted her. She shut off the television and
turned to Ren. "Can you take us to the Republic?"

Chapter 44

Ren dropped them in the alley behind the soon-to-be-renamed Modern Republic Broadcast Services building. Tully entered the code on the staff elevator, and they stepped inside. As they rode to the top floor, Jacob rubbed the back of his neck. "So first we ask Miranda to help us make a copy and then we get them to broadcast it?"

Maya nodded. "Exactly."

When the elevator doors opened, Tully led the way to Miranda's desk. Miranda rose in surprise. "Petulah? You really shouldn't be—" She put her hands to her lips and motioned for them to enter Mr. Doyle's office.

As soon as they were inside, she closed the door. "What are you doing here?" She waved her hand in front of her nose. "And what's that smell?"

"First, I told you to call me Tully last time we spoke. Second, we need your help. And third, we hid between bags of manure to get here. Any other questions?"

"Sorry, Tully. How can I help?"

Tully motioned to Maya. "Show her the cassette."

Maya put the cassette on the desk. "This shows proof of how the reconditioning process is hurting kids. We thought we could broadcast it, along with the audio tapes of Abigor threatening Tully's dad. It's the only way we can be safe."

Miranda picked up the cassette. "I'm sorry, but we can't broadcast this."

"Can't or won't?" Tully stepped toward Miranda and shot her a fiery look.

Maya stepped between them. "It can help us bring out the truth about what happened to Mr. Doyle. Don't you want that?"

"You don't understand. We aren't able to broadcast anything until new management takes over. And it looks like Apex is going to beat out Giovanni Industries. And if Apex takes over—"

"They'll bury it all." Tully slumped into her dad's chair. "We're screwed."

"But what if we could help Giovanni Industries gain control?" Maya turned to Jacob. "Like if the Council knew about the tapes, or Abigor's threats and Apex's involvement?"

Jacob shook his head "There's no way we could even talk to the Council." He began to pace the room and then paused. "But what if Mr. Giovanni knew?"

"Yes." Maya turned to Miranda. "Do you think you could get Mr. Giovanni to talk to us?"

Miranda thumbed through the rolodex on the desk and pulled out a card. "We can try." She hurried across the room to a monitor on the wall, flipped a switch, and returned to the desk. "We'll request a video call." She picked up the phone and dialed. "Hello, Stacy? It's Miranda from MRBS, I have an urgent call for Mr. Giovanni. Can you put it through on video please?" She locked eyes with Maya and then spoke into the receiver. "Thank you." Miranda nodded and then placed the phone on speaker as an image lit up on the monitor.

On the screen, a portly man with a dark comb-over sat at a golden desk. "Hello, Miranda. I've been meaning to express my condolences. So unfortunate what happened to Fitz."

"Thank you, Mr. Giovanni."

"You said you had an urgent call for me?" He leaned in toward the camera. "Is that Doyle's daughter? I thought she was—"

"Yes, it's her. She and her friends have some information that might be of interest to you."

Maya stepped into view of the camera holding the cassette. "We have proof that children were being harmed at the Apex Enterprises reconditioning center and at the Arc. At least one girl was killed. Apex and Abigor threatened Mr. Doyle when he found out. We think they had him killed."

"Killed? I thought it was suicide?"

"My dad would never kill himself." Tully approached the monitor. "We have the threats on tape. And proof of them torturing kids on video. You could bring down Abigor and Apex along with him."

Mr. Giovanni sat back in his chair, stroking his chin. "Well, maybe not completely destroy them, but enough bad publicity to turn the Council in my favor, I'd suppose. How much you want for it?"

"We don't want money." Maya ignored Tully's icy glare. "We just want your assurance that once you gain control of MRBS, and a seat on the Council, you make it public."

"No problem, I was planning to do that anyway."

"And ensure that the Arc is shut down."

"I can't make any promises, but I'll do my best. You have my word. I'll send my courier over right away to collect the tapes. Anything else?"

Tully walked up to the camera. "Yeah, bring back the pepperoni explosion pizza. Can't believe Gino's took it off the menu."

Mr. Giovanni laughed. "I'll see what I can do." The screen went black.

Maya turned to Miranda. "Before you send the tapes, make two copies of everything. Send one copy to Mr. Giovanni and the other to Abigor with a note saying that if he comes near us or Huruma, we'll make it public. We'll take the originals back to Huruma."

When they arrived back at Huruma, night had fallen. Maya climbed out of the truck and turned to Ren. "I think we should still head to the other settlement. At least until we know we are safe. What do you think?"

"Makes sense. We'll need some supplies for the part we have to make on foot, so I'll load up the truck. Can you go make sure the new kids know we're heading out soon?"

Maya nodded and joined Tully and Jacob as they headed towards the tents. When they reached Evie's tent, peals of laughter greeted them from the interior. Maya paused outside the tent. "I'm going to check on the kids."

"Cool. I need a shower." Jacob headed up the path.

"I'll join you." Tully followed behind him.

Jacob turned and grinned at Tully. "I thought I wasn't your type."

"Not in the shower." She smirked. "Obviously." She shoved him out of the way and walked ahead.

Once Maya entered the tent, K ran towards her. "What do you think?" She spun around in her bright pink dress.

"It's beautiful." Maya smiled and walked toward the bed where the twins and the older girl were rummaging through a pile of clothes.

Q sat on the other bed in his coveralls watching them with amusement. "Hi, Maya. Come sit with me."

Maya sat beside him. "How're you doing?"

"Oh, I'm fine. Ms. Celia told us we would be leaving soon for another settlement."

"Yes, that's right. Just to be safe. We should be able to come back here soon. And maybe even get you back to your family. Don't worry."

"I'm not worried." He smiled and picked up a plate of cut apples from the nightstand. "Want one?"

"Thank you." She bit into the apple, savoring its sweetness. Q took a piece and broke off half to eat before slipping the other half in his front pocket. She smiled gently at him. "It's okay. You aren't at the Arc anymore. There's always enough for everyone here."

"I know." He shrugged and reached into his pocket. Cradled in his hand sat a tiny mouse nibbling on the piece of apple. "I brought him from the Arc."

Maya reached out and stroked the mouse's furry little head, her heart full. "I'm sure he's glad you rescued him."

"Me, too." He broke off another bit of apple for the mouse and then looked up at Maya. "Can you help me find some new clothes?"

"I'd love to." Maya got up and scanned the bed, finding a small green T-shirt for Q.

"I just remembered, I need some new clothes, too." Jacob stood in the doorway with a grin. "Any chance you could help me?"

She knew his smiles like the back of her hand, but this one brimmed with a self-assurance she'd never seen before. Maya handed Q the shirt. "I'll be right back." She turned to Jacob. "Come with me. I have something of yours."

Maya led Jacob to their tent and motioned for him to sit down. She dug under her pillow and pulled out his scarf. "You left it in the truck when you saved me. I meant to give it back to you before."

"Did I? I guess I didn't need it."

Maya sat beside him and placed it around his neck. "Maybe you don't need it, but I kinda like it."

"Really?" His hands rose to the scarf as he glanced down at it.

"Yes. It's part of who you are." A wave of happiness surged through her as she sat back and smiled at him. "And who you are is more than enough. We're all more than enough."

Epilogue

MAYA CLUTCHED THE BINOCULARS. They should be leading out the prisoners any minute. Ren sighed. "We can't keep doing this. Don't you think you would've seen him by now?"

Ignoring the question, Maya shifted in the dirt beneath her. The embankment provided the perfect cover despite its lack of comfort. Her neck and elbows ached, but it didn't matter. Ren nudged her. "Hey, I'm serious. We can't keep driving out here. If just one of the guards spot us—"

"Sssh!" The guard pulled open the hatch to the underground chamber and the prisoners began to clamor out of the hole into the sunlight, shielding their eyes. She'd witnessed their frail bodies and ragged clothing emerge from the ground countless times, but the image still jarred her.

Peering through the binoculars, she scanned the line of prisoners as the guards shuttled them to their work-stations. When a guard shoved a young man forward, he tumbled to the ground, his body so emaciated that it would take a miracle for him to rise. As a guard approached him with a gun, Maya mouthed, "Get up."

Please get up.

She had seen what guards did to prisoners who couldn't get up. Instead of a helping hand, they got a bullet to the head. Her stomach dropped as a scraggly prisoner with a long beard crouched down to assist the young man. Pressing the binoculars against her face, she squinted to get a better look.

Dad?

About Mitra De Souza

Mitra has loved to write for as long as she can remember. In elementary school, she used to tape her short stories to the back of her chair for her classmates to read. She is drawn to stories that encourage people to view the world from a new perspective. When she lived in Trinidad and Tobago, she authored a series of children's books published by a local NGO to foster empathy and promote animal welfare. She currently resides in San Diego with her husband, two kids and two big rescue dogs who think they're still puppies. When she isn't writing, she loves walking on the beach, laughing uncontrollably with her kids, and continuing her quest to find the perfect mango.

You can read more about Mitra at https://mitradesou za.com/